Praise for

THE Wild Parrots OF Telegraph Hill

"*The Wild Parrots of Telegraph Hill* is not your Aunt Nellie's backyard bird diary. Instead, it's about loving nature wherever it's found. It's about loving yourself wherever you're found."　　　　*—Santa Cruz Sentinel*

"Charming debut . . . A pleasure and an education."　　*—Kirkus Reviews*

"In this appealing, heartfelt account of one man's attempt to bond with wildlife, the author tells how he made friends with a flock of birds and in the process found meaning in his own life."　　　　*—Publishers Weekly*

"This lovely book on finding one's way through interacting with parrots will be very popular among animal-loving readers."　　　　*—Booklist*

"By falling in with a flock of wild parrots, Bittner has learned more about a real parrot society than those of us studying wild or captive parrots could ever hope to learn. *The Wild Parrots of Telegraph Hill* makes essential and delightful reading for anyone with an interest in the complex lives of intelligent and engaging wild animals . . . and inspires readers to find nature and peace in whatever place on the planet they happen to occupy."　　　　—James D. Gilardi, Ph.D., director, World Parrot Trust

"I went walking up the Greenwich steps on the east side of Telegraph Hill one afternoon, seeking the sky and a moment of breath, and ran into Mark Bittner, for whom, in turn, a flock of wild-flying parrots appeared. It was a liberating moment, right on the Hill where I had lived and worked some forty years earlier. And now here's Mark's full story. I think of Thoreau saying, 'Give me for my friends and neighbors wild men, not tame ones. The wildness of the savage is but a faint symbol of the awful ferity with which good men and lovers meet.' Ferity, wildness, fierceness— of *goodness*? of *lovers*? This instructive, surprising, sweet book shows how and why (and I'm honored to be one of the parrots in the trees)."
　　　　　　　　—Gary Snyder, author of *Turtle Island* and
　　　　　　　　　　　　Mountains and Rivers Without End

A LOVE STORY . . . WITH WINGS

THREE RIVERS PRESS
NEW YORK

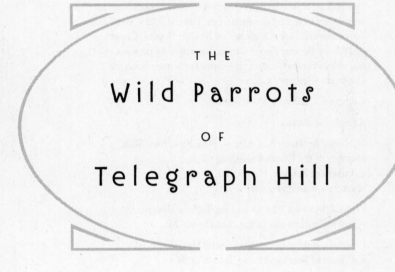

THE Wild Parrots OF Telegraph Hill

Mark Bittner

Grateful acknowledgment is made to *Perseus Books Group* for permission to reprint excerpts from "Painted Rice Cakes" from *Mountains and Rivers Without End* by Gary Snyder. Copyright © 1996 by Perseus Books Group. Reprinted by permission of Perseus Books Group in the format of a trade book via Copyright Clearance Center.

Published by Three Rivers Press, New York, New York.
Member of the Crown Publishing Group,
a division of Random House, Inc.
www.crownpublishing.com

THREE RIVERS PRESS and the Tugboat design are
registered trademarks of Random House, Inc.

Originally published in hardcover by Harmony Books,
a division of Random House, Inc., in 2004.

Printed in the United States of America

Design by Barbara Sturman

Library of Congress Cataloging-in-Publication Data
Bittner, Mark.
  The wild parrots of Telegraph Hill : a love story . . . with wings /
Mark Bittner.—1st ed.
  1. Bittner, Mark. 2. Irving, Judy. 3. Parrots—California—San
Francisco. 4. Telegraph Hill (San Francisco, Calif.)—Biography.
5. San Francisco (Calif.)—Biography. 6. Homeless persons—
California—San Francisco—Biography. 7. Women motion picture
producers and directors—California—San Francisco—Biography.
8. Couples—California—San Francisco—Biography. I. Title.
  F869.S36T45 2004
  636.6'865—dc22   2003015097

ISBN 1-4000-8170-X

10 9 8

First Paperback Edition

For the flock

ACKNOWLEDGMENTS

This book and the experiences that it describes could never have happened without the help and encouragement of many people. I'd like to thank John Aikin, Howard Ashlock, James Attwood, Adah Bakalinsky, Jane Bay, Cheryl Bentley, Brinley Best, Joe Bishop and Lisa Leonard, Patrick Brennan, Roberto Bruno, Patricia Cady, Chris Carlsson, Kathleen Carr, Jeffery Chinn and Mary Nelson, Kyle Chiu, Jacquelyne Cordes, Gerry Crowley, Richard Cuneo, Hank Donat, Art and Marshall Dong, Dorothy Dong, Tom Eby and Denise St. Onge, Barry Edghill, Peggy Ensminger, Sybil Erden, Jann Eyrich, Joe Fields, Chuck Galvin, Kimball Garrett, Leigh-Ann Gerow, Jamie Gilardi, Loretta Giuliotti, Victoire Grassl, Maria Groppi, Larry Habegger, Shawn Hall, Gayle Hampton-Smith, Alan Hopkins, David Kennedy, A. T. Kippes, Ross Lai, Lori Lancaster, Susan Leahy, Mark Leno, Laura Lent, Laurie Leonard, Dave Long, Nate and Betsy Lott, Ben Margot, Margo Metegrano, Howard Munson, Barbara Oplinger, Peter Overmire, Sylvia Portillo, Mike Radke, Allan Ridley, Sark, Ed and Shirley Schaffnit, Richard Schulke, Louis Silcox, Jim Stevens, Gary Thompson, Laurel Wroten, Edna Yarbrough, Paul Yglesias, Jamie Yorck, Pattie Yost, and the officers and members of the Telegraph Hill Dwellers.

Special thanks go out to my father, Clyde Bittner; my mother, Jenny Bobst, who, regrettably, did not live to see completion of the book; my sister, Beth Lyons; and to Daniela Cossali and Natalie Cooper.

For help in getting the manuscript ready for publication, I want to thank the publisher of Harmony Books, Shaye Areheart; my editor, Teryn Johnson; my agent, Candice Fuhrman, and her associate, Elsa Hurley; readers Gardner Haskell, Berenice Jolliver, Irvin Jolliver, and Linette Jolliver; and my copy editor, Jim Gullickson.

My biggest thank-you goes to Judy Irving, who has read, without complaint, every revision of this manuscript, made corrections and suggestions, and listened to me patiently when I was just thinking out loud.

To those I've forgotten, my sincere apologies.

CONTENTS

THE
Wild Parrots
OF
Telegraph Hill

Introduction

I'm standing on the front deck of an old cottage on San Francisco's Telegraph Hill. The cottage, vine-covered and frail, is nestled within the immense and chaotically lush gardens that tumble down the hill's steep eastern face. Just to my right is a large cage containing three lime-green parrots with cherry-red heads. On top of the cage, another parrot prowls at liberty. In my left hand, I'm holding a cup filled with sunflower seeds. Clinging to the cup's rim are two more parrots who are making quick and expert work of the seeds. There are parrots on my right hand, on my shoulders, and on my head.

In front of me, on the limbs of a tall shrub, are another dozen or so. They watch me with eager eyes as I pass around a handful of seeds. One of them, determined to get my attention, flaps his wings furiously, causing the thin branch he's perched on to bounce up and down. Five more parrots eat from a small pile of seeds on the deck railing. To my far right, a gang of fifteen crowds around a large, seed-filled dish that sits on the thick growth of ivy climbing over the railing corner. Another ten sit on the power lines above me. In all, I'm surrounded by more than fifty parrots.

The birds on the lines start up an insistent, staccato squawking that grows louder and more anxious as those below gradually join in. A group of tourists, their faces lit with fascination, stop to stare. The squawking is getting so loud that one of the tourists has to shout his question.

"Don't you ever lose any?"

"They're not mine," I shout back, laughing. "They're wild."

"Wild? . . . Are you serious? Wild parrots in San Francisco?"

Before I can answer, the screaming hits a tremendous peak, and the entire flock bolts. In the scramble to leave, a few of the birds nearly collide with the startled, ducking tourists. The parrots continue to scream as they fly on stiff, frantic wings through a gap in a row of trees and disappear from view.

Yes. Wild parrots in San Francisco.

A Rolling Stone

The first time I saw them was on Russian Hill at a housecleaning job. I was on my knees, dusting an end table, when I noticed four brightly colored birds clinging to a small feeder that hung just outside the living room window. At first glance, I didn't know what I was looking at. Then it dawned on me: They were *parrots*. The birds must have sensed my excitement, for they immediately fled. I jumped to my feet and ran to the window, but the only trace of them that remained was the swinging feeder.

A few weeks later, I was astonished to see the same four birds again, this time in a tree that grew just outside the place where I was staying on Telegraph Hill. They were crawling around the tree's bushy limbs and eating its tiny cones. Completely bewildered, I walked as close to them as they would allow. I'd never known much about birds, so the parrots raised questions that I had no idea how to answer: How had they gotten to San Francisco? Were they someone's pets? What species were they? How could they stand the cold? The last question puzzled me most. San Francisco's weather is generally moderate year-round, but I assumed that anything less than a hothouse environment would kill a tropical bird. Maybe they weren't parrots. I'd always thought of parrots as large birds, but these were only about a foot long, nearly half of which was their tail. They did have the bright colors of a parrot, though—green, with a red head, and red patches on the shoulders of their wings—and like parrots, they had hooked beaks, which were comically large. Their eyes were so expressive that even from a distance the birds struck me as personable and intelligent. There was something goofy about their eyes. It was as if they concealed the punch line to some joke.

All of a sudden, I saw their good humor vanish. They stopped eating and began scanning the area with eyes that now bulged in alarm. They pulled their feathers in tight against their bodies and their breathing became labored. One of the four uttered a few low squawks, and they all took off in a noisy and sloppy panic. I looked around the garden, but I didn't see anything that I thought should have frightened them.

Over the next few weeks, the four parrots continued to pass through my neighborhood. Because they squawked constantly in flight, I always knew when they were coming. The moment I heard them, I dropped whatever I was doing and ran outside to watch. They were different from other birds—so different that it was difficult to think of them as birds at all. They seemed more like monkeys. Sometimes they'd perch on the power lines and, for no apparent reason, scream like lunatics. They also liked to hang upside down. Occasionally I'd see two of them dangling side by side and shrieking hysterically while trying to bite each other in the face.

I learned later that the parrots were visiting my neighborhood because of the many trees that grew there. I didn't know trees any better than I did birds, so I asked Helen Arpin, the woman who lived on the floor above me, the name of the tree from which I'd seen them eating. She said it was a juniper. There was another tree that the parrots liked even more, an Asian fruit tree called the loquat. I already knew the loquat. When the parrots weren't eating its fruit, they often napped in it. Loquat leaves are broad and long, nearly as long as the parrots. The birds' feathers and the tree's leaves were similar enough in color that when the birds perched on the inner branches, they were almost perfectly camouflaged. Even when I knew for certain they were in there, they could be difficult to spot. Eventually, they'd pop their bright red heads out of the treetop, and I'd have them in sight again.

I'd popped my head out of the top of a loquat tree once, and it had gotten me thrown out onto the street.

Sixteen years earlier, in the spring of 1974, my home was a broken-down VW van parked in San Francisco's North Beach neighborhood. I was twenty-two years old and leading the life of a dharma bum, a term coined by the poet Gary Snyder that means "a homeless seeker of truth." I'd met Alan, the van's owner, the previous spring when I was living in Berkeley. Alan was a hippie jeweler and street vendor, and I was a street musician. He liked my music, and we became acquainted. But my musical career had come to an abrupt end, which is why I was living in his van.

When I was a young boy, I'd had the usual ambitions—private eye, baseball player, astronaut—but when I turned fourteen I began to recognize that I was different somehow and that I was never going to have a "normal" life. So I switched to what I thought a more appropriate occupation; I decided to become a Great Novelist. I liked writing, but I kept making the same unsettling discovery: Every writer whose work I admired had ended up alcoholic, poverty-stricken, crazy, or suicidal. Since not even one of them had been a healthy and sane human being, I made what I thought was a better career choice: rock-and-roll musician.

Rock and roll was at its creative peak and looked extremely attractive to me. I thought I could transfer my love for writing from books to songs, but it didn't work out that way. Although my love for music was genuine, inside I simply didn't feel like a real musician. My doubts about my sincerity brought on an inner conflict that began to nag at me. I refused to deal honestly with the problem, however, and my refusal paralyzed me. I couldn't find the will to pick up my guitar. Eventually I reached the point where I either had to make a real move or abandon my goal.

I was living in Seattle then, and I knew that if I wanted to hit the big time, I'd have to move to another city. I never had any doubts about which city it should be: San Francisco. I felt attracted to its particular flavor of bohemia. I pictured San Francisco as being filled with artists living in funky little houses and studying Zen. Timid about moving there directly, I decided to test the waters across the bay in Berkeley first. But even though I managed to make a living playing music, it did nothing to alleviate my doubts. My psychological stress kept growing until one day I freaked. I had no choice other than to give it up.

I'd devoted myself so exclusively to this one goal that when it collapsed, I had nothing to fall back on. I couldn't see anything else I wanted to do. It was an extremely dark period for me. I got so far down that I could barely function. One night I started having vaguely suicidal feelings, and after debating it at length, I decided I should call the Suicide Prevention Center. The man who answered the phone sounded harassed.

"Jeez, man. You picked a really bad time to call. Could you just hold on until morning and call back then?"

I paused, said "Sure," and he hung up.

Then, as though fortune were looking out for me, my sister, Beth, came to town. She'd decided to move to San Francisco and had stopped in Berkeley to look for me. I told her what had happened, and she offered to put me up until I could pull myself back together.

In those days, when one's life was at such an impasse, people often turned to Eastern religions. I'd always believed in inner exploration, but I tended to regard people who'd "gotten religion" as cop-outs. The only spiritual struggle that mattered to me was that of the artist. Someone had once asked me what my religion was, and I'd told him I was a Taoist. I knew nothing about Taoism, of course. I had a superficial idea of it as being about following your own path without having to endure a bunch of rules and ceremonies. I didn't even think of it as a religion, really, which to my mind made it a good thing. So it was an easy step for me to take a more serious look at Taoism. It had a good reputation within bohemian circles, and I considered myself first and foremost a bohemian. I started reading the *Tao Te Ching,* Taoism's main text. While most of it was incomprehensible to me, some of it made beautiful sense. I liked the down-to-earth aspects of its spirituality. As I read it, I got more and more drawn in. I felt challenged by it, enough so that I started reading other spiritual books: the *I Ching, The Analects of Confucius,* the Dhammapada, the Upanishads, the Bhagavad Gita, and the works of Rumi. I even read the Bible. I also started trying to meditate. At first, sitting was extremely difficult for me. I was so restless that I couldn't keep still for more than a few minutes at a time. But gradually I got better at it and learned to sit for longer and longer periods.

Five months after taking me in, Beth decided to move on. It had been a period of intense inner struggle and discipline for me. I was finally dealing seriously with my questions: Who am I? What am I doing? Where am I going? Having started down that path, it felt dangerous to stop. I needed some cubbyhole where I could continue. I'd been a complete recluse while living with Beth, and the only other person I knew in San Francisco was Alan. When I told him about my situation, he offered to let me stay in his van. I jumped at the chance.

The van was parked on a concrete slab in front of the North Beach apartment building where Alan lived. Unfortunately, one of his neighbors was not at all sympathetic to lost souls struggling to sort out their lives. To Maureen, I wasn't a dharma bum; I was just a plain old bum. Whenever she went out or came home, she'd see me sitting in the back of the van doing God-knows-what, and it was driving her up the wall. But I didn't know that.

I fasted a lot that spring—sometimes for spiritual reasons, sometimes because I didn't have any money. In order to eat, I'd been slowly selling off my possessions, but I was running out of things that anybody wanted to buy. Free food made me happier than anything else in the world.

Now, just outside the van grew a loquat tree. The fruit of the loquat is a small, juicy yellow ball. I'd never eaten loquats before, and I thought they were delicious. As the fruit on the lowest limbs ripened, I picked and ate it. Once I'd eaten all the fruit within reach, I started climbing the tree. As the days passed, I climbed higher and higher, until one morning I reached the top. Maureen was washing dishes and happened to glance out her kitchen window at the very moment my head popped into view. My sudden, jack-in-the-box appearance first frightened and then infuriated her. It was the last straw. She ran next door and demanded that Alan kick me out of the van. Alan didn't want to do it, but he had no choice. That evening he gave me the bad news.

It was a heavy blow. I'd had no inkling that there was any problem. The books I was studying insist that it's an error to shirk hardship, no matter how severe the hardship might be. You have to put your trust in the intelligence and benevolence of the Path, which is the course your life takes if you allow events to unfold naturally. If I was to be something more than a dilettante, I had to apply what I was studying to my life. But that seemed to mean heading out onto the streets, and I didn't want to go. Having no idea what else to do, I simply continued living in the van, hoping that a solution might appear before the ax fell.

It didn't take Maureen long to figure out that I was stalling. One morning she dragged Alan down to the van and demanded that he make me leave. Wanting to delay the inevitable for as long as possible, I asked her if I could consult the *I Ching* first. She threw up her hands at my idiocy, but allowed me this last request.

"Okay. But then you *have* to go."

I pulled out my three Chinese coins and threw them into the air six times, writing down the number indicated by each toss. I looked in the index to see which hexagram I'd received, turned to the page in the book, and began reading slowly and carefully. Alan and Maureen stood at the sliding side door and watched me in silence. I felt like a zoo animal. After a few minutes had passed without a move on my part, Maureen grew impatient.

"Well? What does it say?"

I'd received the thirty-third hexagram, "Retreat," with special emphasis on the first line.

AT THE TAIL IN RETREAT. THIS IS DANGEROUS.
ONE MUST NOT WISH TO UNDERTAKE ANYTHING.
In a retreat it is advantageous to be at the front. Here one is at the back, in immediate contact with the pursuing enemy. This is dangerous, and under such circumstances it is not advisable to undertake anything. Keeping still is the easiest way of escaping the threatening danger.

I had no idea what to tell her. It seemed impossibly rude to read it out loud. So I summed up the oracle's counsel in what I thought to be a diplomatic manner.

"It says that for the time being I should do nothing."

Maureen tilted her head curiously to one side, trying to make sense out of my words. Suddenly, her face flushed and she began shouting angrily at Alan.

"Do nothing? What does he mean, *do nothing?* Is he leaving? Is he *leaving?* You have to make him leave! *Now!"*

I didn't want to cause Alan any more trouble. I gathered together my few remaining possessions and, avoiding their eyes, climbed out of the van and headed silently toward the street.

It was a beautiful spring day—fresh, clear, and warm—but I was only dimly aware of it. All my attention was focused on trying to keep the lid on my growing panic. I felt that I should stop somewhere and try to calm down. Two blocks down the street was Washington Square, a big, tree-lined lawn. I threw my backpack and sleeping bag to the ground and sat down. The square was dotted with small groups of neighborhood people sunning themselves, chatting, and throwing Frisbees. I wanted to walk up to somebody and ask for help, but I didn't know what to say. Relaxing on the grass wasn't doing me any good. On the contrary, my anxiety had only grown. Then I noticed a man rooting through a trash can for something to eat. Was that where I was heading? The thought drove me right back onto my feet. I grabbed my gear and set out on a restless circling of the neighborhood, looking for a door to safety.

After a couple of hours of aimless walking, the hunger in my belly began to distract me. I had to figure out what to do. I couldn't steal, and panhandling was out of the question. I'd tried it once in Berkeley, just as an experiment, and the first person I approached had spit in my face. I could have called my parents, and they would have helped, but I needed to find my own way. While thinking over my dilemma, I spotted a nickel laying at the base of a parking meter. I took the coin as a cue and started hunting for more. After an hour of trolling the gutters, I'd gathered enough change to buy a roll from a nearby bakery.

Having pacified my belly, my thoughts turned to the question of where I was going to sleep. It had to be a place in which I'd be completely hidden. I wasn't worried about getting beaten up; I felt more threatened by the humiliation of someone finding me asleep in an alley. The only patches of shrubbery I'd seen so far were in Washington Square, and they weren't thick enough to conceal me. I roamed the neighborhood for several more hours, but nothing looked suitable. By late afternoon, my hips and legs ached from fatigue.

The odd thing is that only a year earlier, if someone had told me that I'd be penniless and living on the streets of North Beach, I would have found it *reassuring*. Back then, I had an idealistic—you might say romantic—view of life on the street, which was tied to an idea I had about consciousness. Since I was a young boy, I'd been fascinated that

I could see and hear and have thoughts. I believed that there were levels to the mind higher than what I experienced in my day-to-day life, and I'd developed an elaborate theory about how one attained those higher levels.

There seemed to be an archetypal story: As a youth, the artist inevitably reached a crisis point. When that happened, the correct, time-honored thing to do was to hit the road. It could be the highway or the street; it didn't matter. The important thing was that he abandon all his old comforts and means of support. He had to descend to the bottom, where he was forced to come face-to-face with his fears. At that point, utterly alone and reduced to his essence, he met his muse, a beautiful woman whom he loved and who loved him. He then had a life-altering experience that kicked open the door to the mind's most magical levels.

I found corroborating evidence in works like Jack Kerouac's *On the Road,* Bob Dylan's "Like A Rolling Stone," Walt Whitman's "Song of the Open Road," and Henry Miller's account of his life on the streets of Paris. When I discovered the Van Morrison album *Astral Weeks,* all the loose ends came together for me. Most of the songs take place on the backstreets of Belfast, Northern Ireland, and they depict romantic love as something profoundly mystical. Then I came upon the poet Arthur Rimbaud, who was probably the source of this idea of squalor as the path to becoming a visionary. He'd certainly gone farther than anyone else in trying to live it out. So I was convinced that there was a more-or-less secret fraternity of enlightened bohemian artists. I wanted to be one—I believed it was the highest thing you could be—but I had strong doubts as to whether I would ever find the courage to take the risks. Reading about the disastrous course that Rimbaud's life took made me think twice; still, not to try was to be for all my life a failure. So I'd kept inching my way toward the street.

When I started meditating and reading Eastern philosophy, I saw that what I'd been trying to suss out had nothing at all to do with art. It was, in fact, a skewed version of the homeless monk's quest for enlightenment—Gary Snyder's dharma bum. But the dharma bum doesn't seek the bottom; he's a mountain climber. The gutter as the source of enlightenment had been an invention of the artists. One reason I'd encountered the idea of homelessness as leading to wisdom was that the artists I loved had been interested in Eastern philosophies. But the homeless seeker is a universal archetype, not specifically Eastern, so traces of the character appear naturally in the work of anyone looking for a deeper awareness. That I was able to recognize any of this was no consolation, though. It had all been a big misunderstanding! I didn't want to be a dharma bum. I wanted to have a girlfriend and to be happy.

North Beach sits on the lower part of Telegraph Hill's west slope, and before night fell, I found a suitable place to sleep in shrubbery on the hill's summit. The next morning, I crawled out of my sleeping bag, dusted myself off, and made my way back down to the streets. Although I'd been living in North Beach for seven months, I'd been a hermit the entire time, so I didn't know the neighborhood very well. When I was growing up, it had been a legendary place—the home of the Beats, the Greenwich Village of the West Coast. Many of the heroes of my youth—Jack Kerouac, Allen Ginsberg, Gregory Corso, Lenny Bruce—had walked or still did walk its streets. City Lights Bookstore, one of bohemia's holiest places, is in North Beach. When I was growing up, the hippies were happening, but I got into the Beats, too. Culturally, I fell somewhere in between the two. I felt the Beats were too down sometimes, while the hippies were too light and airy. But those were the extreme ends. At the center, I saw them as essentially one movement.

I started my day once again by looking for coins in the gutter along Grant Avenue. Grant is a narrow street lined on both sides with three-story Edwardians. The top two floors contained the apartments and cheap residential hotels where the locals lived, while the ground floors had small shops, bars, restaurants, and cafés. North Beach is where San Francisco comes to party, and the evening before, as happened almost every evening, there had been crowds of people eating and drinking and dropping the change that I was now scrounging for. As soon as I'd gathered the twenty-five cents I needed to buy a roll, I hustled over to the Italian bakery. Curiously, the woman who took my order began walking up and down behind the counter, stopping at the different bins and filling a large bag with breads and pastries. She had a strong Italian accent, so I assumed she'd misunderstood me. When she returned, I gave her the twenty-five cents. She handed me the bag and then moved on to her next customer. I was flabbergasted. I hurried out of the bakery, afraid that she'd made a mistake and would realize it before I made it out the door.

I went straight to Washington Square, sat down on the grass, and examined the bag's contents. I couldn't believe what she'd given me. It wasn't even day-old bread; it was fresh stuff. It had been awhile since I'd been able to eat my fill, so I gorged myself. Then, for the first time since getting kicked out of the van, I allowed myself to relax a little.

The bag of bread lasted me an entire day, but the next morning I had to figure out again how I was going to eat. It had worked two days in a row, so I started hunting for change. I hit pay dirt—a quarter—and returned to the bakery. A different woman served me this time—another Italian—and again I asked for a roll. To my astonishment, she went through the same routine as the woman of the day before: looking through the different bins and filling up a large bag with breads and pastries. There were five middle-aged Italian women who worked in that bakery. Over the next few weeks, I discovered that all but one of them were good for that bag. The nicest one was Maria. She was dignified and gracious in an Old World sort of way. She had a big heart, and she always smiled when she dealt with me. The bakery women had one unspoken rule: I couldn't just come in and ask for the bag. I had to buy at least one thing. During my first weeks on the street, I depended on them for my survival. If they were aware of it, they never let it show. They always treated me the same way they treated their other customers.

The kind treatment I received at the bakery was a surprise because one of the very first things I learned on the street was that I'd become invisible. People looked past me as though I didn't exist. But if I ever wanted a little attention, all I had to do was enter a place of business. Some places were more tolerant than others. Cafés that were busy, noisy, and only had counter service provided the most anonymity, and I started spending part of my day in them. Besides needing a break from the wind and sun, there was always the possibility that I might get lucky with a meal. I got tossed out of one place for not spending any money. One of the other cafés, though, was a godsend. Like most North Beach coffeehouses, Caffe Malvina was owned by an Italian, a Sicilian immigrant named Franco Bruno. Franco was a quiet man, and one of the kindest people in the neighborhood. Occasionally customers would leave behind partially uneaten meals, and, if people at nearby tables were sufficiently distracted by their newspapers or their conversation, I'd pick the food off the abandoned plates. Franco knew what I was doing, but he never said anything to me. Every now and then, he'd need someone to run an errand, so he'd ask if I'd like to earn a meal. I saw him help others, too. He never made a big deal out of it. Years after Franco died, his son told me that Franco was from a middle-class family that had fallen on hard times during World War II. After the war was over, he'd come to America, worked hard, and lifted himself up by his bootstraps. But he wasn't contemptuous of those who hadn't done that. He had enough wisdom to recognize that poverty was simply a fact of life, not something inherently shameful.

The people who gave me the most trouble were my fellow, native-born Americans. All my life I'd been treated as just another white, middle-class, regular guy; so it was a matter of disbelief for me that I was now generally despised as one of the hated homeless. Even a lot of the supposedly hip people looked down on me. Some folks went out of their way to be rude. One hot day I was uncomfortably thirsty, so I pumped up my courage and entered a bar. I asked the bar owner—a distinguished-looking, white-haired gentleman—if I could have a glass of water. He tilted his head back and looked down at me through his bifocals.

"You got some ID?"

He seemed serious, so I dug my passport out of my backpack and handed it to him. He examined it skeptically and then handed it back.

"We don't serve water here," he said. Then he turned and walked away.

The longer I was on the street, the more important it became to conserve my energy. It was tiring walking all the way up Telegraph Hill every night. Right next to Caffe Malvina was a narrow alley, Cadell Place, and I was spending so much of my day in the café that the alley was beginning to look inviting as a place to sleep. With the passage of time, I no longer felt quite so strongly the stigma of being homeless. I had to sleep *somewhere,* so it might as well be in the alley. I slept in Cadell Place for a couple of weeks without any problem, until one morning I was awakened by a persistent rapping on my feet. I stuck my head out of my sleeping bag and discovered two cops looming over me. One of them was hitting my feet with a baton. He gave me an exaggerated smile and started talking in a mock cheerful voice.

"Good morning! How ya doin', pal?"

He paused, giving me a chance to clear the fog out of my brain and understand what was happening.

"Guess what. I got news for you. You're not gonna be sleepin' in this alley anymore."

He paused again to study the effect of his words. I just lay there frozen and stared at him blankly. His voice then turned mildly threatening. "If I find you here again, you're going to jail." With that, he and his partner turned and left.

I jumped out of my bag and quickly started pulling my gear together. I'd barely stepped out of the alley when some hippie-looking guy stopped me.

"Hey, man. You oughta go to the roof of the Tower Hotel. That's where everybody else is sleepin'."

"Where's the Tower Hotel?"

He pointed to the corner. "Turn left on Grant. It's halfway up the block." He gave me instructions on where to go once inside the building and assured me that I wouldn't have any problem. Then he continued on his way.

I'd walked past the Tower Hotel's entrance many times, but it was so anonymous that I'd never noticed it. The door was locked, so I hung around and waited for someone to exit the building. A few minutes later, the door swung open. It was a guy my own age. We both looked pretty much the same—shoulder-length hair, beard, and blue jeans—the only differences being that I was slightly dirty and carrying everything I owned. That I was "street" didn't faze him. He held the door open for me, and I started up the stairs. I tried to move with absolute silence, but stealth was pointless: At the top of the staircase I had to walk by a small group of tenants who were talking in the hallway. As I passed them, they gave me quick, indifferent nods and went on with their conversation. I continued to the end of the hall and went up a back staircase that climbed in darkness to a small rooftop hut. There, I opened a banged-up metal door and stepped back out into the morning light. At the far end of the roof stood a group of men laughing and passing around a bottle of wine. They greeted me, and then, like the folks in the hall, resumed their conversation, leaving me to wander around the rooftop.

While exploring the roof, I had a brainstorm. There was a big pile of old carpets up there and a fifteen-foot-long rope that stretched from the staircase hut at one end to a vent pipe at the other. The carpets were large and heavy, but the rope was thick and taut. I spread out one carpet beneath the length of rope and threw another over it. Then I weighted down the upper carpet's corners with pieces of junk that I found laying around the roof. Less than an hour after my arrival, I had a tent. My rooftop neighbors came over to check out the new place. They all thought it was very cool and funny. Word of my tent quickly spread through the hotel, and it wasn't long before I received a visit from the hotel manager. I was worried I was going to lose my new place, but she just wanted to see what I'd made. She came inside, and we had a friendly chat. April was a veteran of the road herself, and she understood how badly I needed that tent. Without actually saying so, she made it clear that I was welcome to stay.

My arrival on the roof of the Tower Hotel marked the end of the three months that I was literally on the street. But for the next fourteen years I was always just one step away from returning to it. I was committed to a spiritual journey, which, as I understood it, precluded me from taking regular work. And regardless of any philosophical principle, employers want an address and a phone number, and I didn't have either one. I still had to eat, though, and since odd jobs allowed me the most freedom, I accepted them whenever they came my way. It started with running errands. As I made friends around the neighborhood, some had me substitute for them at their jobs. I filled in for dishwashers, café countermen, and bar swampers. There were a lot of single mothers in North Beach, and I baby-sat for some of them. Occasionally I'd paint a room. I cleaned apartments, too. I spent several years teaching myself Italian, eventually becoming fluent enough that I was able to tutor. None of my jobs paid well—in a good year, I'd make, at most, $2,000—but they kept me fed. Since I didn't make enough to pay rent, I lived in a series of nooks and crannies. I slept in a stairwell, a basement, a rooftop laundry hut, a storeroom. Occasionally, I got to house-sit. A girlfriend put me up. Every spring I'd tell myself that this had to be the year that I'd find my real work. If I'd known beforehand how long I was going to be living that way, I don't know that I could have endured it. I was lucky to have friends who accepted my way of life without question.

My biggest regret about that time isn't that I was so poor, but that I stopped meditating. Once ensconced in my rooftop tent, I found that all my momentum had dissipated. I didn't really understand everything that I'd been through at my sister's and in the van. I had thousands of pieces to a big puzzle, and they were all in a jumble. At the time, the only thing I could see to do was to start sorting them out intellectually. So instead of meditating, I went back to thinking on the run. But it was decidedly inferior to what I'd been doing.

I wasn't alone in having lost my momentum. The spirit was fading from the remaining bohemian pockets of North Beach. And it wasn't just North Beach; the counterculture was dying everywhere. There are people who rejoice at that, but I considered it a sad thing. For all of its faults, the counterculture had been a community of people struggling to find an approach to life that was based on something other than materialism. A lot of those same people were now withdrawing to their apartments and losing themselves in their television sets. A new generation was moving into North Beach, which went from hippies to yuppies. Few people in the new crew had much awareness of the neighborhood's past. North Beach was close to the financial district, it looked cool, and that was all that mattered to them. Because they had money, rents soared. Even a funky little residential hotel room got beyond the reach of a lot of the longtime neighborhood people. Over the next few years, most of my old friends—my support system— were forced out of San Francisco. I had to wonder how much longer I could continue living there.

One spring, just as I was about to lose the storeroom I was sleeping in, my life took a completely unexpected turn. A friend told me about an ad she'd seen. An elderly woman, Maxine Parish, was looking for someone to clean her house, run errands, and drive for her. In exchange, she was offering a studio apartment next door to her home. We met, and Maxine liked me, so I got the position. The studio was a huge improvement over where I'd been living. It had a toilet, a shower, and electricity. But the best part of the deal was its location in the gardens on Telegraph Hill's east side.

Telegraph Hill rises out of the northeast corner of the peninsula on which the city is built. It's the corner that represents San Francisco to the rest of the world. The base of the hill's southern flank is only two blocks from the first of the downtown high-rises. At the hill's southwest corner is Chinatown; along its west slope, North Beach. On the north side lies the tourist sprawl of Fisherman's Wharf; on the east side, the old piers of the port.

When Europeans first arrived, Telegraph Hill was largely barren. The soil was rocky and sandy, and the only things that grew in it naturally were grasses, wildflowers, and scrub. The hill was originally larger and more gently contoured than it is today. When the gold rush of 1849 got under way, San Francisco became an important port, and because ships bringing supplies had little cargo for the return trip, rock was cut from the hill's east face to provide ballast for their departure. The hill received its name in 1850 when a semaphore, a tall pole with two arms attached to the top, was placed on the hill's summit. A lookout would adjust the position of the semaphore arms, relaying to the townspeople below that a ship was arriving and what type it was.

In the 1850s, San Francisco's population exploded. The hillside above the piers was soon covered by a patchwork of immigrant, working-class neighborhoods. There were a few nice cottages for ship captains and the like, but most of the homes were cheaply built shacks and shanties occupied by the longshoremen, stevedores, fishermen, riggers, and warehousemen who worked the waterfront docks. Few of the buildings lasted long. Some were too flimsy, while others fell down the cliffs after being undermined by the quarry operations below. The quarrying continued until 1914, well after the need for ship ballast had passed. All the blasting and digging left most of the hill's east side too steep for roads, and except for one street, Montgomery, the only way of moving around the area was along a network of wooden staircases and dirt paths. It was little more than a slum. There was trash everywhere, and sewage flowed through open ditches. Hill residents kept pigs, chickens, and goats. There were even gangs.

In the 1920s, the cheap rents and magnificent views of San Francisco Bay attracted the city's bohemian artists. Then, in the 1930s, as has happened time after time, the artists' presence made the place attractive to people of means. Streets were paved, the old cottages were renovated, new apartment buildings went up, and many of the artists got priced out. In 1933, the hill was crowned with one of San Francisco's best-known landmarks: Coit Tower. It's the most beautiful use of concrete I've ever seen, with twenty-four vertical rows of fluting and a series of arches cut into its top at the observation deck. It reminds me of a Greek column, but with softer aspects that make it seem as though it came out of a Maxfield Parrish painting. It has a serene, semiclassical air that lends the hill a sense of timelessness.

The tower is 180 feet tall, and to make sure that it would always rise well above the surrounding trees, it was set on a 32-foot base. The city also passed an ordinance that protected the tower from ever having any tall structures built near it, so that today the buildings on Telegraph Hill retain a more human scale than those in other parts of the city.

The most wonderful aspect of the hill's east side is its immense gardens. Two long staircases, a block apart, climb the hill from bottom to top. The lots on either side of each staircase have been planted so that today there exist two wide corridors of garden stretching up the hill. My new home was on the more northerly of the two staircases. Technically, the staircase is Greenwich Street, but for the length of its 387-step, two-block-long ascent, Greenwich is only five feet wide and open only to foot traffic. Locals call it the Greenwich Steps. The staircase is bisected by Montgomery, and I was moving into Greenwich's lower block, which still had many of the old shacks and cottages. The combination of old homes and massive gardens gave the neighborhood a magical quality that matched the image I'd had of San Francisco when I was living in Seattle. It was easy to imagine that behind each door lived a writer, a painter, or a Buddhist.

The studio was a single room jerry-rigged into the lower half of what my neighbors usually called a cottage but was, in reality, a two-story shack. No one knows when it was built, but it begins to appear on maps as early as 1886. The cottage was built on a slope in such a way that two vertical support beams were needed to hold up its northeast corner. This created an open space beneath the cottage that was twenty feet long and twenty feet wide. At some point before 1910, this lower area was floored and walled off. The room had been uninhabited for several years, and the first time I opened its door, I was hit with a strong smell of mold. There was no insulation, and I could feel moist earth behind the walls. The carpet was imbedded with mildew, and the closet was so damp that it was unusable. The bathroom walls were covered with sheets of mold. There were cobwebs everywhere. The building had no real foundation, so the walls were lined with cracks. The circuit breakers blew and the plumbing backed up. Most people would have considered it unlivable, but I thought it was paradise. After years of living at the extreme margins, I finally had a secure place.

Above me, on the main floor of the cottage, lived Helen Arpin. Having lived in the cottage for nearly thirty years, Helen was one of the hill's old-timers. When I moved in, Maxine warned me that her tenant was crusty and somewhat argumentative. In Helen's view, people were either right-wing Republicans like herself or socialists. Once she was escorting around North Beach some out-of-town friends who decided they wanted to visit the famous City Lights Bookstore. She took them there, but refused to set foot inside "that communist bookstore." Politically, Maxine was somewhere to the left, figured that I was, too, and she asked me to avoid getting into political conversations with Helen. I did, and she turned out to be a good neighbor.

In spite of her age—she was almost ninety—Maxine disliked depending on others, and she made few demands on me. Most of the time I was free to do whatever I liked. Shortly after I moved in, someone gave me a bicycle. I was tired of San Francisco—I hadn't been outside the city limits in years—so I was thrilled to have the means of getting away. I became a cycling fanatic, eventually building my strength to the point that I was taking daylong rides of eighty and a hundred miles. The studio had a small front deck, and my favorite way to recover from a long ride was to sit outside and watch the garden's birds and butterflies. I especially liked the hummingbirds. They were fearless.

Sometimes one would hover right in front of my face. The main attraction for me, though, was the parrots.

I saw the first group of four parrots in 1990, two years after I moved in. In October of the same year, their numbers increased to around a dozen. I didn't know what to make of it. As the population grew, so did their racket. They were extraordinarily feisty, and fought with each other almost constantly. Most of it looked playful, but there were occasions when it seemed to take a more serious turn. They'd go at each other on the power lines, breast to breast, flapping their wings to maintain balance while jousting with their beaks and screaming maniacally. They were expert climbers. Using their beaks as a third hand, they could shinny up tree limbs with impressive speed. I used to watch them climb one tree, whose berries grew right at the tips of thin, erect limbs. As the parrots neared their goal, their weight bent the limbs completely over, and they ate the berries while hanging upside down.

Just before Christmas that year, an unusual cold spell hit the Bay Area. It rarely freezes in San Francisco, but one night the temperature fell to twenty-eight degrees. As it grew colder, I started worrying about the parrots. I'd been impressed by their tenacity, but it seemed to me that an actual freeze would surely be their doom. The flock usually flew in from the south around dawn. I got out of bed just before the sun rose and went out onto my deck to wait and watch. The sky was absolutely clear, and there were small patches of ice everywhere. I'd never seen ice in San Francisco. I was briskly pacing back and forth, hugging myself to keep warm, when the sun peaked out over the East Bay Hills. At that very moment, I heard the flock's intense screams break through the still, cold air. The sound rang out more militantly than usual, as though they were proclaiming a glorious victory and chastising all doubters.

Mansion on the Hill

I worked for Maxine for four years. During the last two, she began having serious memory lapses. She lived alone, so her friends worried about her. A cousin tried to persuade Maxine to accept a live-in caretaker, but she refused. Because I was a man and not a family member, there were limits to the kind of help I could provide. And even when I could help, she often insisted on doing things herself. One afternoon, a week before Christmas, she walked down to North Beach to buy some liver for her cat. On her way back up the hill, she made a wrong turn and wandered into an unfamiliar neighborhood. A little later, a passerby found her lying in a driveway with a broken shoulder.

The day after her fall, Maxine's cousin Edna flew up from Shreveport, Louisiana, to take charge of Maxine's affairs. The two cousins already had an agreement in place that should it ever become necessary, Edna would act as Maxine's legal guardian. The doctor told Edna that Maxine was probably suffering from Alzheimer's, and that she shouldn't be living alone. Edna couldn't take her cousin to Shreveport, so, having no other alternative, she put Maxine in a San Francisco nursing home. Edna needed someone to live in the big house behind my studio while she consulted a lawyer about the estate, and asked if I was willing to do it. I wouldn't be staying there long, she warned me, just for the few months it would take to resolve some legal issues so the house could be sold. To add to my new level of comfort, Edna gave me the keys to Maxine's car. She even left a credit card for gas. Everybody kept telling me how lucky I was when, in fact, I hadn't been more miserable in years.

I was feeling stagnant in every area of my life. Shortly after moving into the house I'd started reading *Zen Mind, Beginner's Mind,* by the Japanese Zen master Shunryu Suzuki-roshi. I liked the book, but I couldn't make much sense out of it. It frustrated me that after twenty years I still had such large holes in my understanding. I would never have real control over the course my life took until my understanding was good, but my practice was nonexistent, and Suzuki-roshi was continually making the point that understanding comes only with practice. I heard him, and I agreed, but I couldn't overcome my feeling of inertia. Edna was concerned about my apparent lack of direction, and kept phoning to ask what my plans were. I had no idea what I was going to do, but I didn't want Edna worrying about me. I told her I had several plans I was working on, that it was just a matter of deciding which one was best. Her calls kept reminding me that I'd soon be losing the security of the estate, and I felt so squeezed by the uncertainties of my situation that I finally threw myself into another urgent round of self-examination. I started meditating again.

I felt that I needed to make some decisions immediately. What did I really need? In a few days, I settled on a list of three things that I believed I couldn't do without. First, I needed a mate. I was forty-two years old, and that I still hadn't found the woman with whom I wanted to spend the rest of my life was beginning to haunt me. But how could I be with another if I couldn't even support myself? So my second wish was easy and long-standing: the means to support myself—work that I loved.

Although my first two wishes are common to most people, my third was a bit less so. By birth, I was urban—but just barely. I'd grown up in western Washington State, on the border between suburbia and farmland. My favorite childhood memories are of my family's camping trips, especially those we took to a cabin that my grandmother owned in the Gifford Pinchot National Forest. It's a wilderness area in the Cascade Range, thick with Douglas fir and home to cougars, bears, and deer. The air was thinner, and the place had a purity and superreality that I loved. My musical ambitions had pulled me away from nature and into cities. I'd been living in San Francisco for twenty years now, and I didn't see what more I could possibly get out of it. I was fed up with cities. I wanted mountains, rivers, and trees again. I wanted to experience wild nature.

I had no clear path to any of my goals, but I believed that inner struggle in and of itself would bring me what I wanted. Besides meditating, I got into a big self-improvement program. I quit drinking coffee and alcohol and became a strict vegetarian. I started studying yoga from a book. I eliminated all diversions: television, magazines, music—anything I did simply to kill time. There was one change that was more difficult than the others. I had a few friends left in North Beach from whom I distanced myself. It wasn't that I disliked them—they'd been good to me—but in order to survive on the street, I'd had to be obliging. Always careful not to say anything that might offend anyone, I'd ended up with a different personality for almost everybody I knew. But I wanted to make a strong stand in my life, and to do that I had to be who I really was. So I cut off everyone with whom I'd developed a character that was false. And because affability had become such an ingrained characteristic, I had a hard time being myself with women who interested me; so I made a vow not to cut my hair until I found my mate. I figured that whatever way my hair grew, it was an aspect of who I really was, and the woman who loved me wouldn't care whether it was long or short.

Months passed, and there wasn't a single development toward any of the things I wanted. I responded by increasing the time I spent meditating. I was very disciplined and utterly humorless. More weeks went by and still nothing changed. I started feeling frustrated, and then angry. Except for going out to do an occasional odd job, I was always alone inside the house. I started breaking down into tears almost every day—huge, hot drops like I'd never felt before.

I couldn't spend every hour of every day wrestling with my problems. Occasionally, I had to get away from them. One of the pleasures that the house offered me was a new perspective on the parrot flock. The house was above and just behind my old studio, at a point where the hillside begins a steep drop down toward the Greenwich Steps. I felt like I was living on a high precipice. Sitting at the dining room's north-facing windows, I was slightly above and about thirty feet away from where the parrots perched on the power lines along Greenwich. I could see now that nearly all of them were in pairs. The flock population had increased to around twenty, and their excitability had grown with their numbers. Sometimes they'd start up an intense bout of screaming that would go on and on until they left the garden.

Another pastime was browsing the bookshelves. The house was filled with hundreds of books. One day I came upon a book that gave me a start. It was Roger Tory Peterson's *Field Guide to Western Birds,* the first hardbound book I ever owned. My grandmother had given me a copy when I was eight years old. This was the same edition, too, with the same greenish-blue cover and dark blue drawing of a swallow. It was an eerie feeling to hold that book in my hand again. Long ago I'd gotten into it enough to choose a favorite—the cedar waxwing— and then I put it away. It stayed on my shelf for years, though. Occasionally, in an idle moment, I'd lie on my bed and leaf through it. The text was a series of lists, information on size, markings, voice, range, and the like—uninteresting reading for a young boy. Mostly, I looked at the drawings.

Seeing the book reminded me of a time ten years earlier, when I'd first started wishing I could leave San Francisco and move to the country. At the same time, I'd been trying to develop an interest in poetry. My two interests led me to Gary Snyder. He was one of the main Beat poets as well as an important figure within the hippie counterculture. He'd had a lot to do with the Western interest in Zen Buddhism, having gone so far as to study in a monastery in Japan. After he returned to the United States, he moved to California's Sierra Nevada foothills, where he became one of the leading voices in the environmental movement. Over the years, I'd become disillusioned with most of the lead figures of the counterculture. But I'd attended several of Snyder's public readings in San Francisco and left each one feeling respect for him. Unlike a lot of alternative culture types, he was a mature man, an adult.

I took my reading of Gary Snyder very seriously. I tried to understand each idea, agreeing with this one, disagreeing with that one, carefully considering the others. In *Turtle Island,* he points out that human beings have always known the intimate details of any landscape they've inhabited—the animals, the flowers, the trees. But Americans arrived as invaders and rushed across the continent without ever really settling in. Snyder was saying that we needed to slow down and get to know the land. The more I read him, the more zealous I became about leaving San Francisco.

One day, while reading *The Real Work,* a collection of interviews with Snyder, I came upon this statement: "The city is just as natural as the country, let's not forget it. There's nothing in the universe that's not natural by definition. One of the poems I like best in *Turtle Island* is "Night Herons," which is about the naturalness of San Francisco." His words made me uncomfortable. There was an implication for me that I caught immediately: If I were really sincere about knowing nature, I'd start right where I was living. He'd even named as his example the very city that I wished to escape. It was a pure, organic idea, the kind I always want to follow out. Still, I tried to ignore his point. My opposition wasn't rooted in any deeply held principle. It was more a lack of imagination. I simply couldn't picture myself walking around North Beach observing, for example, its bird life. That wasn't experiencing nature, it was *bird watching*. And anyway, as far as I knew, they were all pigeons, sparrows, and seagulls—birds that seemed unworthy of serious attention. The only other animals I'd seen were cats, dogs, and the occasional rat or raccoon. All the trees were planted—not natural—and most of them looked barren and forlorn to me. I kept returning to my original complaint: I was tired of the place. I had the nagging sense that Snyder was right, though, and that if I were sincere I'd begin my study in San Francisco. But I never found an approach that felt creative to me. My enthusiasm for learning about the natural world waned then, and I gradually quit reading Gary Snyder.

Sitting on the shelf next to Peterson's guide were two more birding manuals and a pair of binoculars. I wondered if I should give birding another try. It seemed like it might be more interesting to me now. The garden attracted a wide variety of birds: blue jays, hummingbirds, doves, and a bunch of others that, although I had no idea what they were, seemed faintly exotic. I'd even seen an owl once. There were the parrots, too, of course, but they weren't native, so I thought I probably shouldn't pay much attention to them.

I kept the binoculars and the field guides on the sill of the dining room window, and every time I saw a bird, I'd try to identify it. It turned out that most of the birds I'd thought sparrows were actually house finches. The blue jays were technically scrub jays, and the doves were called mourning doves. Most of the hummingbirds seemed to be of the species known as Anna's, but they were so quick I couldn't be sure. Once I'd learned to identify the garden's most common birds, I began looking up the more unusual species. I saw Townsend's warblers, kestrels, mockingbirds, northern flickers, towhees, hooded orioles, and white-crowned sparrows, among others. There were surprisingly large numbers of crows and ravens, but I had trouble telling them apart. I could never remember which had the straight tail and which the delta-shaped tail.

Identifying birds was all right, but not nearly as absorbing as I'd hoped. Whenever I got bored with it, I'd turn the binoculars on the parrots. They were always good for a laugh. They would fly into the garden with their nutty urgency, a united, harmonious group. Then, the instant they landed, fights would break out. Sometimes while fighting they'd get tangled up in each other's feet and fall from the lines, struggling to disengage before both birds crashed to the ground. They were affectionate with one another, too. Pairs had long preening sessions, at the end of which they'd puff up their feathers and sit cheek to cheek.

The mystery of how they got here was still eating at me. I asked people who'd been in the neighborhood for a long time what they knew, and everybody had a different answer. They'd come from a ship docked at the port; they were smuggled birds who had escaped from a downtown warehouse; a pet store had burned down, and the birds were released; they belonged to a couple who got transferred to New York and couldn't take the birds with them, so the couple let them loose from the top of Telegraph Hill; smugglers released them from their helicopter when the feds closed in on their secret drop-off point. Some told me they'd been around only for the four years I'd been seeing them, while others insisted that they'd been here at least twenty. Everything people told me was so contradictory that I starting wanting to know at least one thing about them that was true. Now that I was accustomed to the routine of bird identification, I thought that at the very least I should be able to determine which species they were.

One evening I went down to a bookstore, sat on the floor, and started leafing through a parrot book. I had a clear mental image of them, and for more than an hour I compared photographs until I narrowed it down to one species: the cherry-headed conure. What was a conure? Did that mean they weren't parrots? But this was a book about parrots, so they must be. The book noted that the cherry-headed conure was from southwestern Ecuador and northwestern Peru and gave information on its size, weight, and appearance, but had little else to say.

I was pleased with myself for having figured it out. Nobody else I'd talked to knew what they were, so it felt like a personal triumph of sorts. Two days after my big breakthrough, I was at the dining room windows trying to identify native birds when the parrots flew into the juniper tree near my old studio. It was an unusually foggy and windy day. San Francisco fog is usually high—like rain clouds—but this day it almost touched the ground. The wind was blowing the fog through the juniper branches in beautifully patterned swirls, and as I watched, my eye landed on something that astounded me: a parrot with a *blue* head. He was the same size as the other parrots and, except for that blue head, entirely green. He was strangely cool and mystical looking, not all tropical and fiery like the cherry heads. Moments later, I was stunned to see yet another blue-headed parrot. *Where were all these parrots coming from?* As soon as the flock left the garden, I hustled back down to the bookstore and compared photographs in the parrot book again. The two new birds were called blue-crowned conures.

After seeing the blue crowns, I didn't find it quite so astonishing when just a week or two later I discovered a third species. There were around half a dozen of this new parrot. They were slightly smaller than the others, and entirely green. I studied their appearance carefully and made another trip to the bookstore. As near as I could tell, the new birds were white-eyed conures. They were strange birds who had a peculiar thing going with the cherry heads. I'd often see a white-eyed conure walk up to a cherry head, puff up her head feathers, and stare intently at the larger bird. The cherry head often seemed annoyed, but eventually he'd take the beak of the white-eyed conure into his own and start jerking her head up and down. It was hysterically funny to me. The white-eyed conures obviously loved having their heads jerked, since they begged the cherry heads to do it again and again.

My ignorance about the crazy white-eyed conures lasted only a few days. I found a book specifically about conures, and reading it I realized that the birds were not white-eyed conures, but baby cherry heads. The bizarre behavior was the babies begging to be fed and the parents regurgitating food into their beaks. The idea that the parrots were breeding in San Francisco would have seemed preposterous to me, so I'd never even considered the possibility.

I was getting so bored with identifying the native birds that I was on the verge of hanging it up. Then one afternoon I stopped at the local grocery and, on a whim, bought a bag of wild bird seed. Maybe if I could entice the birds to come closer they'd interest me more. When I got home, I filled a large clay bowl with seeds and set it out on the fire escape. Standing in the kitchen, I'd have a good view of any bird that came. Two days later, I got my first house finches, who were soon followed by the mourning doves. I watched them eat, but I wasn't sure what I was supposed to be looking for. I thought the house finches were okay, but I didn't like the mourning doves at all. There were dozens of them, and they all looked dim-witted to me. They were gluttons—big, fat eating machines. I didn't get interested in what was going on out there until the scrub jays showed up. They were more colorful than the other two species, and they had a wily look in their eyes that I liked. Whenever they left the bowl with a seed, they emitted a laughing/shrieking cry that sounded as though they thought they'd just pulled off a great heist. The bag of bird seed contained mostly millet, with a bit of sunflower thrown in. Since the scrub jays preferred the sunflower seeds and I preferred the scrub jays, I bought a new bag containing just sunflower seeds. I assumed the mourning doves would be unable to open the larger seeds, and then I'd be done with them, but I was wrong. Since they couldn't open the shells, they simply swallowed them whole. The mourning doves continued to dominate the bowl, and my interest took another nosedive. I decided to let them finish off the bag of sunflower seeds and that would be it.

But then, one October afternoon, I was standing in the kitchen eating an apple and staring idly at a pair of scrub jays perched on the bowl when one of the parrots flew over to see what the jays were eating. My heart jumped. I'd never seen the parrots anywhere near a house, so it had never occurred to me that they might come. Not wanting to frighten him, I stood absolutely motionless and watched as he dug into the seeds. A minute later, the first parrot was joined by two more. The rest of the flock was out in the garden perched on the long boughs of a seventy-foot-tall deodar cedar. When they started making noise, the three parrots on the bowl were quick to rejoin them. Moments later they all left the garden. I felt giddy about the visit from the three parrots. This was the feeling I'd been hoping to get from the native birds. I wondered if they would remember the seeds and return to the bowl. I went down to North Beach and stocked up on sunflower seeds just in case.

The next day, the entire flock landed on the fire escape. All twenty-six of them. I was ecstatic. It had been years since I'd felt that kind of joy. The day before, when the first three came to the bowl, I'd been about ten feet away from them. Since they'd been comfortable with that, I carefully maintained the same distance now. The flock started coming every day, and each time they did, I'd move a step or two closer to the Dutch door that led to the fire escape. After about a week, I was right up against it. I slowly eased myself down to the kitchen floor and sat in front of the lower window to watch. I did not go unnoticed. The parrots kept one eye trained on me at all times. Whenever I made even the smallest motion, they bolted instantly and in unison back to the trees and power lines. After a few minutes of cautious waiting, they would return one by one to resume their feasting and fighting.

The scene at the bowl was chaos. They were screaming furiously and running all around the area directly in front of me. They had large, floppy feet, and I got a big kick out of watching their clumsy, plodding runs across the fire escape floor. Their colors were luminous. The green had a shimmer that was almost psychedelic, while the red was a bright fire-engine red. I was struck by their eyes again. In a lot of the native birds I'd seen, the iris was nearly as dark as the pupil, which made the eye appear empty and impassive. But the cherry heads had a light iris, and the black pupil stood out distinctly. I could see their emotions, which were shifting constantly from playfulness to curiosity to rage. Fights were breaking out everywhere. A bird would jump up on the lip of the bowl and lunge at the bird next to him, stabbing him with his beak if there was any resistance. They used their beaks on one another quite freely. Birds perched on the bowl were often attacked from behind with a bite on the leg or wing, or a yank on the tail. The bitten bird would scream loudly and fly away. I was totally captivated. It was like watching the Three Stooges, only much funnier.

A Joyful Encounter

It was never my intention to make a big·thing out of watching the parrots. But I found all the noise and commotion so entertaining that I kept coming back to the window for "one last look." The more I watched them, the more curious I became. I was seeing some very strange activity out on the fire escape. I wanted to understand what was going on, but to do that it looked like I'd have to sort out the individual birds, which seemed impossible. They were so restless and high-strung that I couldn't imagine ever being able to keep track of them all. Even when they were holding relatively still, all the adult cherry heads looked alike to me. So did their babies. Out of the entire flock of twenty-six birds, I was able to positively identify only the two blue crowns. Their blue heads made them easy to recognize, of course, and the two birds were so different in size that I could tell them apart from each other.

I think the larger of the two would have stood out even in a flock of blue-crowned conures. There was something magnificent about him. He had a regal presence that exuded intelligence. Unlike the cherry heads, he wasn't the least bit playful. He was gentle and reserved. He was a handsome bird, and because I was able to recognize him so easily, he was the first member of the flock I named. I called him Connor because it sounded like *conure*. The cherry heads were not as impressed with Connor as I was. In fact, they barely tolerated him. Although he was slightly larger than the cherry heads, Connor was a poor fighter, and whenever he approached the seed bowl, the cherry heads would drive him away. There was another thing about Connor that intrigued me: On his left leg he wore a silver band. It had engraving on it, but from where I sat it was much too small to read. I thought that if I could get a look at that band, it might tell me something about the flock's origins.

The other blue crown was Connor's opposite in every way. She was skittish, with a mousy face and cautious bug eyes. The weakest member of the flock, she'd retreat from even the mildest threat with an injured-sounding squeal. She wasn't especially attractive, but she had a sweet and shy demeanor that quickly endeared her to me. I named her Catherine, after an unrequited love. I knew from what I'd read that it was impossible to determine the gender of either a blue crown or a cherry head by appearance. So to say that Connor was male and Catherine female were just guesses. But their behavior seemed to fit traditional ideas of the sexes. Connor was the leader of the two, and Catherine was devoted to him. Whenever they perched together, she would give him a thorough grooming, and on cold days she huddled against him for warmth. Connor and Catherine always had to wait for the others to finish eating before they were allowed on the bowl. But the cherry heads often flew out of the garden before the two blue crowns had gotten their turn, and since the pull of the flock was always stronger than their hunger, they often left without eating. I kept wishing there was something I could do to help them.

After a week or two, the flock settled into enough of a routine that the jumble of parrots became a little less confusing to me. As they grew more accustomed to my presence, they stopped demanding that I sit so still. Occasionally, I'd make a move that startled them and they'd take off for the power lines, but they always returned after just a minute or two. I noticed that some birds jumped on the bowl at the start of the feeding and stayed as long as they liked, while others had to wait for a spot to open up. I also discovered that at least five cherry heads had silver leg bands like Connor's. While the leg bands made it easier to distinguish some of the individual cherry heads, I was also beginning to recognize other, more subtle differences.

Sonny had such a distinct look that once I identified him, I never confused him with any other bird. His face was hawklike and he had a crack in his beak that ran from the tip to halfway up the center. Most of the parrots had round, friendly looking eyes, but Sonny's were slightly almond-shaped, which gave him an aspect that was similar to a scrub jay's—skeptical and cunning. But the most notable thing about Sonny was that he was a bully. The cherry heads fought among themselves almost constantly, but most of it was just squabbling or play fighting. Sonny's attacks, on the other hand, were often cold-blooded. As the weaker birds roamed the fire escape waiting for their turn at the bowl, he wandered among them, ruthlessly assaulting any bird without a nearby ally. Because of his "broken nose" and outlaw behavior, I thought of him as a parrot mafioso, so I named him after Sonny Corleone of *The Godfather*.

Despite his aggressiveness, Sonny was not allowed on the bowl with the stronger birds, although he clearly considered himself the equal of any parrot in the flock. On several occasions, I saw him stake out a position four or five feet from the bowl and bide his time. He'd stand there acting oh-so nonchalant, and then, with a sudden burst of energy, charge toward the bowl, ready to take on any bird that challenged him. It was a ridiculous sight. Parrots have short, stiff legs and long toes, and it made me laugh to watch his squat body and floppy, pigeon-toed feet trying to run as swift as the wind. The instant Sonny began his charge, two or three parrots would hop off the bowl and go intercept him. He was never a match for them, and he'd have to retreat.

Another cherry head who emerged out of the initial chaos was, like Sonny, one of the banded birds. Eric was gorgeous. He had more red feathers than any other parrot in the flock. While the cap on most of the cherry heads stopped in the middle of the top part of the skull, Eric's continued halfway down his neck. He also had a large red area around his chin—something that was completely absent in many of the cherry heads. Even the red patches on his wings were fuller. I named him after Eric the Red, the Viking. He certainly had the fierce pride of a Viking. Few birds ever hassled him, and when they did, they suffered swift retaliation. Unlike Sonny, though, Eric was generally benevolent, and seemed to be respected by the others. He always perched in the same place, the area where the bowl's lip pressed against two vertical railing bars. It was the most coveted spot because whoever perched there was actually outside the bars, and thus had a direct escape route. The other birds had to fly up and over the railing on their way out. Given the deference shown him, I wondered if Eric might be the flock's leader. But do parrot flocks have leaders? Was there a pecking order?

Answers to such questions were hard to come by. I wandered through the city's bookstores searching for information on parrots—especially parrots in the wild, and specifically on the two species represented in the flock—but I had little success. Most books dealt with parrots only as pets. I was looking for a science book that would explain in detail what the cherry-headed conure was all about, something that said, "When they do this, it means that." But the few ornithological books I found were disappointingly superficial.

I went into pet stores hoping to learn something about the flock's origins. I thought they'd be eager to talk, but few of the pet-store owners had much interest in my questions. Some even seemed to disapprove of the wild flock's existence. Eventually it occurred to me that there had to be a scientist studying the flock. How could there not be? Its presence was too bizarre. But how would I find this person?

In late November, while leafing through the newspaper, I saw a front-page photo of three cherry-headed conures perched on a power line. The headline read: PARROTS ADD GREEN TO CITY'S LOCAL COLOR. I dove into the accompanying article with the expectation of finally having the mystery solved. But no such luck. Some of the information I knew to be inaccurate. One source for the article had made the same mistake I'd made, misidentifying the baby cherry heads as white-eyed conures. The article also said that the flock roosted (slept) near Dolores Park in the city's Mission District. Dolores Park is about four miles southwest of Telegraph Hill, and the parrots were flying into the gardens from that general direction every morning, so it made some sense.

A major source for the article was the curator of birds at the San Francisco Zoo. He'd seen the parrots in Dolores Park, and he provided an explanation for their ability to survive in San Francisco. The weather wasn't an issue at all. While San Francisco isn't tropical, it's still mild enough for parrots. The real issue, he said, was the availability of food. A lot of nonnative tropical and subtropical foliage had been planted in the city's gardens, and this, along with seed from bird feeders, enabled the parrots to find food year-round. The article also contained a new detail that added to my confusion regarding the flock's history. The parrots had appeared on Telegraph Hill in Armistead Maupin's book *Tales of the City*. Since Maupin's book was written in the mid-1970s, this supported the claim that the flock had been in the city for at least twenty years. But I still couldn't quite believe it. Something didn't add up. One thing the article did make clear was that no one was studying them. That seemed so odd to me.

When the parrots first began coming to the fire escape, I kept the bowl outside all the time, and I made sure it was full whenever I left the house. I wanted them to be able to count on it. But that was putting a huge strain on my small income. Not only was I feeding the parrots, I was feeding all the other birds in the neighborhood. I didn't mind the house finches and the scrub jays so much, but the mourning doves were driving me crazy. So I started putting out the bowl only when the parrots arrived.

On clear mornings, through the living room windows, I could see them coming from about a quarter mile away. They flew in a disorganized stack, like a swarm of bees, with individual birds veering sideways, up and down, and sometimes falling off the back. Their wing beats were distinctive—stiff, shallow, and frantic—and I learned to recognize them at a glance. In spite of their graceless appearance in flight, they were surprisingly swift. At around two or three hundred yards out, I'd begin to hear them. They always sounded as though they were arguing over which way to go. As the parrots neared the garden, they'd stop their screaming and awkward flapping and become silent, graceful gliders. As they dropped from the sky, they curved their wings downward slightly, holding them rigidly in place. Sometimes I could see the wind buffeting them as they descended, but they held staunchly to their intended flight paths, executing some magnificent swoops and loops just before fluttering down onto the lines. At that point, I would carry the seed bowl out onto the fire escape, reenter the house, and sit on the kitchen floor to wait for them. They were usually reluctant to make an immediate crossing. They'd have to mull it over first. Eventually, a handful of the braver birds would come, which set off the avalanche of the rest of the flock.

The more I saw of Connor, the more he intrigued me. He often seemed disgruntled about something. In spite of his apparent discontent, he carried himself with a stately bearing. I'd never imagined birds as capable of possessing dignity, but Connor's was so palpable that it was impossible to ignore. Connor and Catherine were still having trouble getting a chance to eat, and I was still looking for a way to help them. One day, I filled a small tray with sunflower seeds and set it out against the doorsill. I had a hunch that Connor would be willing to come that close to me, but that the cherry heads would not. I was right. He came to the tray the moment he spotted it. He was just a foot away from me and seemed completely unconcerned. From a distance, I'd seen that Connor's eyes were different from those of the cherry heads, and I was able to get my first close look at them now. The outer iris was bright orange, and the inner iris—as I'd seen in many of the native birds—was nearly as dark as the pupil. In Connor's case, rather than making him look dim-witted, the dark iris gave him the appearance of inscrutability. He had unusually soft, fluffy-looking feathers on the back of his neck. They were so inviting that as I watched him eat I felt a persistent desire to reach through the glass and stroke him. Seeing that Connor was eating from the tray with impunity, Catherine decided to join him. But while my looming presence didn't concern Connor, Catherine was afraid of my smallest movements. I made a special effort to keep still for her, but it made little difference; she couldn't relax. She hated having to bend down to pick up a seed. She'd jerk her head back up as fast as she could, terrified that the instant I was out of her sight I'd pull a fast one.

It didn't take long for the cherry heads to realize that nothing bad was happening to the two blue crowns, and with twenty-four parrots competing for twelve spaces on the bowl, a few of the cherry heads decided to check out the tray. When they saw that I hadn't killed and eaten the first one brave enough to abscond with a seed, the tray quickly filled up with more cherry heads, who booted off Connor and Catherine. I hadn't anticipated that. The tray was a foot long and six inches wide, and since one of its long sides was flush against the building, only three sides were available for perching. If I pushed the tray out a little, that would open up the second long side. But any bird who perched there would be right up against the window with its back to me. I had a hunch that this would be too much for the cherry heads, but that Connor might find it acceptable, and again I was right. A few days later, Catherine swallowed her terror of the new setup and joined him.

With two feeding stations, things calmed down considerably. I continued to identify individuals and give them names. I discovered that both Eric and Sonny had mates. Eric's mate was another of the banded birds. I named her Erica. I thought Sonny's mate should have an Italian name. I thought "redheads, Lucille Ball, Lucy," which led me to Lucia.

One of the regulars at the tray was a baby. Some of the babies had developed their first specks of red feathers, which made it easier to identify them. But again, more than any marking, it was this baby's face and demeanor that I recognized. He was a handsome and very cool customer who seemed to take special pleasure in sunflower seeds. When he was eating, nothing could disturb him. No matter how wild the commotion around him, he was single-minded about working on the seed in his beak. Sometimes he'd close his eyes and shudder and sigh as though he were in a state of bliss. Because he was so cool, I named him Marlon, after Marlon Brando.

As we got deeper into winter, the feedings became longer and more frequent. The flock was spending more and more time at my place, often remaining on the fire escape even after they were done eating. I loved watching them go up and down the fire escape railing bars. Parrots have long, dexterous toes that function much like our fingers. The beak served as a third hand, and they could ascend the bars with ease. They were amazingly swift and machinelike about it. A bird would climb, one foot reaching over the other, while simultaneously pulling on the bar with her beak, attacking the bar from a different side with each pull. I saw pairs climb the bars side by side and in unison, both birds making the same move at exactly the same moment. To descend, they simply loosened their grip and slid like firemen down a pole, retightening their claws just nanoseconds before hitting the bottom. Dangling from the west end of the fire escape railing was a five-inch-long metal hook that was used to keep the door open. The hook was very popular with the babies. They'd reach down and pick it up with their beaks, then drop it and watch it swing. Occasionally, a baby would crawl down to the hook's end and just hang there while the others jabbered at him, demanding that he stop hogging the hook.

One of the more entertaining aspects of parrot watching was listening to them. They were compulsive noisemakers, and the noises

they made sounded as though they sprang out of a deep well of silli-
ness. Sometimes it seemed to me that the birds knew they were being
ridiculous, but were keeping a straight face about it. I didn't understand any of their noises until one day I recognized the call to leave.
All the birds who'd had their fill and wanted the flock to move on
would start squawking, trying to win agreement from the others. Sometimes they couldn't convince a sufficient number of their flock mates,
and the effort would peter out. But when they succeeded, more and
more birds added their voices until the whole flock was absorbed into
the frenzied, rising scream: "Let's go! Let's go!" Usually, they split the
instant the entire flock hit a certain pitch. Sometimes, though, there
was an interval during which they were all revved up but still holding to
their perches. It was similar to the moment when a heavy rocket has
reached full thrust but hasn't left the ground yet. Suddenly, screaming
thunderously, they would all leap into the air and fly out of the gardens,
usually heading north toward Fisherman's Wharf. I watched them until
they rounded the hill and disappeared from view.

My bicycle turned out to be a very useful tool for learning their
territory. I ran into them frequently on my rides, most often at Fort
Mason, a small military base that was in the process of being con-
verted into a park. A lot of trees and bushes grow there, so it's a popular foraging spot for all kinds of birds. It's right on the waterfront,
about a mile west of Telegraph Hill. I assumed that the four-mile
flight from Dolores Park to Telegraph Hill was already an arduous trip
for them, so it seemed reasonable to conclude that Fort Mason was
the outermost boundary of their territory. I was quite surprised to
hear one morning while riding into the Presidio—another former military base and yet another mile west—the familiar squawking of two
parrots in flight. I had stopped and was scanning the bright morning
sky when the green bodies and blue heads of Connor and Catherine
suddenly sailed overhead. They were flying very fast, and heading
even farther west. It amused me that I was more than two miles from
home and seeing wild birds that I knew personally. I wondered if they
recognized me.

The discovery I made on the bike that excited me most happened near Dolores Park. One morning I was on an errand in the Mission District just four blocks east of Dolores, when I thought I heard a lone parrot, a straggler, flying above me. I still had some doubt about Dolores Park being their roosting spot, so I braked to a quick stop right in the middle of traffic. I didn't care; I had to see that bird. It was around twenty feet above me, and it was clearly a parrot. There was no mistaking that sound. I threw my fists into the air and laughed. I loved solving their mysteries.

If I had the radio on too loud, or I was taking a shower, and didn't hear the flock's arrival, they took it upon themselves to fly to the fire escape and squawk for my attention. I'd come into the kitchen and find them peering through the window. When I carried out the seed bowl, they still flew back to the lines in an obligatory panic, although it seemed more like a habit now rather than real fear. But soon, instead of going all the way back to the lines, they started retreating just to the east end of the fire escape. I never did anything more than set the bowl down and come back inside. I never lingered or even looked in their direction.

Connor began having more trouble with the cherry heads. For some reason, he abandoned his place against the window, deciding that he preferred the tray's narrow east end. This infuriated the cherry-head couple whose spot it had become. Instead of acquiescing, though, Connor become uncharacteristically stubborn. It was the cause of my first entry into flock politics. One day, as he and Catherine approached the tray, I began shaking my finger at the two cherry heads coming up behind them. Catherine took off, but once again I felt an intuitive certainty that Connor would not be alarmed, that he'd understand I was trying to protect him. I was right: While the two cherry heads lunged threateningly at Connor—stopping just short of an actual attack—he kept eating, extremely ill at ease, but clearly aware that I was holding off the pair.

For several days the cherry-head couple continued to crowd Connor and act as though they were going to bite him, but they were kept away by my wagging finger. Then one of them decided to call my bluff. As Connor walked toward the tray, the cherry head ran up and boldly attacked him. The bird then wheeled around and looked me straight in the eye. His message was unmistakable: "What are you going to do about it?" To the cherry head, the real issue was no longer Connor himself, but my intervention on his behalf. He seemed bewildered by it, and wanted to know how far I was willing to go. All I could do was laugh. They *understood.*

After that altercation, Connor's troubles grew. At one feeding, Sonny mugged him. He had Connor down on his back and was about to inflict some real harm when Connor managed to struggle free. Connor and Catherine were having such a hard time getting any seeds that one day I had the thought that he and Catherine ought to come by without the flock so that they could eat in peace. The next day I found the two of them perched all alone on the fire escape railing, patiently waiting for me to bring out the bowl. I was beginning to wonder if Connor and I were telepathic. After that, they started coming on their own almost daily. And even when they showed up with the flock, they often stayed behind after its departure.

Throughout that fall and winter, I rarely missed a day. Rain or shine, I saw to it that the bowl was out there for them. They were coming by three or four times a day, and their trust in me kept growing. Now when I stepped out with the bowl, many of them didn't even bother flying down to the fire escape's far end. Yet as much as I longed to stop and feel their presence, I thought it best to be in their world as briefly as possible.

One clear and warm morning in early spring, I went out onto the fire escape to take in the view of the bay and found that I wasn't the only one out there. Five feet down the railing, all by himself, stood Sonny. It was an awkward moment—for both of us—but he didn't fly away. As mean as he was to the other birds, I liked Sonny, and I wanted to put him at ease. So I feigned nonchalance. I greeted him casually, as if my being out there with him were a common event. Then I turned away, rested my hands on the railing, and took in the view just as I'd intended to do. After a minute or two, I made an idle comment about what a beautiful day it was. I turned to see if Sonny was still there. He was, but he looked uneasy and suspicious. I turned slowly and went back into the house.

Later that day I found out why Sonny had been alone: He and Lucia had been kicked out of the flock. It became apparent when the flock was feeding on the fire escape, and the two outcasts were heard approaching from the north. Whenever the parrots heard stragglers flying in from a distance, they erupted into a shrill trumpeting sound that announced their location: "We're here! We're here!" As Sonny and Lucia approached, the flock responded with its "incoming" call, but it was imbued with distinctly hostile overtones: "Stay away! Stay away!" Sonny and Lucia kept coming anyway, so a small group flew out to head them off. Sonny and Lucia landed on a limb of one of the garden's deodar cedars, where a furious fight broke out. The fighters were in a tumble, wings and beaks thrusting and jabbing, as they erupted into their most intense version of a parrot scream. (I call it *psychogobble* because it sounds like turkeys who have completely lost their minds. When the parrots psychogobble, two birds sound like four, four like eight, eight like sixteen.) As soon as the fighting began, the rest of the flock scrambled over to the deodar and joined in the frenzied screaming. Sonny and Lucia had no choice but to retreat.

After the outcasts' withdrawal, the flock returned to the bowl, but it was not a happy feeding. Everybody was extremely worked up about what had just happened. Their eyes were wild, and they were even more vocal than usual as they ate. Sonny must have picked on the wrong bird, or maybe the flock simply got fed up with his behavior. Whatever the cause, Sonny and Lucia were kept in exile for another two weeks and then gradually permitted to rejoin. For quite some time afterward, though, Sonny had to be deferential in his encounters with the others.

Around the same time that Sonny was having his problem with the flock, I started having problems with a neighbor, Harvey, who lived in the apartment just below me. One day he started making noises, in an attempt to frighten the parrots away. At first I didn't understand what was going on, but when I did, I was livid. We had quite an angry confrontation. He told me that his door to the fire escape contained a set of louvered windows, which he liked to open to air out his apartment. He complained that the slats were catching seed hulls, feathers, and bird shit, which were then falling into his apartment. I asked him why he hadn't complained to me first, but he wouldn't give me a straight answer. He wanted me to stop feeding them. I wouldn't agree to that, but I had to tread carefully since Harvey held a big card in the situation. Edna viewed my interest in the parrots as eccentric but harmless. But because Harvey was a renter, I knew she'd order me to stop if he made a single complaint. After a couple of tense discussions, we came to an agreement: I could continue to feed the flock, but I had to look down first to see if his louvered windows were open. If they were, I couldn't put the bowl out. I was disappointed that I no longer had absolute freedom with the birds, but it was the best deal I was going to get.

It didn't take long. One morning the flock arrived, and I looked down and saw that the windows were open. I was going to have to refuse my little friends. I'd never done that before. Parrots have keen eyes, and they could see me through the windows. When I didn't come out immediately, they started calling to me. When I didn't respond, they kept calling and calling. I felt lousy about ignoring them, but I didn't dare break my agreement with Harvey. Conceivably, I could lose my caretaker job if I did.

An hour later, the parrots began filtering out of the garden. Eventually, they were all gone, except for Connor. He was still sitting out on the fire escape railing and peering expectantly into the house. Connor was my favorite, and I wanted his affection. Each parrot had his own style of eating. Connor's way was to step down into the bowl with one foot while leaving the other up on the rim. He usually stayed in that position, so the empty hulls dropped right back into the pile of seeds. Since he never left any mess, I decided it would be safe to put the bowl out just for him.

Connor had been eating for no more than two minutes when ten cherry heads came swooping around the corner of the house and landed on the fire escape railing. I was in a terrible bind. The cherry heads were right above the bowl, all set to drop down and start eating. If I let it happen, I was going to catch hell from Harvey and Edna; but I hated the idea of deliberately scaring them away. I had to make a quick decision. The only thing I could think of was to open the door and step out aloof and relaxed, like I'd been with Sonny. This time I'd be even closer—just a foot away—and I knew I'd frighten them into leaving. But I hoped my nonchalance might lessen their terror. I turned the knob, gently opened the door, and eased my way outside. I moved toward them in slow motion, expecting them at any moment to bolt away in a panic. But they didn't budge! I was so astonished that my legs started trembling. There I was, surrounded by my little green-and-red friends, none of whom seemed the least bit bothered by my presence. They all had their heads cocked and were staring at me softly with cautious, puzzled eyes. "What's the matter? Why won't you feed us?" So many impressions were racing into my eyes and mind from so many directions that I couldn't focus on anything. The magic of the moment did not alter the fact that I still had to keep the parrots away from the seeds. Certain that they'd be unwilling to come that close to me, I sat down right next to the bowl. I needed to give my shaking legs a rest anyway. It remained a standoff—a most pleasant one. They stuck around a few more minutes and then gave up and flew away. As soon as the parrots were gone, I went out of my mind from the thrill of the encounter. *Friends with wild animals!* I couldn't believe my luck.

A Question of Trust

There was a stairwell running through the fire escape's center, which left a foot-and-a-half-wide inside passage against the building. At the next feeding, I chose this narrow passageway as my new spot and sat down to watch. It was magical being out in the open air with the parrots and hearing the immediacy of their squawks and screams. They talked to each other constantly. They were making a lot of low croaking sounds that I hadn't heard from inside. I loved listening to the rustle of their feathers and the flutter of their wings as they flew around the fire escape. The only bad thing about my new position was that I was uncomfortably cramped. I was shoved right up against the wall of the house, which was hard on my back, but at least I was able to dangle my legs down into the stairwell and rest my feet on the stair steps. The parrots accepted the new situation with their usual condition: no movement. The instant I scratched an itch or flexed a stiff leg muscle, they fled to the safety of the power lines. After a few days of this, I started telling them in advance what I needed to do, pointing slowly to the area that I was going to scratch or move before I did. Happily, it made a difference: They stopped bolting every time they saw me twitch.

Naturally, I wanted even closer contact. It became my goal to have one of the birds perch on me. The parrots were constantly flying past me, either retreating from or heading toward the bowl. Often a bird would cross paths unexpectedly with a rival, which would require an abrupt change of course and, perhaps, a collision with some other bird, or else a hasty perching. My hope was that during all the maneuvering, one might choose to land on me. One place where they often did make emergency landings was the stairwell handrail. The handrail was level with my forehead and only inches from me, but I ignored any bird who landed there. It seemed smart not to make a big deal out of it. I'm sure that they stuck around longer because of it. Our closest contact came when a parrot landed next to my feet on the stairwell step. She put a foot on the toe of my boot as if to climb up on it, but then thought better of it and flew away.

After three weeks, the joy I felt at being outside with them had faded. The confinement of the tight space and the flock's demand that I remain relatively still was causing me back pain. One day, I couldn't take it anymore. I stood up in the middle of the feeding and moved down to the east end of the fire escape. I wanted to retreat anyway and figure out my next step. The birds who weren't eating often roamed the railing, sometimes coming quite near me. I usually had a few sunflower seeds in my pockets, and, as a joke, I'd occasionally offer them to passing parrots. Any bird to whom I offered one would give me a startled look and hustle on by—which is exactly what I'd expected. Then one day, before running away, a bird I'd offered a seed seemed to think it over first. I'd thought that hand-feeding them was out of the question, but the bird's hesitation made me wonder. Maybe it would be possible. Maybe Connor would do it. So I started encouraging every bird who wandered by me to take a seed. But no one was willing to try, and Connor wouldn't come anywhere near me.

After several days, one of the cherry heads paused and seriously considered my offer. I moved my torso back as far from him as possible and extended my right arm, a seed sticking out from my fingertips. I was in a very uncomfortable position, and the bird was in no hurry to make a decision. After awhile, my arm began to tremble. To keep it from shaking, I had to hold my elbow with my left hand. My discomfort kept growing while the parrot patiently sized up the situation. Finally, his neck began to stretch out toward the seed. He moved so slowly, it was nerve-racking. I forcibly held my body stiff and still as his beak came closer and closer. Abruptly, he snatched the seed and waddled off with it, disappearing into the crowd.

I had to keep a lid on the pleasure that exchange gave me. The parrots disliked it when I was anything other than matter-of-fact, so I was in the habit of restricting my emotions when I was outside with them. Besides, I'd spent six months watching them several times a day from inside the kitchen and another month sitting out on the fire escape with them, so it was all beginning to feel normal to me. The bird came back two more times for seeds later in the feeding. For some reason, the name *Noah* popped into my head. I probably meant *Adam,* thinking of him as the "first bird," but I got my biblical names mixed up. I made a mental note of the pattern of red in Noah's cap so that I could recognize him the next day.

It wasn't until after the flock left the fire escape that I began to take in what had happened. I'd always been fascinated by stories about relationships between humans and wild animals. It seemed to me that if I were patient enough, there might be no limit to how close I could get to the parrots. I liked the idea of cultivating a close friendship with one of them. I fantasized having a parrot friend who came into the house for visits, for food, and for long pets, and who knew that he was free to leave whenever he wanted. My neighbors had been making jokes, comparing me to Saint Francis. I'd read stories about sages and saints making friends with wild animals. Maybe it was all allegory, but I could imagine the conditions that would allow such a thing to happen. A real saint is someone who through prolonged, deliberate effort has purged himself of every trace of selfishness and aggression. I reasoned that wild animals, not having the neuroses that human beings do, might be able to perceive directly the authentic friendliness of such a personality. On the other hand, if a person was at a spiritual level where he or she was still capable of thinking how wonderful it would be to catch one—even if there was no real intention of acting on that thought—the bird would sense it, and it would set a limit on the closeness of the interaction. I wasn't a saint, but I saw that there was a continuum I could work in. So it became my goal to have a close friendship with a single parrot. I knew that I would never harm the parrots, but how could I convey that? How does one win trust? I'd never given it any serious thought.

At times, all of us sense a poetry in the universe—strange coincidences that speak to us in a strong way. In my life away from the parrots, I was beginning to have doubts about my path. Although I believed in the existence of the spiritual plane, I wondered now whether it was benevolent and considerate of my needs. I'd devoted twenty years of my life to this idea, and I felt like I was wasting away. It seemed cruel. A spiritual path has to be reliable and genuinely good-hearted. How else can you trust it? At the same time that I was struggling with my spiritual doubts, I was obsessing over a woman whose trust I wanted. A few years earlier I'd fallen in love with her. We barely knew each other and, hoping that I'd finally met the one I'd been looking for, I'd gone overboard and frightened her away. I was willing to let go of her, but I wanted the opportunity at least to explain myself, to let her know that I wasn't a bad guy. But she didn't trust me and wouldn't let me anywhere near her. So in a very clear way, this issue of trust was being mirrored back to me in my experience with the parrots. I saw that to win trust, you have to be *trustworthy*—not simply most of the time, but constantly. The first time you cut even the smallest corner, doubt enters, which is corrosive to trust. This was a big revelation to me. To some it might seem too simple to be a revelation, but, as with every virtue, the profundity is in the difficulty of practice. The issue of trust arises wherever there is temptation. Parrots are obviously tempting to some people. They've been taken out of their free and natural lives, locked in cages, and sold to those who have desired their beauty and personality. I wanted them to know I wouldn't do that.

The next day, Noah didn't come to me immediately, but he did come. I'm sure he saw the advantage of taking seeds directly from my hand: He no longer had to fight for a place on the bowl. Noah's red cap still had little green gaps in it, which indicated to me that he was one of the babies I'd seen the previous October. That made Noah one of the "wild ones," a bird who I was certain had never been a pet. He was cautious about the experiment, and so was I. I had no idea whether what I was doing was dangerous. I'd heard of parrot fever—although I had no idea what it was—and I was a little concerned about that beak. Its size was intimidating enough, but it also had a small, razor-sharp, V-shaped point extending down from the middle of the upper beak and fitting neatly into a notch in the lower beak. It was a very nasty-looking piece of work. What if Noah suddenly went completely berserk and attacked me? He did, in fact, bite me that day—but they were just soft little nibbles. He licked my fingers as he nibbled. He wanted to know what I was made of. Was my skin hard? soft? rubbery? He seemed to be gauging what it would take to cause me pain, but he made no attempt to actually hurt me.

Noah was particular about the way I handed him seeds. Afraid of my open palm, he would accept a seed only if I held it by my fingertips. At first he wouldn't eat in my presence. He'd take the seed to the other end of the railing, eat it, and then come back for another. By the end of the feeding, though, he trusted me enough that he'd planted himself in front of me and was taking seed after seed from my hand.

A few days later, I spotted Marlon standing near the fire escape ladder and peering over at Noah and me. He was obviously curious about what we were doing, and I was pleased to see his interest. After he'd watched us for awhile, I casually offered him a seed, which he took without hesitation. I was surprised at how easy it was. That got me thinking. I'd noticed a frisky elusiveness in Noah's personality that made me doubt that he was the right bird to fulfill my aim. Marlon seemed more straightforward: He wanted to eat. I also felt more affection for Marlon than I did for Noah, and it made sense to choose a bird I liked. After taking his first few seeds, Marlon started nibbling curiously on my fingertips, just as Noah had done. It was a pleasant, ticklish sensation to feel him dragging his dry, rubbery tongue over my skin.

Marlon was the constant companion of a bird I called Murphy. I'd named Murphy in honor of Maxine's brother, Jack Murphy, who was the original owner of the house I was living in. In spite of the male name, though, I suspected that Murphy was female. Like Noah, Marlon and Murphy were both a year old. I knew that cherry-headed conures didn't mature sexually until around the age of eighteen months, so it seemed likely to me that they were siblings. Anything that Marlon did, Murphy imitated; so I soon had three parrots eating from my hand.

Passing out seeds one at a time from my fingertips got old for me fast. I started to insist that they eat from my open palm. They accepted the change, but it led to a complication. Noah and Marlon turned out to be rivals, and they were constantly lunging at each other, trying to bite. They were so insistent about fighting that I was worried one of them might accidentally get me instead. No one had bitten me yet, but I dreaded the prospect. I'd read that some pet parrots had the strength to crush finger bones. What might a wild one do? My solution was to separate them with my feeding hand, forcing them to eat from opposite sides of my palm. That led to an unexpected and pleasant outcome. Not only did they stop fighting, they also started leaning their chests right up against my hand. Before that they'd avoided touching me. I'd had tail feathers brush against me, but when taking seeds they'd always been careful to arch their necks up over the side of my hand. I'd imagined their bodies to be somewhat cool, but they were surprisingly warm.

It wasn't long before a fourth cherry head began hanging around my little gang of three. I'd been aware of this bird for months. You couldn't help but notice him. He had ugly patches of bare skin all over his throat and skull. I assumed he got them from fighting, so I named him Scrapper. Then one day I saw Scrapper perched next to his mate, who was in even worse shape than he was. She still had her head, wing, and tail feathers, but, except for a few random tufts of white down, the rest of her was completely bare. Her skin was pink and bumpy, like a plucked chicken's, and she had a dirty yellow circle of down surrounding her bum hole, or *cloaca*. She looked terrible, and didn't seem to care. I named her Scrapperella. My best guess was that Scrapper and Scrapperella shared some kind of skin disease. Although Scrapper came by every day to watch me feed the other three, he refused to join in. He was never frightened by my hand when it came near him, but if I stopped to offer him a seed he'd go hide behind a ladder strut or fly away. Sometimes it seemed like he was watching over Marlon and Murphy. I wondered if he was their father. Maybe he was making sure they weren't in any danger.

The bird I really wanted to feed was Connor, of course. Whenever we made eye contact, I'd hold out my hand to show him that it held seeds, but he wouldn't approach me. He and Catherine were still coming by without the flock to be fed separately. Because they weren't noisy fliers like the cherry heads, I was often unaware of their arrival. Connor took it upon himself to let me know they were waiting. At first, he'd squawk quietly and politely; but if that didn't produce the bowl, he'd get a little louder and more demanding. If that still wasn't enough, he'd raise the volume until he was shrieking hysterically. Sometimes he sounded like his voice was on the verge of breaking, and I'd worry about the neighbors getting annoyed. My main concern was for my downstairs neighbor, Harvey, but for some inexplicable reason he'd completely retreated. He never made another complaint, and he allowed me to feed the flock whenever I wanted.

Since Catherine was seldom allowed on the bowl when the flock was present, she often served as the "watch parrot." While the others ate, she stood guard—on the lines usually, or in the juniper. Nearly every feeding had a watch parrot whose duty it was to scream out alarms whenever she saw danger. Catherine saw danger everywhere. When I first started coming out on the fire escape, I was one of those dangers. She zealously alerted the flock to my presence—which was, of course, already obvious to everyone. It took her a long time to accept me being out there. Catherine often sent out alarms that the flock would ultimately choose to disregard, but not without having to expend some energy first. They'd bolt from the fire escape, see that her concern was trivial, and then wheel back to continue eating. She never lost her job, though. Despite her low standing, Catherine did have one superior quality. I remember her as the flock's most accomplished flier. She'd swoop low into the garden and turn tight corners with a swiftness and grace that distinguished her from the others.

After several weeks of observing, Scrapper finally accepted my offer of a seed. He wasn't as enthusiastic as the others about being hand-fed—he was strong enough to get on the bowl whenever he wanted—but he became a regular anyway. I was hand-feeding four birds now, and my pockets couldn't hold enough seeds to last an entire feeding. I started bringing the seeds out in a plastic cup. The new object—like all new objects—frightened them initially, but seeing that it held the seeds, they made peace with it quickly.

None of the birds would perch on me or let me touch them, but I could see that their trust was growing. The sweetest result of their confidence was that after a feeding ended, instead of flying back to the lines and trees, they often remained on the fire escape to groom and play. I'd sit down on a ladder step and watch them. Marlon was so comfortable that he once took a nap right in front of me. He was just a foot away, standing on one leg, the other tucked up under his belly, his eyes closed, as he ground his beak contentedly. The parrots had many little moves and habits that I found endearing. The large nostril holes in the beak are covered by a band of flesh called the *cere.* The cere has small openings directly over the nostrils, and I'd often see a parrot stick a long toenail all the way inside and dig around, sneezing as he pulled it out. Couples often scratched in sync. Both birds would stand on one leg and, at precisely the same moment, begin rotating the other. Their legs moved so fast that they disappeared in a blur. They usually finished simultaneously, too. Sometimes during a mutual preening (called *allopreening*) one of the birds would pause for an instant, rapidly clatter his upper and lower beak together, making a sound like castanets, and then go back to work.

Not long after Scrapper joined Noah, Marlon, and Murphy, Connor began wandering down to my end of the fire escape. He consistently declined my offer of a seed, so it was probably just a matter of Connor wanting to expand his room to roam. He actually looked irritated whenever I attempted to hand him a seed, but I never stopped trying to entice him. Then one afternoon, while feeding my gang of four, I saw Connor climbing up one of the vertical railing bars near my right leg. He was about halfway up when I stuck my hand in his face, a seed protruding from my fingertips. He hesitated for a moment and then abruptly snatched it from me. He looked exasperated. Nevertheless, he continued up the bar and took his place on the railing as my fifth hand feeder. He was even more relaxed about taking seeds than the four cherry heads. The band on his leg was tantalizingly close. But the lettering on it was tiny, and he wouldn't permit me to set my face close enough to read it. He insisted that I keep some distance, both physically and psychologically. Having won Connor over to hand feeding, I stopped encouraging any other birds from the flock. I wanted to focus on cultivating my relationships with these five. I hoped that out of this group, I would find my wild parrot friend.

Unfortunately, my hand feeders weren't interested in cultivating anything more than their appetites. The only touching that all five allowed was beak strokes. Marlon and Connor sometimes allowed me to brush my hand up against their chests, but if I managed more than two or three strokes, they bit me. Marlon's bites were swift and hard, although not nearly as damaging as I'd feared. He didn't even break the skin—although his bites did hurt. Connor's bites were slow and polite, but firm. If I touched the chests of the other three, they either pulled away from me or flew off. Scratching their necks—something I'd been told that pet parrots adore—was out of the question.

As summer approached, I noticed an odd thing happening with the flock. Instead of coming to me three or four times a day in a large group, they were coming to me all day long in many small groups. They kept me busy. Toward the end of the day, I'd see larger groups, but never the entire flock. Some birds seemed to have disappeared entirely. I had no idea what was going on, but there was never a day that I didn't see my hand feeders, and since my attention was entirely on them at this point, I didn't concern myself much with the others.

I was so comfortable with my little gang of five that I started getting overly familiar with them. Prior to this, I'd always been respectful and slow-moving around them. But now my movements were becoming brusque and my tone of voice glib. One day, I was being presumptuous with Marlon and Murphy. It was subtle, but they sensed my state of mind, and they didn't like it, so they pulled away from me. I caught what was happening, paused, adjusted my attitude, and slowly offered another seed. I was rewarded for my consideration. As my hand came forward, Murphy lifted a foot and wrapped her long toes around my finger. Her toe bones were tiny and fragile, with very little meat on them—just a tough gray skin covered with tiny knobs—but her grip was electric and surprisingly firm. It was the first time one of them made deliberate physical contact with me. I'm sure she was simply trying to keep my hand from moving on to Marlon. It wasn't a measure of love, but of trust. That was good enough for me. I was flattered.

As Marlon matured, he started changing from that cool little bird I'd known as a baby into a big hothead. He nipped at me almost constantly. At first, I didn't mind too much. In a sense, it was another piece of flattery. It was the kind of bite the parrots gave each other, one that grew out of familiarity rather than hostility. Sometimes Marlon would be angry with Noah, but would bite me instead. At other times, it was simply the spontaneous upwelling of cherry-head feistiness. Marlon was more easily irritated than most, and one bird seemed to go out of his way to get a rise out of him. Rascal would dangle upside down from a ladder strut and stare down poker-faced at Marlon as he ate from my hand. Marlon kept glancing up at Rascal, growing more and more incensed as Rascal continued to taunt him. Finally, Marlon couldn't take it anymore. He'd spring up furiously after Rascal, who then fled from the fire escape—with great mirth, I'm sure. Marlon would still be fuming when he returned to eat and lash out at the first thing that came near him—usually my hand.

After awhile, I started getting irritated with Marlon's constant biting. It always hurt, and sometimes he even broke the skin. One day, he bit me hard on the index finger. While he still had my finger, I quickly put my thumb down on his upper beak and lifted him up into the air. He flapped his wings to raise his body high enough to place his feet up against my wrist so that his neck wouldn't bend. I set Marlon back down immediately and waited to see his reaction. It all happened in a flash. What I'd done was completely out of character, and Marlon looked bewildered by it. He seemed to be trying to decide whether to fly away or ignore it. Seeing his indecision, I offered him a seed, which he took, and the issue was dropped. But it was a gross violation of my effort to win their trust. Even worse was the fact that I'd been planning the caper for several days. Truth is, I wasn't trying to stop Marlon's biting so much as I simply wanted to hold him. But by doing that, I'd ruled him out as my close bird friend. Marlon had become so temperamental that he didn't seem a likely candidate anyway. We remained on good terms, but there was always an element of friendly parrying between us. I took Marlon on a few more "rides" when his biting got out of hand, but he eventually got wise to me. Instead of taking the entire width of my finger into his beak, he opened just wide enough to pinch the skin, which he then gave a painful little twist.

While there was something in Marlon's makeup that allowed me to indulge in mischief, I was reluctant to do anything that I thought might even vaguely annoy Connor. But I couldn't stop looking for ways to get closer to him. Around his feet on the railing were small piles of debris—splintered shells and dropped bits of seed kernel. I started brushing the piles away with my finger, coming near his toes, but not actually touching them. When Connor didn't like something, he could make a recognizable frown. At first, he closely followed the course my finger took, glaring at it when it made too close an approach. He came to accept it, though, as a harmless eccentricity—just so long as I didn't touch his toes.

I remember that summer as idyllic. The experience was still fresh, and my days were bright and relaxed. Even when the parrots weren't around, I'd hang out on the fire escape waiting for them. I was well above any obstructing buildings, and the view was superb. I felt like I had a box seat at the opera. I could see for miles and miles across the expanse of the bay to the rolling brown hills on the distant northern horizon. I learned to spot the parrots from the moment that they were just specks over Fisherman's Wharf, a half-mile away. I could detect their squawking when it was just the faintest element in the great background of urban clamor. As the days passed, the parrots and I became increasingly casual with one another. I remember one time when Marlon had his back to me and was staring down at something in the garden. It was his turn for a seed, so I tapped him lightly on the wing—something I'd never done. Marlon turned around, took the seed, and then looked away again. A moment like that would satisfy me for days.

Throughout the summer, the flock numbers grew progressively thinner. I still didn't recognize many individuals, so I couldn't tell who or how many were missing. Then, in early August, I started seeing slightly larger groups again. Some of the birds looked terrible. They were skinny, and the tips of their feathers were coated with some kind of hard black grease.

Around the time that the birds started reappearing, another cherry head began hanging out near my band of hand feeders. She was a sweet-looking thing, so I lured her into the group. I named her Martha, after a girl I'd had a brief crush on in high school. She was very gentle for a cherry head, and a little more timid than the others. She wouldn't come to me every day, and she never stayed for the entire feeding. Just a couple of weeks after she started taking seeds from me, Martha showed up looking woozy. Her head hung to the side, and she was having trouble staying on her feet. Over the next few days, she became more and more clumsy. She was having trouble flying now, too. The other parrots were pecking at her, trying to keep her away from both the bowl and my hand. In spite of the flock's hostility, Martha adamantly hung on as a member. I kept trying to get seeds to her, but I didn't have much luck. The other birds wouldn't let her near me. I had some concern that this might be parrot fever, and I wondered whether I was at risk. But I never altered my behavior on account of it. One day Martha didn't show up. I never saw her again. That stunned me. Up to that moment, my experience with the birds had been nothing but fun—a child's dream come true. Somehow, it had never occurred to me that one of them might die.

Mandela

One night toward the end of summer, I had a dream about the parrots. In the dream, I went to answer a knock on the front door and found a huge crowd of baby cherry-headed conures. They were large birds, taller than me and built like penguins. The moment I opened the door, they began a slow, steady march into the house, advancing shoulder to shoulder in an endless line. As they passed, they knocked into me as though I didn't exist. I struggled to stay on my feet, but I was finally overwhelmed, flailing my arms as I fell over backward.

An hour after waking, I heard the flock arrive. I looked out the dining room window and found them perched on the power lines waiting for me. I carried the seed bowl outside, set it down, and walked to my position at the east end of the fire escape. As soon as I turned to face them, I sensed something out of the ordinary. Then I saw it: a baby—all green. He was perched on a slack, gently swaying telephone line and had to work to stay upright. I was startled to see him. I thought that all baby birds *fledged* (left the nest) in spring, and when I hadn't seen any then, I decided that the previous year must have been an anomaly. I was surprised by his size. I'd imagined the babies to be as small as parakeets, but he was nearly as large as an adult. The only obvious differences were that he had no red cap, much darker eyes, and a slightly smaller, more snub-nosed beak. When the flock came to eat, he remained behind on the line. I was so engrossed with the baby that I barely paid attention to the birds eating from my hand. Every now and then he'd take a clumsy step or two down the line, but mostly he perched silently and looked around the garden with dopey baby eyes.

While studying him, I was distracted by a flash of bright green out in the garden. I looked up just in time to see a second baby jump from a limb of the deodar cedar and fly toward the lines. She made an awkward landing near the first baby, and then the two were joined almost immediately by a third. I was dying to know who the parents were, but the three fledglings kept their distance, and none of the adults went anywhere near them. After the flock left, I picked up the bowl and carried it back into the house. Only then did I remember my dream.

Over the next few days, six more babies made their debut. Out of the total of nine, Eric and Erica had three, Guy and Doll had two, and Sonny and Lucia had four, one of whom disappeared just days after fledging. I was eager to get a closer look at one, but the parents prohibited them from coming to the fire escape. So while the adult birds ate, the babies passed the time chewing and playing on branches and lines. Once the parents had eaten their fill, they flew back to their babies, who begged to be fed. The begging sound was something like a chuckle or a lamb's bleat. Of all the sounds the parrots make, it's the one I love most. To feed, the mother (or father—both parents share the duty) bounces her head up and down to bring food up from her *crop* (a small pouch above the stomach) and into her mouth. She then takes the baby's beak into her own and, while rapidly shaking the baby's head up and down, regurgitates. The baby squats, wings held out from his sides, and lifts his head straight up to receive the food. Afterward, he keeps his wings held out and puffs up his head feathers while he nods and trembles, bleating ecstatically.

Around two weeks after fledging, the babies were finally allowed on the fire escape, and I got my first close look. Like all babies, they had a cherubic appearance that was adorable. Although still incapable of cracking open the shells, some of the chicks were allowed to sit in the middle of the bowl (something no adult was ever allowed to do), where they imitated their parents by sweeping their beaks back and forth through the pile of sunflower seeds. Occasionally, a baby would wander down to my end of the fire escape, but the parents always flew over to shoo it away.

In the days just before I saw the first babies, I'd been telling myself that it was time to stop messing around with the parrots and get down to business. When I first moved into the house, Edna told me that I'd be staying there two or three months at most. I'd been caretaking a year and a half now, and while there didn't seem to be any movement toward clearing up the estate's legal issues, she was calling every month or so to tell me that things could change at any moment and that I should start looking for a new situation. I took her warnings seriously, but the arrival of the babies put all my attention back onto the flock. It isn't often that one gets the opportunity to observe wild baby parrots, so I chose to stick with it another week or two to see what they were like.

Before I stopped feeding the flock, I called Dan Paine, the man whose house I'd been cleaning on the day I first saw the parrots. I hoped he might be able to answer the questions I had about the flock's origins. He told me that he'd started seeing a single cherry-headed conure around 1984. The bird would come by late in the afternoon and perch ten feet from his window. Dan assumed it was an escaped pet, and he started talking to it, encouraging the parrot to come to him. But the bird refused. Concerned that it might otherwise starve to death, he began putting out sunflower seeds, which the parrot accepted. The bird came by daily for three years. Then, one day, a second cherry head showed up with it. The two birds were regulars at Dan's feeder until the summer of 1989, when the second bird vanished. Dan thought it had died, but several weeks later it reappeared looking haggard and filthy. A month and a half after that, the pair showed up at his feeder with four babies in tow. Two of the babies disappeared shortly thereafter. That's what I'd seen in the spring of 1990: the two parents and their two surviving offspring. Dan moved just a few months later, so that was all he knew of the flock's beginnings.

Although I still had to contend with Armistead Maupin's story of parrots on Telegraph Hill in the 1970s, Dan's story added weight to my feeling that the cherry heads had been around for only a few years. I also understood now why so many of the parrots had disappeared in late spring: The females had gone to sit on their eggs. And the birds that had looked so skinny and dirty were those same females shortly after coming off the nests. I also knew now, with certainty, the sex of some of the individual birds. Scrapper had been at the fire escape uninterruptedly throughout the summer, but during that same time I hadn't seen Scrapperella at all. It was the same for Eric and Erica, Sonny and Lucia, and Guy and Doll. I'd guessed the gender of each bird. Only the last three couples had brought out any babies, so not all the females had been successful. I wondered about Connor and Catherine. Neither one had disappeared that summer, so maybe they weren't male and female. But I'd seen them mating in the spring, and Connor had taken the male position. I'd also seen Connor feed Catherine, which is courting behavior in adults. But their genders were going to have to remain a mystery. It was time to put an end to the diversion and get serious about my life.

By mid-October, the babies were getting the hang of opening shells. Some were allowed on the lip of the bowl, which was making it even more crowded. For half of the flock, there was little to do other than preen or explore until a place opened up on the bowl. One morning, I saw Mandela, one of Sonny and Lucia's babies, coming down the railing to where I was feeding Connor, Marlon, Murphy, Noah, and Scrapper. I'd been hoping to lure a baby into my group of hand feeders—although I doubted the parents would ever allow it. He came close enough for me to offer him a seed, but before I could do so, the hand feeders chased him away. They weren't trying to protect the baby; they just didn't want to share. Mandela was not to be put off, though. He stayed on the railing, a few feet away, and stared at me. Suddenly, he fluttered up into the air and plopped down onto the cup in my hand. Then he started to eat from it. His two front toes were clutching the rim, and his rear toes were actually resting on the back of my hand. I was elated. I'd been waiting nearly six months for one of the parrots to land on me. I brought the cup right up to my face so I could go eyeball-to-eyeball with Mandela, and he wasn't the least bit afraid. His eyes were confident and relaxed. He even got feisty with me. He didn't like me reaching into the cup to get seeds for the others, and each time I did, he'd bite my fingers. Before the feeding ended, I looked to the bowl to see what Sonny and Lucia thought of all this. They showed no concern.

The next day, Mandela came again to eat from the cup. Soon after he landed, his sibling, Chomsky, trundled down the railing to watch. Chomsky seemed eager to join Mandela, but apparently he felt stymied by the difficulty that Mandela's presence on the cup added to a clean landing. After some hesitation, he jumped into the air and flew to the top of my head. I could feel his sharp toenails digging into my scalp as he walked around surveying the situation. I had to work to suppress my laughter. After resolving whatever concerns he had, Chomsky fluttered down onto the rim of the cup. I now had two parrots biting my fingers.

From that day on, Mandela and Chomsky were regulars on the cup. All my resolve to stop feeding the flock vanished. I felt as though I might be close to fulfilling my wish to have a close parrot friend, and although it seemed risky, I decided to stick with it just a little bit longer. I thought that if I were to invest time in cultivating a friend-ship with a particular bird, it should be one of these two babies. A young bird would probably be more open to a close approach than an adult would be. Of the two, I liked Mandela more, but he was biting me a lot. Chomsky was gentler and seemed better suited tempera-mentally. But neither baby showed much interest in a serious relation-ship. They came to accept my reaching into the cup for more seeds, and they allowed me to rub their beaks with my nose, but that was as friendly as they got. I was not allowed to touch them with my hand.

One of Guy and Doll's babies wanted to join Mandela and Chomsky on the cup, but the two siblings were adamantly opposed. So the other baby took an original approach: He jumped up on my right wrist and began eating the seeds in my palm. He was a slightly different shade of green than the other parrots. He reminded me of a Granny Smith apple, so I named him Smith. At first, I didn't think Smith's position was going to work out, since every time I needed to reach into the cup to get more seeds I had to turn my wrist over. But it turned out not to be a problem. He learned to walk my wrist in the same way that one walks a log floating in water. Later, he refined his technique. Whenever he saw me about to drop the handful of empty shells, he readied himself by clamping down on my sleeve with his beak and then surfed my wrist as it turned inside the jacket.

That the three babies could perch on me with impunity had a star-tling effect on the rest of the flock. Within a matter of days, there was a mass migration of parrots over to my end of the fire escape. For rea-sons that I still don't understand, most now found it more desirable to eat from my hand than from the bowl—so many, in fact, that I had a hard time keeping up with their demands. They were spread out all around me, on the railing in front and to my right and on the ladder steps to my left. Feedings became riotous. Some of the old touching taboos fell. They were tugging on my sleeves, and hooking my palm with their beaks and pulling on it from opposite directions. Several got into the habit of trying to prevent my hand from moving away by tightly gripping one of my fingers with a free foot. To get to the seeds, they leaned their necks and chests against my hand without restraint. I was so busy that it was difficult to focus on individuals. I had to start leaving little piles in front of each bird as I went around. Connor was kicked off his spot on the railing and moved down to a horizontal rung six inches below. He exacted his revenge, though. He started running little guerrilla operations, biting the toes of the birds perched just above him. They had to watch him constantly. A few weeks later, Connor abandoned the railing entirely and began standing at my feet, demanding that I leave his pile of seeds there. I accommodated him. Meanwhile, Catherine remained over at the bowl, which had plenty of room now. Only about a third of the flock was still eating from it.

Each bird that ate from my hand was very particular about where it perched during feedings, so I was having a much easier time identifying individuals. The new situation required me to make a quick study of flock politics. I had to keep an eye on a number of different situations. There was usually some cherry head making an advance on Connor's pile of seeds, and whenever one did, I put a foot between them. If Guy's pile of seeds on the ladder steps wasn't constantly replenished, he'd push a weaker bird away from hers. As Smith rode around on my palm, I had to make sure that some bird on the railing—usually Marlon—didn't reach out and pull for all he was worth on Smith's head feathers. I tried to maintain privileges for my original five hand feeders, but Noah got lost in the shuffle, and I wasn't able to keep track of him for several months.

Although those big beaks were quite capable of lacerating my skin, most of the parrots were consistently gentle with me—except for Marlon. He was developing a remarkably full red cap for such a young bird, and the hot red of his head feathers mirrored his growing belligerence. A couple of times I saw him get into fights in which he actually ended up dancing on his opponent's back—like a flamenco dancer. Marlon was biting me constantly, and it nearly always hurt. Although I was careful to restrain it, more and more often he was arousing real anger in me. One day, I finally lost my temper. I bent over and yelled right in his face: "Goddamn it, Marlon, stop it! Stop biting me! I'm sick of it." I immediately regretted what I'd done. I expected the flock to take off in a panic, but nothing happened. Nothing at all. The parrots know their biting hurts, and they didn't really expect me just to stand there and take it. Marlon looked self-conscious about being the center of attention. He acted as though I were exaggerating. His demeanor seemed to say, "Big deal. I bit you. So what." But he was clearly embarrassed. He wouldn't look at me.

Back when I had to watch the birds from inside the kitchen, they'd bolt for reasons that sometimes seemed unrelated to my movements. Now that I was out with them and they'd lost most of their fear of me, they were still bolting. I began to notice that the bolt was often preceded by the parrots tilting their heads to one side and training their eyes on the sky. At the same time they were making a low, questioning, cawing sound. One day I finally saw what they were staring at: a hawk. It was just a tiny dot high up in the sky, but they were all focused on it. Once I learned to recognize the hawk warning sound, I always knew to look for one. It turns out that San Francisco has lots of hawks. I began to see them almost every day. I'd lived there for more than twenty years and had never noticed them. They weren't always high up; sometimes they swooped down low through the garden. If a hawk came too close, the watch parrot would send out an alarm, a strident and nasal "Yak, yak, yak, yak, yak, yak" that continued on and on until either the hawk vanished or the flock bolted.

Connor didn't always respond to the cherry heads' alarms. He demanded clearer evidence of danger before he would stir himself. Sometimes the jays would try to clear out the parrots by shrieking a false alarm. The flock would take off, see they'd been fooled, and then wheel around and sprint back to the fire escape. For me, it was one of the most beautiful moments. They'd all be racing straight at me, looking as though they were going to collide. At the very last moment, they'd drop their tails and fan out their wings in order to break their speed, and all of my vision would be filled with a mass of green parrot bodies gently fluttering down onto the railing.

I got to witness some very unusual behavior out on the fire escape. One of the most intense experiences was when I got to stand in the middle of a flock scream. I heard them do this in the trees a lot, but to be in the middle of one was something else. They all stopped eating and for no discernible reason begin screaming as loud as they possibly could. It lasted at least ten minutes without any letup. Their eyes were wildly enthusiastic, and their little chests heaved with the effort. The volume was overwhelming. I stood there waiting for it to stop, but it went on and on. Whenever the screaming began to subside, one of them would raise his own volume until the others joined in again with renewed zeal. They looked both utterly serious and completely silly. I was so charmed that I started laughing, and couldn't stop. Then, as abruptly as they'd begun, they all fell silent and resumed eating.

There was another common behavior that I found downright spooky: the *display*. It often began the moment that a mated pair landed on the railing. Without unfolding them, they'd pull their wings away from their sides and constrict their pupils. The pair would then rotate in unison a half circle, pause, rapidly expand and contract their pupils several times, rotate another half circle, pause, flash their eyes again, and so on. Usually there'd be several couples along the railing all doing it at once, each bird in sync with its partner. They looked like little space aliens.

One afternoon that November, the parrots were grooming and play- ing on the lines after a feeding. I was watching from the fire escape when I heard one of them start to scream in a way I'd never heard before. But I understood immediately: The parrot was afraid for its life. The bird was on the ground—a place they never went—in the vacant lot between my old studio and the house next door. My line of sight was obstructed, so I ran back into the house and out onto the east balcony, where I thought I could get a clearer view of what was happening. I still couldn't see the bird, but I did see a neighbor's cat running away from the area that the screams were coming from. The cat did not have the parrot in its mouth, but the bird was still hysterical. I sprinted back into the house, out the front door, and down a narrow path that led to the Greenwich Steps. When I got to the vacant lot, I found an outraged and terrified baby clinging to a trampled iris. It was Mandela. His beak was open wide, and he was flashing it around menacingly as he screamed out his threats. The beak intimidated me, but I had to do something; I couldn't just leave him there. So I scooped him up and stuck him inside my jacket. I was afraid that he was going to start ripping into my belly, but he shut up immediately and crawled toward my shoulder. I started back to the house, quite aware that the entire flock was perched silently on the lines above and watching me.

Back in the house, I opened my jacket and set Mandela on the rug. I was struck right away by the contrast between this bright green and *alive* bird and the drab, brown, civilized room he was sitting in. I was so used to being out among them that I kept forgetting they were wild. Mandela was in shock. He tried to walk, but kept falling over. His right wing was drooping low, as if it were broken. I tried to imagine what might have happened. The parrots never go to the ground, but they are exuberant fliers, and they often swoop low and then soar up high. Mandela must have been at the bottom of his arc when the cat knocked him out of the air. There was a struggle afterward, and little Mandela had won. He struggled silently across the dining room floor, searching for a place to perch. Although I was worried about him, I was excited to have one of the parrots in the house. I had no idea what I was going to do with him. What if the wing was broken? I wasn't sure if a broken wing could heal. And how could I possibly afford a trip to a veterinarian?

Earlier in the year, a neighbor, Jackie, had taken care of a baby scrub jay who'd fallen out of a nest, and she still had the cage she'd kept him in. I called her up and explained my predicament, and she brought the cage right over. I felt funny putting one of the parrots in a cage, but Mandela settled into it without objection. His limp wing was getting caught underneath the perch, so I kept lifting it up and setting it back on top. I wanted him to know I was there to help him. I made an offering of sunflower seeds, which he cracked, but let fall from his beak uneaten. I promised him that I wouldn't keep him, that I would do everything within my power to return him to the flock. I carried the cage upstairs to my bedroom and set it on the night table. He crawled up into a corner of the cage, and, clinging to the bars with his toes and beak, went to sleep. I put a towel over the top and went back downstairs to sit and marvel at this new turn of events. Although I didn't have any money, I made an appointment with a veterinarian anyway, and just hoped that somehow I could work out payment. I also decided that I should start keeping a journal.

The next morning, when I took away the towel, Mandela was still clinging to the side of the cage. He seemed a little frightened now. When the flock flew by, he put out a loud, ringing call, but otherwise he was quiet. The appointment with the vet wasn't until the next day, so I thought we should take the time to get better acquainted. All he wanted, though, was for me to leave him alone. When I reached into the cage, he bit me hard. He hated the cage now and kept trying to squeeze through the bars. When the flock came through a second time that morning, he became frantic, climbing around the cage in circles. Just before the afternoon feeding, I set Mandela's cage near the dining room window so he could watch. During the feeding, I held up the cup with Chomsky on it so that Mandela could see his brother. After the flock left, I came back inside and opened the cage door. Mandela leaped out and tried to push through the glass. He was a very unhappy baby. Throughout the day, his family—Sonny, Lucia, Chomsky, and Stella—made several visits alone. They seemed to be looking for him, but I wasn't sure if it was a good idea to let Mandela see them. I was worried it would add to his anxiety. In the evening, his mood brightened; he started taking seeds from my hand and did some acrobatics, walking around while hanging upside down from the top cage bars.

Helen, the woman who lived above me in the cottage, had emphysema, and I'd been running errands for her the past several months. When she heard about Mandela, she insisted on paying for the trip to the vet. Mandela was completely relaxed during the ride over, so much so that it seemed as if he'd spent his whole life riding around in cars. The X rays showed that the wing wasn't broken. The vet told me that Mandela probably had some nerve damage, and that there was a good chance for a full recovery. I told her I wanted to return Mandela to the flock. She said to keep him caged for a couple of weeks, and then to let him fly around the house for a few days before I released him. She also told me that I should, by all means, let him see his family. It was important to keep them bonded. I should also leave him outside as much as possible to keep him acclimated.

As soon as we got home, I put Mandela's cage out on the east balcony. None of the parrots had ever gone to that side of the house, but when the flock came to eat, Sonny and Lucia saw Mandela and flew to the east balcony railing. They ended up spending most of the day near his cage. Even when the flock left, they stayed behind, leaving only to get food for themselves and their two other babies. I hoped they understood that I was trying to help Mandela. Maybe I was being overly sensitive, but it seemed to me that the flock was acting slightly standoffish toward me.

Over the next few days, Mandela and I settled into a routine— something parrots love—and he began to trust me more. He seemed confident and content with his new situation; his eyes were bright and curious again. Not only had he stopped biting me, he wouldn't bite even when, as a test, I offered him a finger and encouraged him to. I was allowed to stroke his beak all I wanted, and he even permitted me some tentative neck scratching. One evening, he demonstrated his climbing skills by shinnying up the slick spokes of my bicycle wheel. I started putting Mandela's cage on the fire escape so that he could be with the flock, and his family continued to come by every day to visit. Sonny was the most persistent, sitting on top of the cage protectively during flock feedings. Sonny had become a hand feeder in the days just before Mandela's encounter with the cat, but he refused to come near me for awhile afterward. As the days passed, his distrust lessened.

Edna was coming to visit Maxine in the nursing home for Thanksgiving, so I had to vacate the house for the nine days she was going to be there. The studio downstairs seemed like the perfect place to let Mandela get used to flying again. The room was small—eighteen by thirteen feet—and it had low, seven-foot ceilings, so I'd have no trouble catching him at the end of each session. I bought some rope and set up an elaborate gym between the two posts that came up through my floor. I was impatient to see him play on my contraption, so I started letting him out of the cage a week before the vet said I should. The wing was beginning to show some strength. Mandela was able to fly in short bursts of a few feet now.

I needed to keep Mandela acclimated, so I continued to put him outside every day. But the only place I could put him was on my front deck, and that was worrisome, since it was vulnerable to cats. But the cage should protect him, I thought, and I'd check on him continually to keep the cats away. Sonny spotted Mandela as soon as I carried the cage out. The studio's deck was too close to the ground for his family to sit with him, so they maintained their vigil on the power lines directly above. Again, it was Sonny who was the most tenacious at watching over the baby. One rainy afternoon, Mandela was sitting on the east windowsill gazing out at the garden when, incredibly, Sonny fluttered down onto the sill just opposite Mandela. He clung to the window and looked at Mandela for a full minute before flying away.

Mandela was now thoroughly at ease with me, letting me approach him as often as I liked. While trying to fly the length of the studio, he'd had to land on my shoulder once, which delighted me. I loved to sit right next to him and watch him do things. He had munchkin eyes—innocent and playful. He was curious about everything. He still wouldn't allow me to pet him, but I kept trying—very gently—and he was becoming less leery of my hand. Our only real conflict was over my insistence that he sleep in his cage. To get him back inside of it, I always had to use gloves. He understood my intention the moment I began putting them on, and I would have to chase him. He always screamed at the moment of capture, but once I had him he didn't hold it against me.

As much as I enjoyed my little houseguest, I was reminded every day that he'd be leaving soon. His flight was improving rapidly. Within a few days, he was flying the length of the room, hovering, and then changing direction. But the wing was still droopy, and he seemed to tire quickly. It looked to be a minimum of two weeks before he'd be strong enough to make the four-mile flight back to Dolores Park. As attached as I was to Mandela, I had a strong stake in seeing him fly free again. I'd made a promise to him, and I intended to keep it.

One afternoon, about two weeks after the cat attack, I put Mandela out on the deck in his cage. Sonny and the rest of his family were, as usual, up on the lines just above him. I went periodically to the long north window to check on him. One time I went to look and found that he was gone from the cage. That was impossible! I looked all around, but I didn't see him anywhere. Then I spotted him: He was standing on the deck only six inches from the cage. I opened the front door and casually strolled outside, but Mandela wasn't fooled. As soon as he saw me, he fluttered up to the lines. His family gathered all around him, excited to have him back. I went inside and got a knapsack and gloves. I wanted to be ready in case he took off and the wing gave out before he'd flown very far. Mandela walked along the power line and disappeared, with the line, into a tangle of tree limbs. A few moments later, I saw him climbing around the branches, with Sonny, Lucia, Stella, and Chomsky close behind. He seemed slightly perturbed by the intensity of their interest. Then somebody let out a squawk, and they all took off. Mandela was flying well—better than I thought possible—but I doubted the wing would hold up for long. I walked over to look at the cage. The only way he could have escaped was through a vacant feed-cup hole that was covered by a plastic slat.

He'd probably pushed the slat up with his beak and then crawled through the hole.

All night long, I ran the possibilities through my mind. Maybe he made it to Dolores Park, but that didn't seem very likely to me. Maybe, as his wing tired, he landed in a tree somewhere, or he crashed to the ground and somebody found him. I imagined him crashing onto a roof or some other isolated spot, the wing completely exhausted. He'd starve to death there. Or maybe he landed on a downtown street—which would have been in rush hour—and was crushed by a car. I got more and more depressed thinking about it. There was nothing I could do but wait and see.

The next day was a bright and sunny Thanksgiving. I intended to spend the entire day, if necessary, standing outside, waiting to see if Mandela was still alive. Late in the morning, I saw a group of four birds land on the lines above the Greenwich Steps. It was Sonny, Lucia, Stella, and Chomsky. They seemed to be looking for someone. Mandela was gone.

Three days later Edna returned to Shreveport, and I was back up in Maxine's house, feeding the flock from the fire escape. I'd been a little depressed about Mandela, and being back with the flock cheered me up. It was raining, and everybody was soaked. Their feathers were all askew, which made it difficult to recognize individuals. Early in the feeding, Chomsky flew onto the cup. I was glad to see that he didn't regard me as his brother's captor. The birds were ravenous, and it was a particularly unruly feeding. After around twenty minutes, everybody, except for Chomsky, went to seek shelter in the trees. I'd been so busy feeding the thirteen birds on the railing that I hadn't had the opportunity to pay any attention to him. I examined Chomsky's head for specks of red feather growth, which most of the babies were beginning to develop now. I saw that he had a little red dot below his right eye just like Mandela used to have. Then I noticed that his right wing was drooping. I looked at the eye dot again and then back to the wing. My God. It was Mandela! He'd *made* it. I erupted into laughter and started yelling his name. He must have known how happy I was to see him. A lump of coal would have known. I rubbed his beak with my nose, and Mandela—who rarely made a sound the entire time he lived with me—cawed back at me lightly. Then he left my hand, flew back to the trees, and rejoined his family.

The ∫cience of It

O ne morning, I was standing on the Greenwich Steps watching
the parrots with a local woman who hadn't known there were
parrots in San Francisco and was seeing them for the first time. The
flock was deep in play—hanging upside down from the lines, chasing
each other, and wrestling. She was so enchanted that for several minutes she couldn't speak or take her eyes off them. Finally, she turned
to me and said, "They don't really seem like birds. They're more like
little people." It was a common reaction among passersby. But science has also had difficulty fitting parrots into a niche. The ornithologist F. E. Beddard wrote: "The determination of the affinities of the
parrots to other groups of birds is one of the hardest problems in orni-
thology." He said that in 1898, and since then the situation hasn't gotten much clearer.

Birds have light, hollow-boned skeletons that disintegrate easily, so fossil remains are rare. The few remains that have been found indicate that the order of parrots is ancient. Current scientific thinking is that parrotlike birds go back around 40 million years. Some ornithologists believe that the parrot's closest living relative is the pigeon, while others see the parrot as being so singular that it has no close living relatives.

There are approximately 330 parrot species in existence today. They come in many different shapes, sizes, and colors. Lengths range from a little more than three inches to more than three feet. While most parrots are primarily green, they can also be red, blue, white, black, gray, purple, orange, and yellow. Most have short necks and large heads, but tail length varies from short to long. All parrots have at least three things in common. First and most obvious is the hook-shaped bill. The second is the cere, the band of flesh stretching across the base of the upper beak, or *mandible.* The cere allows movement of the upper bill in relation to the skull. Because of this flexibility, parrots are able to open their beaks wide. The third common feature is their *zygodactyl* feet. In most birds, three toes point forward and one points back; parrots have two toes pointing forward and two pointing back. The toes are long and have many joints, giving them a strong and agile grip. They can manipulate held objects with remarkable grace and skill. Their funny, pigeon-toed waddle is the result of their long toes and short legs.

Parrots are native to Africa, Australia, southern Asia, Central and South America, and Mexico. Not long ago, the United States had its own native parrot, the Carolina parakeet *(Conuropsis carolinensis),* which ranged as far north as Wisconsin. In 1918, the bird became extinct, exterminated by farmers, who considered them crop pests, by "sportsmen," and by entrepreneurs seeking feathers for ladies' hats.

Parrots live in many different habitats—dry woodland, savanna, and even semidesert—but most live in forests. One reason I had such trouble finding information about parrots in the wild is because so many parrot species are green and live high in the forest canopy.

Scientists have difficulty both finding them and getting close enough to make useful observations. As a result, parrots have been studied very little. I would expect that they make short work of tracking collars, too.

Another reason I had trouble finding scientific information was that the bird I was involved with goes by several different names, and the name I knew—cherry-headed conure—is one that ornithologists never use. *Cherry-headed conure* is used exclusively by the pet trade; ornithologists prefer to call it the *red-masked parakeet.* When I first started seeing references to the red-masked parakeet, I didn't realize that this was the same bird. It wasn't until I'd memorized its scientific name, *Aratinga erythrogenys,* that I made the connection. The word *parakeet* contributed to my confusion. I thought parakeets were the small cage birds I'd been seeing all my life. But *parakeet* is a general term that describes many different parrot species. It's descriptive rather than taxonomic, meaning that not all parakeets are of one closely related genetic group. A parakeet is usually defined as a small to medium-sized parrot with a long tail. (Birds that have the word *parrot* in their name usually have short tails.) The bird that Americans typically refer to as a parakeet is merely one example of a parakeet. Its real name is the budgerigar, or budgie *(Melopsittacus undulatus).* Parakeets are parrots. So are macaws, rosellas, Amazons, cockatiels, cockatoos, lories, and lovebirds.

The word *conure* is derived from an early attempt at classifying the South American parakeets. Originally they were all lumped together in a single genus, *Conurus,* which means "wedge-shaped tail." As knowledge of the differences among the conures grew, the one genus was broken down into six or seven (depending on the system used) genera. *Conure* persists within the pet trade, though, and because of its widespread use there, some ornithologists call our bird the *red-masked conure* or the *red-headed conure;* but I've never seen a scientist use the term *cherry-headed conure.* Unless I'm speaking with an ornithologist, though, I always say cherry-headed conure. It was the first name by which I knew them, so it was well ingrained in me before I learned any of their other names. And I think it sounds friendlier.

By the book, the cherry head is, on average, thirteen inches (thirty-three centimeters) long. Like most parrots, the bird looks compact and powerful. The base plumage is green, with a bright red head and a red edge along the bend of the wing. The amount of red varies widely from bird to bird. At the age of one year, the red cap is small— it usually stops at the top of the skull and just behind the eyes—and contains little green gaps. Birds continue to develop more red with each year's molt. I've read that it can take as many as ten years for the red coloration to develop fully. Males tend to be redder than females. None of these rules are firm, though. Sonny had a small red cap that remained small, while the cap of his mate, Lucia, was larger than his. Marlon developed an enormous amount of red in his first year. Some of the smaller caps have clean lines, while others look like a map of shoreline spits and inlets. I learned to recognize some individuals by memorizing the red-cap map. One bird, Patrick, looked like he had large flames painted on his cheeks. Another bird had a fairly small cap on top, but developed a broad band of red under his chin. Right after a molt, the head feathers are bright scarlet. Between molts, the feathers can become so weathered that they're a dull orange-red. Birds with a lot of red head feathers tend to have fuller patches of red on their wings.

Parrot green has a phosphorescent sheen. Your eyes can play tricks on you if you stare long enough at a single spot on a parrot's body. A feather is a collection of many thin barbs growing out of a central shaft. When the feathers are laid over one another, the barbs form elaborate patterns that shimmer and glow. The hue changes as your point of view changes. Sometimes the feathers look dark green; at other times they have a yellowish tinge. In fact, parrot green is an illusion. The feathers are actually yellow. If you hold one up to a bright light, you'll see that it's true. We see their feathers as green because of the Tyndall effect. The surface of the feather contains millions of microscopic air vacuoles that reflect back the blue end of the light spectrum. It's the same process that makes the sky look blue; light is scattered by dust and water in the atmosphere and reflects back to us as blue. In the case of the parrot, the reflected blue light blends with the yellow pigment in the feather to create the illusion of green. The underside of the wing and tail feathers do not reflect light the same way the top feathers do, and you can see the true color—a grayish yellow. When wet, their feathers turn a dirty brown. On the underside of the wing is a patch of orange-red.

Whenever someone asks me what it was that initially attracted me to the parrots, I always end up talking about their eyes. Because the pupil stands out clearly, it was through the pupil that I saw their keen intelligence and personality. I've never seen mention of it in any book, but there are actually two concentric bands surrounding the pupil. There's an outer iris that's orange-brown, and then another inside that. This inner ring has a metallic color, tending toward a silvery or bluish gray. *Aratinga,* the genus to which the cherry head belongs, means "little macaw," and like the macaws, the Aratinga species have a bare batch of furrowed skin (called the *periophthalmic ring*) that surrounds each eye. In the macaws, the patch is quite large, but in the conures it's small, only slightly larger than the eye itself. The periophthalmic ring of the cherry heads is creamy white.

Other features include a bone-colored beak and skirts of orange-red feathers that hang down over gray legs. In older birds, the bumpy skin often peels away, leaving the legs a brownish pink.

After I'd gone through all the useful literature available in bookstores, I was still dissatisfied. I'd never gotten into the habit of using libraries for research, but one day I decided I might as well see what was available in the local branch. The library shelves didn't contain any books I hadn't already read, so I asked the librarian, Gardner Haskell, if he had any tips. He asked which of the databases in the branch computers I'd searched. I'd never touched a computer in my life, and I had no idea what a database was. Gardner helped me get up to speed. On our very first search, we came up with something that looked like gold, a paper called "The Nesting Ecology of Red-Masked

Conures in Peru, and the El Niño Event," written by Patricia Chavez-Riva. It was a master's thesis sitting on a shelf thousands of miles away at the University of Miami Library. I was thrilled that such a document existed, but dismayed that it was out of reach. But Gardner assured me that I'd have no problem getting hold of it through the interlibrary loan program. For the next few weeks, I felt like a kid waiting for Christmas morning. Finally, the thesis arrived. I was so jazzed that I started reading it on the walk home. My excitement didn't last long. In fact, I was somewhat disappointed. It wasn't the comprehensive species study I'd hoped for. Rather, like most theses, it confined itself to a narrow topic: the effect of El Niño on the cherry head's breeding success. Most of the species information was taken from sources I already knew. The most interesting aspect of the thesis was that it provided me with a clearer image of the world that the birds came from.

The territory of the cherry-headed conure ranges from north-western Ecuador, near Manabí, to northwestern Peru, just south of Lambayeque—a distance of approximately six hundred miles. Laterally, the birds are confined to the narrow coastal strip between the Pacific Ocean and the western Andean foothills. Although the bird is occasionally seen as high up as 8,200 feet (2,500 meters), it usually keeps to elevations below 3,300 feet (1,000 meters). Fieldwork for the thesis was conducted at El Coto de Caza El Angolo, a nature reserve in northwestern Peru that is close to the border with Ecuador. The habitat there, and the primary habitat of the cherry-headed conure generally, is called *tropical dry forest*. It's not rain forest, nor is the cherry head a jungle bird. Tropical dry forest is located in hot lowland areas with distinct wet and dry seasons. Trees are relatively low and more widely scattered than in a rain forest. Most trees are deciduous; in the dry season they lose their leaves entirely. The shrub layer is dense, and vines are common, but ground cover is sparse. One of the most common trees is the ceiba *(Ceiba trichistandra)*. It's an unusual looking tree, with an immense, bulging, bottle-shaped trunk and strangely contorted limbs. It has a cottonlike fruit that the parrots eat. Other common trees are the palo santo *(Bursera graveolens),* the acacia, the laurel, and the fig. In the driest areas, there are cacti. Although tropical dry forest seems to be its preferred habitat, the cherry head is occasionally seen in moister forest—although apparently not rain forest—and in semi-desert. But there is no place where it is seen *often.* Its habitat is one of the most devastated on the planet. There was once continuous dry forest from Esmeraldas in northern Ecuador to south of Tumbes in Peru. But dry forest makes good agricultural land; today, nearly all of it has been cleared, much of it for banana plantations. Current estimates of its destruction range from 95 percent to 99 percent.

Birds are generally described as either sedentary or migratory. Sedentary birds stay year-round in a particular territory, while migratory birds have seasonal homes. The cherry head, on the other hand, is usually described as nomadic. For most of the year, it ranges over a wide territory; but during the breeding season, the bird sticks to a particular locale. Accordingly, the only time that cherry-headed conures visit El Coto de Caza El Angolo is during the breeding season, which lasts from May to July. One reason they breed there is the abundance of ceiba trees. Besides eating its fruit, they use it for nesting. Like nearly all parrots, cherry heads don't build twig and grass nests, but use naturally occurring holes in trees. They like the nests to be high above the ground, and the ceiba is one of the tallest trees in the forest. Although the birds will not start a hole from scratch, they will expand a preexisting hole, and the wood of the ceiba is relatively soft and easy to work on.

Like the cherry-headed conure, the blue-crowned conure comes from a dry habitat. Reflecting its large, discontinuous territory, there are five different races of blue crowns. Connor and Catherine were both of the race *Aratinga acuticaudata acuticaudata,* which inhabits the southernmost end of the range—southern Brazil, Paraguay, Bolivia, and northern Argentina. *Acuticaudata* means "sharp-tailed," and sometimes the bird is called the *sharp-tailed conure.* More often it's called the blue-crowned conure, except by ornithologists who prefer to call it the *blue-crowned parakeet.*

Averaging 14.5 inches (37 centimeters) in length, the blue crown is one of the largest conures. It's primarily green, except for the head—most of which is blue—and the tail feathers, which are streaked with red on the underside. The blue head feathers are somewhat pale; in some lighting situations, they are indistinguishable from the bird's green feathers. The periophthalmic eye ring is snow white. The outer iris is—to my mind—orange, but others describe it variously as pale-red, yellow, and orange-yellow. The blue crown's upper beak is bone-colored with a pink tinge, and narrows to a thin, needle-sharp point at its tip, which is gray. The lower beak is dark gray or black. The legs are a brownish pink.

The blue crown is also nomadic, traveling the countryside in large, noisy flocks until the arrival of the breeding season, when the birds break down into pairs or small groups. Its habitat ranges from dry, deciduous forest to semidesert. In Bolivia, blue crowns have been seen as high up in the mountains as 8,700 feet (2,650 meters), but they generally keep to lowland areas. In Argentina, where they are especially numerous, they're often seen in the pampas. Connor probably came from Argentina. One day, I was able to get close enough to read his leg band: OIW 844. That's a type of numbering system that was once used in quarantine stations in the United States, and it indicated that Connor was an imported, wild-caught bird. In the 1980s and early 1990s, Argentina was the biggest exporter of wild-caught parrots to the United States.

The wild bird trade was—and still is—an ugly business. American importers preferred baby birds, so trappers searched the forests and savannas for nest holes. If the nest hole was easily accessible, the trapper climbed the tree, hacked open the hole with a machete, and threw the babies down to a catcher. If the catcher missed, or the baby landed in the catcher's hands too hard, the baby died. If a nest hole was difficult to reach, the trappers cut the tree down and hoped the babies survived the crash. Survivors were thrown into a box teeming with other terrified baby birds. It's been estimated that out of every ten nestlings taken, six to eight died within the first four days. Besides killing so many babies, the felling of the trees created problems for the remaining flock members. Parrots are particular about nest holes. They have to be high above the ground and of a certain size. They should not face the sun during the heat of the day, and they should have a clear view of approaching danger. Good nest holes are scarce, and every time a tree is cut down, the nest hole is lost forever.

Because of the difficulty in taming them, adult birds were less desirable to the pet trade. But by the 1970s, parrot ownership in developed countries had become so popular that the trappers, who had large orders to fill, started taking adult birds anyway. One method of catching adults was to put glue on a branch that parrots were known to perch on. The bigger operations strung mist nets along the treetops in the forest canopy. Entire flocks were taken this way. Some-times adults were shot, with the hope that the bird would be wounded lightly enough that it would recover.

After "harvesting" the parrots, the trappers took them to holding pens—stacks of wood and wire-mesh boxes. Hundreds of birds were crowded together, and conditions were filthy. Birds were given a cheap gruel, which would soon be soiled by the birds' own excrement. Parrots fought each other for cage space, and some died in the fights. Others died from shock or starvation. One study of Mexican parrot exports estimated that 60 percent of all captured parrots died on the way to the marketplace.

The survivors were put on planes and flown to the United States, Europe, or Japan. In the United States, birds were immediately trans-ferred to quarantine stations, where they spent the next thirty days. The stations were mandated by federal law, but privately owned and operated. Again, large numbers of parrots were crowded together in small cages. The purpose of the overcrowding this time was to detect diseased birds, and to make sure that enough of the others got ill so that no sick bird would slip through quarantine undetected. The pri-mary aim was to keep out carriers of exotic Newcastle disease, an avian virus that can spread easily to poultry and cause enormous losses. Birds that made it through the quarantine period had a small stainless-steel band crimped around one leg. The bands were engraved with three letters and three numbers that indicated which station the bird came through and which shipment it was in. The birds were then sent on to the pet trade. Some were bought by domestic breeders, but most were sold to pet stores.

In the 1980s, biologists and conservationists began to notice an alarming drop in wild parrot populations. Parrot species were becoming more and more threatened both by habitat loss and by capture for the pet trade. The Convention on International Trade in Endangered Species of Wild Fauna and Flora (CITES) lists three levels of endangerment, from high to low, Appendices I, II, and III. Except for the budgerigar and the cockatiel *(Nymphicus hollandicus),* all parrot species are on one of the three lists. Appendix III lists only one parrot, the ring-necked parakeet *(Psittacula krameri).* Both the cherry-headed conure and the blue-crowned conure are on Appendix II, although some believe that the cherry head should be moved to Appendix I (most threatened). In 1990, Robert Ridgely, a specialist on the birds of Ecuador, made the following statement at a conference on the problems posed by the pet bird trade:

"There is no question in my mind that certain species have undergone catastrophic declines in Ecuador over the last fifteen-year period. I would point in particular to Aratinga erythrogenys, which occurred in the thousands in southwestern Ecuador. It was a very common, widespread species in the mid-to-late 1970s. Now it is at a population level where you really have to look for the odd dozen or two, perhaps fifty in remote canyons with relatively low human population density. In 1977 there were thousands of them passing over Guayaquil every morning and evening. If there is one anywhere near there now, I don't know where it is. Indeed, that conure has been very extensively harvested in Ecuador during that period. It is my understanding that they have been smuggled through Peru. I have no information about the current status on Peruvian populations, but I suspect

that they have also been affected seriously by the trade. It's devas-
tating to me that this has been happening. It shows what con-
certed efforts to trap birds over a decade can do to a population."

The United States was the world's largest importer of wild-caught parrots, and conservationists lobbied the government to do something about the problem. In 1992, Congress passed and President Bush signed the Wild Bird Conservation Act (WBCA), which put heavy restrictions on the importation of Appendix I species. In 1993, the act was amended to include Appendix II species, which virtually eliminated legal importation of wild parrots. (Smuggling persists, of course, with smugglers doing such things as drugging birds with alcohol to keep them quiet, and then stuffing them in mailing tubes before passing through customs.)

At the time that the WBCA became law, there were already millions of wild parrots in homes in the United States. Many novice parrot owners discovered that the beautiful and relatively inexpensive parrot they'd bought (cherry heads sold for under $100) really was a wild bird. The birds feared them and hated captivity. Some screamed endlessly, and they bit their owners. Angry and frustrated themselves, some pet owners tossed the birds out windows. As wild birds, the parrots were constantly looking for an opportunity to escape, and many did. There were also handling accidents at pet stores and airports. There is a surprisingly large number of wild parrot flocks in the United States today, and many of them live near airports. In any locale, whenever enough parrots of the same species have found each other, they've begun to breed. One study claims that there are at least twenty-seven parrot species living free and breeding in the United States. I've heard of parrot flocks, large and small, in Connecticut, Florida, Hawaii, Illinois, Louisiana, New York, Texas, Oregon, southern California, Utah, and Washington State. They have succeeded for at least two reasons. First, along with corvids, owls, and woodpeckers, parrots are considered to be among the smartest birds. Second, there is a large amount of food available to them. American cities and suburbs are large, human-built ecologies in which parrots are able to thrive. Gardens and parks are usually designed to have something growing in them at all times of the year. Sometimes the plants are even exotics that are native to the parrot's home territory. That so many different species can thrive outside their native habitat indicates adaptability with regard to diet. They've also learned to use bird feeders. So far, none of the wild parrot flocks have left urban or suburban areas. If they were to venture out of urban areas, they would more than likely starve to death. Birds don't migrate because of cold, but rather because there isn't enough food for them in winter. One of America's largest wild parrot flocks lives year-round in Chicago. Temperature is simply not an issue.

John Aikin, the curator of birds at the San Francisco Zoo, had taken the time to explain to me in some detail why cold wasn't a problem for the parrots. He said they could acclimate with little trouble as long as the change was not too abrupt. Parrots have a layer of warming down feathers that can grow in more thickly if need be. The down layer explanation was one that I'd encountered elsewhere. But one day I realized that it must be simpler than that. Scrapperella, the parrot without any feathers on her breast, ribs, or back, had been through forty-degree temperatures in the rain, and she'd seemed absolutely unfazed by it. Parrots are tough birds.

I telephoned the zoo often for answers to my questions. John's specialty was raptors, but he tried to answer my parrot questions as best he could. It was John who told me that I was wrong about Dolores Park being their roost spot. They were actually roosting in Walton Square, a small park only half a mile from where I lived. John had been at Walton Square for a television interview about the thousands of starlings that one winter were descending upon the square every evening to roost. While being interviewed, he saw that the parrots were there, too, and settling in for the evening. It seemed to me an odd choice for a roost spot, given that the square was right across the street from the first of the downtown high-rises. But the square's proximity to Telegraph Hill explained how Mandela had survived the flight home on the day he slipped out of his cage.

John often expressed interest in coming out to see the parrots, and one day he found the time. I was excited to have an expert on the scene. I set out the bowl, and as John and I stood at the Dutch door, its top half open, he gave me a running commentary on what he was seeing. It was a typically noisy feeding. He told me that one reason parrots scream so much is practical. They're flocking animals, and in a forest only a few trees will have, at any given time, something edible growing on them. When a parrot does find food, he screams so that all the other parrots in the area can know about it, too. I often thought that the parrots' fear of hawks was exaggerated, that the hawks weren't interested in the parrots as a meal, so I asked him if their fear was warranted. He assured me that it was. San Francisco has many more hawks than most people realize, and they will go after parrots. He said he'd once inspected a peregrine falcon nest on the Bay Bridge and found that it was lined with budgie feathers. He said that budgies would be especially easy to catch since, having never been wild, they were completely disoriented when they escaped. His most insightful observation was in regard to Scrapperella. I'd always assumed that she had a skin disease, but John told me she was a feather plucker. And not only was she plucking herself, she was plucking her mate, Scrapper, too. He pointed out that Scrapperella was plucked only in places she could reach, while Scrapper was plucked mostly in places that he couldn't reach. Feather plucking is a common problem with pet parrots. Bored or frustrated, they preen and preen to the point that they eventually start to pull out their own feathers. Once a bird starts plucking, it can be extremely difficult to get him to stop. But it's supposed to be a problem of pet parrots, not wild ones.

I'd looked forward to John's visit. For months, I'd wanted to have a professional talk to me about what I was seeing, and so much anticipation had built up within me that by the time he arrived, I felt a little self-conscious. Once I saw that I was being self-conscious, I got even more so. It kept getting worse, minute by minute, until finally I became tongue-tied. I was completely immersed in what I was doing with the parrots, and I wanted to make sure that I was doing it right. But I was very sensitive to the fact that I had no scientific background, and I wasn't sure what "right" was. John did have a scientific background, of course, and I was aware of the strictures scientists have against giving their subjects names and interacting with them. They say it leads to *anthropomorphism,* which is the ascription of human characteristics to animals. So I had some doubt as to whether John approved of what I was doing. As we were making our good-byes I told him, "I realize I'm probably anthropomorphizing the birds by giving them names and hand-feeding them and all . . ." It sounded so awkward and false to my own ears that I couldn't finish. It was as though I were apologizing to him. John looked puzzled and unsure of how to respond. He didn't have any problem with what I was doing.

Dogen

I had some hope that after living with me in close quarters, Mandela might trust and like me enough to visit—which was naive. He was friendly, but not the slightest bit interested in coming inside. If there was any possibility of it happening, I'd have to bring him along gradually. Getting him comfortable with my hand seemed the next logical step, but now that he was free, he rejected even the tentative petting he'd allowed when he was in my charge. In spite of that setback, there were two charming developments in our friendship. When the flock arrived, they usually landed on the lines or in the trees before coming to the fire escape. I'd look for Mandela, and when I spotted him, I'd pat my arm, and he'd fly straight to me. His wing still drooped, which made precision flight difficult for him. So instead of attempting a landing on the rim of the cup, he often plopped onto my chest and then walked down my arm. The other development—one I liked even more—was that he'd started perching on my shoulder and taking seeds from my lips. He actually preferred to be fed this way. But I could never get the seeds to him quickly enough. Whenever he was ready for another, and my lips were empty or turned away, he'd pull on my beard or bite my ear to get my attention. The ear bites stung— especially on cold days. Some days, instead of eating, he'd sit on my shoulder and survey the fire escape and gardens while I fed the others. He would play with me, tugging on my hair and glasses, and preening my mustache. His siblings, Stella and Chomsky, always perched on the seed cup now, and from time to time Mandela would walk down my arm to join them. Whenever he was on the cup, I couldn't resist giving him a kiss on a wing or his back. I loved the silkiness of his feathers and the warmth of his body against my lips. As long as I didn't overdo it, he seemed not to mind.

But the parrot with whom I had the most physical contact was not Mandela; it was Smith. Since his usual position was to stand on my wrist while eating from my palm, Smith always had his back to me, and I took advantage of it to kiss him. He disliked the kisses, but he was so absorbed in eating that he usually ignored them. Every now and then I'd set the seed cup down and stroke him with my free hand. He usually allowed me to get in a few pets, but, again, only because he was so wrapped up in eating. The other parrots disliked me touching Smith, and if my petting hand was near the railing, the birds perched there would bite it until I stopped. Sometimes Smith became sufficiently irritated with my attentions that he turned around and bit me himself. No parrot bit harder than Smith, and he never gave warning bites. Sometimes I was incorrigible, so he'd get fed up and leave for the bowl, where he could eat unmolested.

Connor was constantly having to fend off various cherry heads trolling for seeds along the bottom of the fire escape. Since Catherine couldn't bear even the mildest threat, she seldom ate with him. And despite the small number of birds eating from the bowl, she'd been unable to hold her own there. After getting chased from the bowl, she overcame her fear of me and began taking seeds from my hand. I felt protective of her. I was constantly on the lookout for any bird who might attack her. She understood what I was doing, and became comfortable enough with me that she started clutching my fingers with her toes while I fed her. My happiest moment with Catherine was the morning that she showed up at the fire escape all by herself. She made one squawk to let me know she'd arrived and then waited. I looked all around for Connor, but he didn't seem to be lurking anywhere. She'd come on her own. Catherine was so timid that she flinched every time my hand came near her, but she stuck it out until she was full. I was touched that she'd had enough confidence in me to give it a try.

Although I'd gotten used to it, I could still be surprised on occasion by the parrots' acceptance of me. Besides being relaxed with them and not violating their trust, I would try to show solidarity by feigning concern at whatever concerned them—barking dogs, runaway helium balloons, distant hawks. It probably made little impression on them—they seemed adept at detecting insincerity—but I enjoyed doing it. Even at the more high-strung feedings, when they were so vicious with one another that they sometimes drew blood, I seldom got bitten. I learned to avoid any parrot, though, with constricted pupils and wings held away from his sides, because that indicated a parrot in a highly excited state. Sometimes they were so wired that I could feel their energy vibrating inside of me well after they'd left.

They were aware of me as an individual, even from a distance. One time, I was away from the house much longer than I'd planned, and I didn't return until well past the usual time of the day's last feeding. There were still four parrots on the fire escape waiting for me, but the others had lost patience and gone away. A few minutes after I began to feed the four remaining birds, I saw the flock coming from the north, on their way to roost at Walton Square. They were high up and working hard (flight always looks like hard work for a parrot), but two of them spotted me and began an abrupt dive down to the fire escape, while calling out to the others, "He's back! He's back!" They recognized me away from the fire escape, too. One day, Helen asked me to sweep the Greenwich Steps. The flock was napping in the loquat tree, which was around sixty feet from the fire escape, and as I passed by them I stopped sweeping to say hello. The moment I greeted them, they all bolted from the tree, flew up to the fire escape, and waited for me to come feed them.

One of my favorite aspects of their character is their taste for bizarre humor. I once saw two of them playing a game in which one parrot clung by his beak to the hinge of a casement window—the kind of window that swings out—while the second, with his back to the first and his toes locked together with him, flapped his wings as hard as he could. Because their feet were locked together, the flapping bird couldn't fly away, and his stationary flight was lifting the body of the bird clinging to the hinge. Both were screaming joyfully. I saw another quirky game after a rain. A group of ten flew to a tree, plopped down onto the outermost layer of leaves, and spread their wings out to dry. One of the parrots—wings still extended—hopped a foot sideways. Then another did the same. Then another and another. It went on like that all around the tree. They looked like Mexican jumping beans. The game seemed spontaneous and improvised. I never saw them play it again.

The first eggs weren't laid until the beginning of summer, but I saw pairs mating as early as May. They were graceless lovers. There never seemed to be any foreplay; the male simply put his foot on the female's back and started grinding away. Both sexes have a cloaca, a small hole at their butt end, that leads to their reproductive organs and waste tract. When the two cloacas touch, sperm passes from the male to the female. Like the year before, I saw Connor and Catherine mating, and again Connor took the male position. Although I was hoping to see some baby blue crowns this time, a breeder I talked to warned me that Connor and Catherine might not be male and female. Two males would engage in sex if no females were available.

Mandela's sister, Stella, wasn't even a year old, and already one of the adult cherry heads was feeding her, which is courting behavior in parrots. I'd never singled the older bird out, and for awhile I referred to him as "Stella's beau." Then he became just "Bo." Stella and her two siblings, Mandela and Chomsky, had separated from their parents, Sonny and Lucia, but the three juveniles were still together. Apparently, parrot etiquette demanded that Bo hang out with all three of them. As the breeding season drew closer, the flock was breaking down into smaller and smaller groups, and Stella, Bo, Mandela, and Chomsky were a constant foursome. One day, I saw Bo and Stella mating on a power line. I'd read that cherry-headed conures don't reach sexual maturity until they're a year and a half or two years old. I wondered if Stella was going to prove the books wrong, but I never got the chance to find out.

At a feeding in mid-May, a parrot made a startlingly clumsy landing on the rim of the seed cup. It was Stella. Her condition shocked me. Her head was tilting to one side and she was wobbling badly. They were the same symptoms that Martha had shown the previous summer. Her head twitched so much that it took her a long time to eat even one seed. When the flock left, she remained behind on the cup rim. She looked dazed and bewildered. I started walking toward the fire escape door, hoping she wouldn't realize what I was doing. But just as I was about to enter the house, she flew away.

Over the next few days, Stella's landings on the cup kept getting sloppier. One time, she just managed to hook the lip of the cup with a toenail. She was hanging from the cup rim, too weak to lift herself, so I had to help her, grabbing the tip of her beak with my finger. She felt limp. It was depressing to see her in that state, and I started thinking up ways to get Stella into the house. I decided to trap her underneath my jacket. I had, at most, one chance, and I was so nervous about blowing it that I had a hard time pulling the trigger. I started bringing the cup slowly toward my body. When I had her right up against my belly, I abruptly shoved her under my jacket. I had her, but I was afraid of pressing on her too hard, so she was able to struggle free. Stella flew away in terror. I felt lousy about having frightened her. To

make things worse, there were a few parrot witnesses, and for my failure, I had to endure several days of mistrust. Stella wouldn't come
anywhere near me after that. Fortunately, she still had Bo to feed her.

A week after Stella got sick, Smith showed up on the lines with
similar symptoms. He looked sleepy, and his head was hanging to the
side. Smith's decline happened more quickly than Stella's. Only three
days after I first noticed that he was ill, his condition became desperate. I went out to feed the flock and found Smith flying around and
around in a circle, trying to find the confidence to attempt a landing
on the fire escape. Exhausted, he veered off course and crashed into
the thin, tangled branches of a plum tree. His torso dangled below his
wings, which were hung up in the branches, making him look like a
tiny scarecrow. After a short rest, he struggled free and resumed his
urgent circling. Finally, at the end of his rope, he broke away and
headed straight toward me. He landed on my head, slipped, and fell
to the fire escape floor. He lay there panting, not moving. After the
mistrust I'd had to go through for trying to grab Stella, I was reluctant
to touch him. But when Connor waddled over and started pecking at
him, I shooed Connor away, picked Smith up, and carried him past
the others into the house. They had no apparent reaction.

I still had the cage that I'd kept Mandela in, and I put Smith
inside it. As soon as I closed the door he became animated, crawling
anxiously around the bars, looking for a way out. Still concerned that
the flock might be suspicious about what I was doing with Smith, I
left him and went back outside to finish the feeding. I was relieved to
see that none of them had lost any confidence in me. After the feeding, I came back inside and found Smith frantically biting the bars of
his cage. When I approached, he abruptly stopped and perched. He
looked like a prisoner of war standing for inspection. Smith was one
of the smallest cherry heads in the flock. He'd been very slow to
develop any red feathers, so except for a few red spots here and there,
he was almost entirely green. His beak was stained purple from some
berry that the flock had been eating, and the feathers surrounding his
beak were caked with dried juice and bits of broken plant parts. He

had a bald spot above his cere, and there was a cut running through it. His chest feathers were sticky and matted, and most of his tail feathers were broken. In spite of his illness and the new and strange circumstance in which he found himself, Smith's demeanor was remarkably calm and self-assured.

I handed him a seed through the cage bars, which he took eagerly. He seemed to have calmed down, so I opened the cage door to feed him. Instead of taking another seed, though, he bit me. I closed the door and resumed feeding him through the bars. Once he'd had his fill, I carried him upstairs to the bedroom and covered the cage with a towel. It looked like Smith might be staying for awhile. I made the same deal with him that I'd made with Mandela: As soon as he was healthy, I would set him free.

The next morning, his eyes were bright and he ate heartily, but he was still unstable. Other than his lack of balance, he didn't really look ill. Maybe it was the berries. I wasn't sure what to do. I'd been excited to have Mandela in the house, but I felt an odd lack of enthusiasm for Smith. Maybe it was simply that the novelty of having a wild parrot in the house was gone, but I'd never found anything in Smith's personality that especially appealed to me. Nor was he particularly good-looking. I thought his beak was too large for his head, and he looked kind of plain. I couldn't afford a trip to a veterinarian, and I wasn't about to ask Helen to pay for another one, so I adopted the policy that I would feed Smith and give him rest, but he was going to have to pull through this illness on his own. I opened the cage door and offered him water, which he drank eagerly. I had a job to get to, so I closed the cage door and left the house.

On the bike ride home, I stopped at a pet store and bought Smith a treat—some kind of seed cluster. When I got to the house, the flock was out on the fire escape making anxious noises, trying to lure me out. I wanted to give Smith his treat before feeding them, but when I tried to hand it to him, he bit my finger again. This time I bled. It was a frustrating moment. I felt pulled to go outside, but the cut was deep and it took me several minutes to stanch the flow of blood. Eventually, it slowed to the point that I could put a bandage on the cut. I went out to feed the birds, but for some reason none of the parrots would come near me. Each bird to whom I offered a seed flew away. Connor was the only bird who would take one, but only after showing a great deal of caution. Finally, I saw the problem: It was the bandage. They hate unfamiliar objects. I tore it off, and everybody relaxed.

Smith had been falling off his perch and into his droppings. His feathers were caked with them. It looked so unsanitary that I was concerned it might hinder his recovery. I'd read that some pet parrots like to be sprayed with a mister, so I sprayed him, hoping it might stimulate him to clean himself. But it only frightened him. He sat on his perch soaked and shivering. I noticed a bit of shit on the rim of his water dish, so I reached into his cage—cautiously this time—to clean it off. He completely surprised me by leaping through the open door, flying across the room, and smashing into a window. I ran over and grabbed him with my bare hand, and he sliced open another finger. Twice in one day! I stuck him back in his cage and glared at him while squeezing my bleeding finger. He was listing heavily to his right and trembling. I left him there to shake and went off to tend to my new wound.

The next morning, Smith was sitting up straight, but he was still shaking. Every few minutes he'd fall off his perch and have to climb back up onto it again. After one fall, he stopped to scratch his head. A healthy parrot balances on one foot while scratching with the other. They balance easily, and can hold the position for as long as they need to. Smith was too unstable to do anything more than quick, brief scratches. If he'd merely been drunk on berries, the effects would have worn off by now. I clearly had a sick bird on my hands.

Thinking that fresh air might do him some good, I carried the cage out onto the east balcony. A little later, the flock showed up, and Smith's sibling, Jones, flew over to visit with him. They talked back and forth for awhile, and then Jones left. Smith called out to him in a tone that was distinctly anxious, so Jones turned around and flew back to the railing. For twenty minutes, Jones kept leaving and returning in response to Smith's cries. The commotion attracted the attention of the rest of the flock. More parrots flew to the railing to see the caged flock member. Each time a group revved up to leave, Smith would crouch and spread his wings. At the very moment the birds left, he'd leap to the cage bars and hang from them. When the flock left for the day, I brought him back inside. He was still trembling.

I decided that he was simply going to have to get used to my hands—it was too difficult to deal with him otherwise—so I offered him another seed as a peace offering. Quick as lightning, he opened up a third wound. This one was even worse than the other two. He had me intimidated now. I went upstairs to put on another bandage and pulled out of storage the heavy gloves I used for winter bicycling.

The next day, curious to see how well Smith could fly, I took him down to the studio. He was even weaker than I'd supposed. When he flew, he went sideways or even backwards, zooming off on unintended tangents, bouncing off the walls and furniture. After each failed attempt, he stood on the carpet looking dazed and helpless. I put on the gloves and picked him up. As I was putting him back in the cage, he bit me repeatedly, furiously, and even with gloves on the bites were painful. When I carried Smith back up to the house, there were some parrots on the lines calling out to him. He climbed the bars excitedly and squawked back at them. Back in the house, I set the cage down, and saw that he was leaning heavily to his right again. I didn't like the look of it. Of the two perches in the cage, he'd preferred the upper, but now he was confining himself to the lower. His head was hanging again. When he walked across the cage floor, he kept falling over.

I was still puzzled by my indifference toward Smith. I wanted his problem to just go away, but he'd been with me four days now, and not only was he not getting any better, he seemed to be deteriorating. He was having so much trouble staying on his perch that he gave up trying to mount it. I was beginning to think he might not last the day. At mid-afternoon I found Smith on the bottom of the cage, his head in an extreme list. To keep it upright, he was resting the tip of his beak on the cage floor. He was trembling heavily. Suddenly, he looked like he was going. He was struggling to keep his eyes open. As he faded, I felt tears coming. I fought to suppress them, and my head ached from the effort. I pleaded with him: "Come on, Smith. Don't die. Hang in there. Come on. Please don't die." I kept thinking about my decision to leave the responsibility of healing up to Smith himself. I'd been so cavalier about his illness. I vowed to him that if he pulled through this, I'd take better care of him. Just please don't die. *Please.*

He heard a parrot squawk outside and lifted his head weakly. Then he laid it back down on the bottom of the cage and trembled some more. His eyelids kept drooping. He seemed to be giving in to unconsciousness. My eyes were so blurry with tears that I couldn't see. I'd just launched into another urgent plea for him to hang on when he stood up, climbed onto his perch, and started eating from his seed dish. I couldn't believe it. Either it was a miraculous recovery, or I'd been disturbing his nap.

Regardless, I'd made a vow to do my best for Smith. I'd noticed that every time he got excited his condition worsened, so my first decision was to isolate him as much as possible from the flock. I carried the cage up to the bedroom, closed the curtains, and then went straight down to the public library, where I checked out several books that contained information on parrot health care. It was a subject that up to that point I'd completely neglected. Each book emphasized the same thing: Give a sick bird heat. They have a high metabolism and lose body heat quickly. I remembered that just a few days before I'd seen a heat bulb in the back of a closet. I got it out, hooked it up to a portable fixture, and set it up in front of his cage. I placed a towel over the cage to keep the heat in, and added a thermometer so that I could monitor the temperature. The moment I switched on the lamp, Smith looked up, got out of his prone position at the bottom of the cage, and climbed to the top perch to bask in the heat. He stopped trembling. His response was so immediate that it cheered me.

I thought he deserved a more distinctive name. I was still struggling with *Zen Mind, Beginner's Mind,* the book by Shunryu Suzuki-roshi, and as difficult as I found the book, I enjoyed it. Even when I didn't understand what he was talking about, Suzuki-roshi's good heart and humor came through to me. I wanted Smith's new name to honor him, but I didn't think that Suzuki sounded like a good name for a parrot. I tended to prefer names with two syllables, but roshi is a title, so that didn't work either. Throughout the book, Suzuki talks about the Zen master Dogen, whose spiritual lineage he was descended from. I liked the name *Dogen,* so Dogen it was.

Everything Changes

It was difficult to get a sense of a young bird's gender, and since I named most birds when they were babies, a lot of males ended up with female names, and vice versa. Not long after naming Dogen, I started thinking that he was actually a female, which turned out to be true; but by the time I was certain of it, she'd been "Dogen" for so long that I never considered giving her a new name.

Little by little, Dogen's health improved. She had bad days when her head hung and she trembled, but the heat lamp always brought her back. Because my housing situation was so tenuous, I was eager to get her healthy enough for release. Nothing worried me more than the possibility that she wouldn't be ready before I had to move. What would I do then? I couldn't carry her from house to house or, if the worst happened, around the streets with me.

While Dogen seemed on the way to beating her illness, Stella was finally overcome by hers. Two weeks after she first showed up sick, she disappeared. I'd thought her condition had stabilized, and since Bo was at her side I'd even become optimistic about her chances for surviving. But birds are notorious for concealing illness, so she may have been in worse shape than she looked. Stella wasn't the only missing parrot; Murphy was gone now, too. Marlon was still coming around, but he was always alone. I considered the possibility that Marlon and Murphy were a mated pair, and that Murphy had gone to nest, but it seemed remote. When I first noticed them together, both birds were only eight or nine months old, so I thought it more likely that they were siblings.

Things took yet another bad turn when Chomsky showed up ill. His symptoms were the same as Martha, Stella, and Dogen's: head tilt, poor balance, erratic flight, and awkward landings. Chomsky's illness was troubling. It made me wonder if the parrots were contracting a disease to which, as nonnative birds, they had no resistance. Something like that might destroy the entire flock. And there was another possibility. I knew that some people detested the parrots. Some couldn't stand the noise, while others had a doctrinaire hatred for all nonnative species. I'd met a tree trimmer who told me he'd once seen a bird-watcher cursing the parrots, shouting that they should all be shot. Maybe someone was trying to poison them.

Dogen's attitude toward me was beginning to soften. Although she still hated being handled—she'd yowl like an angry cat and bite my gloves furiously—I was spending so many hours a day with her that she was getting used to my presence. I spent entire days lying on the bed, alternating between watching her and reading. She was finally beginning to clean herself. Her balance was still poor, so instead of preening her chest while perched, which a healthy parrot would do, she lay on her back on the bottom of the cage. She had other workarounds for her instability. When a parrot stretches, he raises a leg and fans out and tenses the wing and tail feathers on that side.

Dogen couldn't do that, so she stretched while lying on her belly. Apparently, she was studying me just as much as I was studying her, for she was beginning to learn my routines. Each night, before turning out the lights, I made certain preparations, which I always performed in a particular order. One night, she saw me reach through the curtains and open the window. Understanding where my movements were heading, she scurried up to her perch to sleep. I had an intuition that she felt some delight—not that it was bedtime, but that she'd known what was going to happen next.

I was beginning to feel real affection for Dogen. Much of it grew out of the new respect I had for her. I was impressed that despite living in a completely alien environment, she held herself with such confidence. She never cowered. She always acted as though she were the master of whatever space she inhabited. Even when she suffered from tremors, her eyes were clear, bright, and untroubled. I wanted us to be friends, so I worked on winning her over. I offered her all kinds of special foods: corn, grapes, strawberries, bananas, kale, rice, even tofu. She liked the grapes, kale, rice, and tofu, but not the corn, strawberries, or bananas. Whenever I opened her cage door now, she was eager to see what new treat I'd brought her. I gave her toys, too. She enjoyed a wooden spool and a used-up toilet paper roll. I had to take the latter away from her, though, after finding her stumbling around the cage with the roll stuck over her head. Since parrots nest in holes, I thought she might like a hiding place. I took an old shoe box, cut a hole in one end, and placed it upside down in her cage. Dogen loved the box, and she spent many hours inside of it. But the result was that I saw less of her. To lure her out, I'd hold a sunflower seed up to the cage bars. She'd crawl out of the box, take the seed, and then creep backward into the box to eat it. Thinking that I was making real progress toward winning her confidence, one day I opened the cage door to hand her the seed, and she gave me her worst bite yet.

I used to read pet parrot magazines in order to cull the occasional bit of information they contained on parrots in the wild. I found the magazines irritating, though. They pushed a set of rules that I thought were priggish: *Always* clip your bird's wings; *never* let him sit on your shoulder; *don't* let him eat seeds, and so on. One article said that the best way to tame a bird was to scold him severely for bad behavior and to praise him lavishly for good. I'd always loathed that kind of approach, but I felt that I had to do *something* about the biting. It was driving me nuts. So I decided to give the method a try. I made Dogen a simple T-stand—a cross stuck in a flowerpot—put my gloves on, and set her on it. Once her rage at being handled had subsided, I took off the gloves and put a bare index finger right in front of her legs. When Dogen reached down to bite it, I bellowed at the top of my lungs, "NOOO!" She drew back, startled. Once again I put my finger in front of her legs, and she tried to bite it. I hollered at her. I kept repeating the process until she finally chose to ignore my finger. I left it there and started sweet-talking her like crazy. I did this over and over until she had it down cold.

One afternoon, out on the fire escape, Mandela got into a tussle with Mozart and Mendelssohn, Eric and Erica's offspring from the previous year. The moment the fight began, Bo flew over to help Mandela push the two siblings off the railing. Having routed Mozart and Mendelssohn, Bo and Mandela flew to the lines, where they perched side by side. Bo started bouncing his head up and down and looked like he was about to gag. This was all very familiar to me now. Bo was preparing to feed Mandela. After feeding, he put a foot on Mandela's butt and began pushing on her with his pelvis. So Mandela was a female, too! I'd often suspected as much. When Mandela lived with me, I'd kept referring to her as "she" in my journal. I thought Mandela and Bo looked good together. I was curious to see if their relationship would change mine and Mandela's.

I started to allow Dogen time out of her cage, and although she'd regained some of her ability for controlled flight, she seldom took advantage of it. Whenever she did fly, it was usually just to the windowsill. To keep her calm, I'd been leaving the curtains closed, but she easily figured out how to get through them. The sky had a power-ful effect on her. Whenever she saw it, she'd lean forward and extend her wings as if she were about to launch herself into space. Her wings would tremble from her desire to fly free. I allowed her to go to the window as long as she didn't get too worked up by what she saw. One afternoon, Bo and Mandela spotted her on the sill. They flew to the window just opposite where Dogen was standing and clung to the molding. Dogen's enthusiastic screams bounced off the window and filled the bedroom. Bo and Mandela squawked and pecked at Dogen from the other side of the glass, and Dogen pecked back at them. I was concerned about a relapse, but the situation was so charming that I had to give it a chance. There was an armchair set against the wall, and the top of its backrest was just level with the window's lower sill. I kneeled on the cushion and placed my arms on the back of the chair. Dogen was waddling up and down the length of the sill, yakking at her flock mates, trying to figure out how to escape. Each time she passed my arms, she gave me a bite, but not one of them hurt.

After Mandela and Bo left, I took Dogen down to the dining room in her cage. I was handing her pieces of kale though the open cage door when I got distracted for a moment. While I was looking away, she jumped out of the cage and flew straight into the dining room window. Her momentum hadn't been strong enough to hurt her, and before I could get to her, she'd flown off to the living room. I was uncomfortable with Dogen flying free in the house. I got a towel out of the bathroom and went into the living room, where I found her perched on one of the high sills. I waved the towel at her to try to scare her down—a big mistake. She flew across the living room and then upstairs. My discomfort with Dogen flying free turned to alarm when I remembered that I'd left some upstairs windows open. I ran up after her in a panic. If she got out, she was a goner. I frantically herded her away from the windows, scaring her half to death in the process. As I slammed the windows shut, Dogen flew back down-stairs. I found her standing on the dining room floor, exhausted and terrified. I gently put the towel around her, picked her up, and put her back in the cage. She was panting heavily. The panting turned into sneezing, and then a desperate and mournful honking sound. She no longer looked like the master of her surroundings. She looked like a fragile and sick little bird. I felt a wave of pathos wash over me. Once her breathing had slowed down, Dogen crawled back into her box. To make peace, I offered her a sunflower seed, which she accepted. I also offered to let her take a piece out of my finger, but she gave me only a light, perfunctory bite. It was clear to me now that she was nowhere near being ready for release. I didn't want another incident like the one we'd just been through, and knowing that she'd be molting again in just two or three months, I decided that for her own safety, I should have her wing feathers clipped.

I couldn't bring myself to do the job—I'd never done it, and I was afraid Dogen would hate me for it—so I called Jamie Yorck, the owner of Spectrum Exotic Birds. Jamie had been helpful to me in the past, answering questions and giving me good deals on seeds, so I asked if he'd mind clipping Dogen. He said, "No problem"—but there was. As he clipped her, Jamie and I were talking, and I think he forgot that Dogen was not his usual customer. She bit him until his fingers bled. The clipping was a freebie, so I felt terrible, but Jamie was cool about it. He'd been bitten before.

When Dogen and I got home, I set the cage down on the living room floor and opened the door. She came right out. I was surprised at how quickly she accepted the fact that she couldn't fly. She flapped her wings hard a few times, but when nothing happened, she shrugged it off and began exploring the living room floor. I went into the kitchen to heat up some curried rice, and when I returned Dogen was still checking the place out. I sat down on the couch with my dinner and watched. Although her legs were still clumsy from her illness, she was clearly enjoying herself—scurrying under the coffee table, climbing a wicker footrest, and shinnying up a lamp cord. Her explorations stopped, though, when she noticed the black bowl on my lap. She knew what it was, having seen me eat from it many times. She ran across the floor, took my pant leg in her beak, and clawed her way up to my lap. Once there, she dug into the rice with enthusiasm. She was especially partial to the pieces of onion and picked through the rice in search of them. I put my fork down and let her have at it. When she was finished, I fully expected her to jump back down to the floor, but she stayed put. She looked funny and sweet standing there on my lap, her beak coated with sticky grains of rice. I felt some kind of anticipation coming from her, but she wouldn't look at me, so I didn't try to touch her.

For several weeks, Connor had been acting unusually aggressive—picking fights and winning them. One day, Connor and Catherine got into a fight with a cherry head who'd been after Connor's pile of seeds, and it turned into all-out war. The head feathers of all three birds were puffed up with rage, and they psychogobbled furiously while jabbing each other with their beaks. Connor and Catherine had the cherry head two against one, and they came out on top. I laughed at how tough they'd been. Later in the day, at another feeding, I noticed Catherine acting a little strange. I took a closer look and saw that one of her eyes was blurry. She seemed a little lethargic, too. As I examined her, I had a brief flashback to a moment right at the end of the fight. I remembered seeing a spot of blood on the cherry head's beak. Was that Catherine's blood? I didn't see any wounds on her.

The next day, the flock's run of bad luck continued. It was raining, and I kept hearing the call of a single cherry head from the fire escape. I was reluctant to go out in the rain to feed just one bird, but he was so persistent that I finally gave in. When I got there, I saw something dismaying. The bird had a large, jagged hole in the middle of his upper beak. He must have smashed into something while flying. His head was wet, so I couldn't identify him. Whoever he was, he didn't seem bothered by his injury, which looked ghastly. I worried that after being so badly weakened, the rest of the beak might crack off. I thought I saw some exposed dark and fleshy material inside the beak that looked liable to infection. When the parrot showed up again the next day, I saw that it was Sam, the bird I thought of as number two in command after Eric. The hole looked just as bad as it had the day before, but Sam acted as though it was no big deal. I called Jamie to ask about Sam's beak, and he told me not to worry about it; the beak would grow out like a finger nail and be as good as new.

I would have thought that the odds precluded any more extreme developments, but then another incredible thing happened. It was the first day of summer, and I was out on the fire escape waiting for the parrots. Off in the distance, I heard and then saw a small group heading my way. Somehow I knew it even before they reached the fire escape: There was a new parrot in the flock. It was a different species, too: a mitred conure.

The mitred conure, or parakeet *(Aratinga mitrata),* is very similar in appearance to the cherry head. It's green with red on its head, but the red coloration is limited to a maroon band across the top of the beak and a narrow mask around its eyes. Mitred conures are slightly larger than cherry heads, and the new bird was larger than any bird in the flock—including Connor. He had a bigger beak, too, and a distinct voice that reminded me somewhat of a seagull. I'm not really sure how from such a distance I was able to recognize that there was a new bird in the flock, but it was probably that voice.

The mitred conure followed the cherry heads to the fire escape and then joined them on the seed bowl. He was nervous and aggressive, lunging at anybody who perched next to him. The cherry heads seemed unhappy about his presence and unsure of how to deal with him. Later in the feeding, he came over to where I was standing and took a few seeds from my hand. He was banded—another wild-caught bird—and tame enough that I was able to get his quarantine band number: CSP 203. A few days earlier, I'd gone to visit a friend who worked at Oliver's Books, and I took the bookstore's name for the bird: Oliver.

I was happy that there was a new bird in the flock, but it didn't last long. When Oliver came the next day, I saw that he had the cherry heads in an uproar. He was sidestepping along the rim of the bowl and kicking off anybody who tried to perch there. A few minutes into the feeding, he came to me again, and when I offered him a seed, the cherry heads on the railing yanked on my sleeve to pull my hand away. They didn't want me encouraging him. When the feeding was over, the cherry heads ditched him. Oliver flew to the garden and perched in the tallest deodar, where he called out forlornly in his strange seagull-like shriek. It seemed to me that both the flock and Oliver would be better off if he were back with his owner. For several days, I bought newspapers and looked through the lost-and-found section, but nobody was advertising the loss of a mitred conure.

Now that Dogen was warming up to me, I wanted to take things a step further. The pet bird magazines constantly admonish owners to say "up" or "step up" each time a bird steps onto a hand. It's to show the bird who's boss. I decided to try their method. I took Dogen down to the studio and placed her on Mandela's old rope gym. You're supposed to start with a stick. I stood in front of her and, holding a sunflower seed in my hand between my body and a stick, tried to coax her to step onto the stick. "Up," I said. "Up, up." Dogen wanted nothing to do with it. She jumped down from the rope and took off running across the floor. I chased after her with the stick and the seed until I had her cornered. I held the seed and stick a few inches above the floor. "Up, up," I said, and she ran away again. I chased her around the room—not intensely, but persistently—for ten or fifteen minutes. By the time the session was over, she'd actually gotten the hang of it.

A few days later, I started working on the next step, which was getting her onto my hand. I held my hand, backside up, between her and the seed and asked her repeatedly to step up. She refused. But I hadn't expected her to get it immediately. We worked on it a little bit every day for several days, and although she was willing to step onto the stick every time it was offered, she was adamant about not stepping onto my hand. I kept repeating "up, up," but she just sat on the rope and looked helpless. Then, at one session, she was in a position to step onto my arm, and did. I thought we were making progress, so

I offered her my hand again, but she still wouldn't do it. Finally, I saw why. Every time she stepped onto my arm, she grabbed my sleeve with her beak to steady herself. But the nerve damage in her legs made her feel insecure about stepping onto the bare and relatively slippery flesh of my hand. I'd been so single-minded about what I wanted that I hadn't paid any attention to what she was going through.

Dogen was enthusiastic about my food, and since it brought us closer, I allowed her to eat from my plate whenever she wanted. One evening, after we'd finished dinner, I got her onto my arm, carried her into the living room, and set her on the back of the recliner. Because it was tall and right up against the living room windows, Dogen liked to perch on the back of the recliner and watch the world go by. After setting her down, I kneeled on the seat cushion and encircled her with my arms. I paused to check her reaction; she seemed relaxed, so I slowly lowered my face toward her until my nose was just grazing the silky feathers on the back of her neck. The parrots have a musty odor that I love. I inhaled deeply, and she sat absolutely still. I caressed her head feathers with my lips, and when she didn't object to that, I started scratching her neck with my finger. Soon I was delicately tracing the contours of all the muscles and joints in her body. I paid such careful and close attention that she allowed me to do whatever I wanted. But birds are sensitive about their backs, and out of consideration to Dogen, I refrained from doing what I wanted most: to pet her with the flat of my palm.

I needed a girlfriend.

Catherine's condition was getting worse every day. Her landings were awkward, and, once perched, all she wanted was to sleep. I thought about trying to catch her, but she seldom came to the fire escape anymore. She spent most feedings out on the lines with her beak tucked into her back. As weak as she was, she still had enough life in her to bite the tail feathers of a mourning dove that came too close once. She seemed to want everybody to stay away. Sometimes she even lunged at Connor when he approached. As Catherine deteriorated,

Connor became more remote psychologically. He sat on the fire escape a lot, staring into space.

Wanting Dogen to get some sun and fresh air, I put her in her cage one day and carried her out onto the east balcony. I brought a book with me and sat down next to her to read. Shortly after I settled into the book, Connor showed up. He landed on the cage and studied Dogen's situation for a bit and then looked at me and started squawking. He was glaring and getting more and more worked up, his voice becoming shrill and hysterical. It was obvious to me what he was doing: He was chastising me for putting Dogen in a cage. Connor knew about cages; he'd been in a minimum of five—a holding pen after his capture, and cages on the plane, in quarantine, at the pet store, and in his owner's home. I was always seeking Connor's respect, so I felt a twinge of regret at having earned his disapproval. At the same time, I was fascinated that he was able to size up the situation and pass judgment on me.

After months of acting meek and deferential, Sonny was gradually returning to form. He was beating up on the other parrots and getting away with it. Sonny and Eric were a constant team that summer, flying the flock's territory together, and gathering food to take back to their mates in the nest holes. If there was a leader in the flock, it had to be Eric. That Sonny was spending the day in his company suggested complete rehabilitation, which turned out to be a good thing for the entire flock.

I'd been expecting that after a few days Oliver would settle down and find his place. But after a week, he still wasn't allowing anybody else on the bowl. No one would stand up to him. For the hand feeders, it wasn't a problem; but for the bowl birds, Oliver was a real nuisance. They would gather in small groups on the fire escape and give each other confused looks. Since they couldn't get on the bowl, they'd fly away and eat elsewhere. It finally got to the point that I started thinking about trapping Oliver and, if I couldn't find a home for him, releasing him somewhere far away.

Small groups of parrots came and went from the fire escape all day long, and Sonny and Oliver hadn't met yet. One day, they arrived in two different groups simultaneously. Oliver was already on the bowl when Sonny pulled himself up onto the rim. Oliver sidestepped over to where Sonny was eating, opened his beak threateningly, and lunged at him. Sonny ignored Oliver and kept eating, so Oliver lunged again. This time Sonny lunged back. After that, each time Oliver attacked, Sonny responded in kind. It was only light sparring, but it was the first time any bird had dared to stand up to Oliver. Seeing that Sonny could not be intimidated—or even impressed—Oliver backed down. When the other birds saw it, they began heading for their old places on the bowl. Eric challenged Oliver, and Oliver backed down again. Then Oliver began to shrink away from every confrontation.

The parrots had adapted so thoroughly to the coolness of San Francisco that heat was the greater problem for them now. At Patricia Chavez-Riva's study site in El Coto de Caza El Angolo, the yearly mean temperature is seventy-four degrees Fahrenheit, so you'd think that eighty degrees would be a piece of cake. But whenever the temperature got that high—a rare occurrence in San Francisco—the parrots held their wings away from their sides and panted like dogs. One day it got up into the nineties, and I worried that the heat would finish off Catherine and Chomsky. Because she was such a sweetheart, and because she was Connor's mate, I pulled for Catherine more than I did for most other sick birds. Chomsky had been barely hanging onto life. I'd tried to catch him twice, and failed both times. My concern about the heat was justified. I never saw either bird again. But Catherine and Chomsky were not the only birds who vanished that day. So did Connor.

I looked for him day after day. I thought he might be tending to an immobile Catherine. But if that were so, why wasn't he coming to me for food? When a neighbor on the nearby Filbert Steps called to tell me that her cat had dragged a green wing into the house, I feared the worst. After a week had passed without a single sighting, I gave up on ever seeing Connor again. And the flock's troubles were still growing.

Eric showed up at a feeding with a glassy eye. I wasn't too concerned about it—they often had small problems that cleared up on their own—but soon afterward Eric vanished for good. I was beginning to wonder if the flock's presence in San Francisco was so unnatural that it was doomed.

That summer was a frustrating time for me in general. I had a long list of complaints. Because the birds were coming by all day long in small groups, I was constantly having to go outside to do another feeding. When they all focused their hunger on me, it could make me physically anxious. They'd be screaming and fighting to get to my hand or my arm, which was all scratched up from their claws, and I'd feel so uncomfortable that I'd just want them to go away. I was worried that they depended on me too much for food. The parrots had dropped thousands of empty shells onto a neighbor's deck and into Helen's backyard. To keep them both happy, I was constantly having to sweep up seeds. Edna had taken a liking to San Francisco, and she often made the trip here from Louisiana not just to talk with lawyers now, but to visit the city. Each time she came, I had to scrub down the fire escape and move my stuff back down to the cottage. I was still depending on odd jobs at an age when I thought I should be doing something meaningful. My responsibility to Dogen was taking up a huge amount of time, and I hadn't done a thing toward finding a new situation for myself. I felt trapped. On hot days, I hated the heat; on windy days, I hated the wind.

Ten days after disappearing, Connor showed up again. He flew in with a small group and landed in his usual spot at my feet. His toes and beak were heavily stained with berry juice, and he seemed a little down, but otherwise he looked the same. With Catherine's death, Connor seemed destined for a life of loneliness. The cherry heads were never going to accept him completely, which would be misery for him; for if I'd learned anything about parrots, it was how social they are. I briefly considered trapping Connor and bringing him inside, but I didn't think it was my place to make that decision. From what I'd seen, I had to believe that any wild parrot would prefer a life of lonely freedom to one in captivity.

In the meantime, the captive Dogen and I were becoming close friends. Day after day, the boundaries she'd set against me were falling. She now allowed me to handle her with complete freedom. I could even put my hand over her back and squeeze her ribs. She loved cuddling with me, and she couldn't get enough head scratches. Whenever I was too busy to give her attention, she'd sit quietly on the living room windowsills and stare outside. Otherwise, we were inseparable. Sometimes she followed me as I walked around the house doing chores. I could hear her toenails clattering across the slick cork floor as she lurched along behind me. She loved to preen me. She'd work on my beard and mustache and around my neck and ears. I let her do what she wanted.

Once, I was sitting in a chair and eating a handful of granola while Dogen was playing on the floor in front of me. I wasn't in a sharing state of mind, and I tried to conceal from her that I was eating. But she saw that I was surreptitiously chewing, so she scrambled across the floor and climbed the length of my body to my shoulder. I'd already finished the granola, but she insisted on pulling my lower lip down with her toes and licking my teeth clean. It was so ridiculous that I started laughing; and when I laughed, she tried to get even deeper into my mouth. Just to see what she'd do, I opened up wide. She stuck her head completely inside and scoured my mouth for crumbs.

I disliked caging Dogen. I locked her in only when I had to leave the house for a long period of time. And there'd always been something distasteful to me about training her. I could see now that shouting at her to get her to stop biting had been unnecessary. If I'd been more patient, she would have stopped on her own. Bo, Mandela, and Dogen's sibling, Jones, still came to the bedroom window whenever they saw Dogen there, and their visits excited her so much that I could never forget where she really belonged. I stopped making a special effort at taming her, and I abandoned the "up" command. I wanted us to be friends, not owner and pet. I let Dogen be who she was, a wild bird, and enforced only the amount of discipline it took to ensure her safety. At night, before going to sleep, I would lay in bed and look at her as she perched on her T-stand. It was a lovely sight—a little wild parrot clutching her perch with both feet, feathers fluffed up, her eyes closed, and making an intermittent grinding sound with her beak, which is the sign of contentment in a parrot.

Two months after I took her in, Dogen's condition stabilized at around 85 percent of full coordination. Her molt was going to start soon, but before releasing her, I wanted to have her checked out by a vet. I was still running errands for Helen, and I'd built up enough credit that she offered to pay. It was too late for the veterinarian to be certain about Dogen's problem, and Helen couldn't afford the battery of tests it would take to get a more precise evaluation. The vet said it was possible that Dogen might have had something viral, but she thought it more likely that she'd eaten something toxic. The vet thought the juveniles might be eating something that the adults had learned to avoid. That made sense given that the problem was occurring just at the time of year that the young were splitting from their parents and losing their day-to-day guidance.

One morning I put Dogen on my shoulder and took her out for a walk. I thought she might like to revisit the garden, so we went down to the Greenwich Steps. As we walked along Greenwich, a woman stopped me and asked me why I had one of the wild parrots. The fire escape was high and set back from the steps—there were only a few short stretches along Greenwich where I was visible—so not many people had seen what I was up to. But Cynthia had noticed. Most neighborhood people loved seeing the parrots free, and anyone who thought I'd trapped one would have been furious with me. So I was quick to explain Dogen's situation.

Cynthia had a special interest in parrots. She had three living with her. She started telling me about her most recent acquisition, a parrot that had been rescued from an abusive home. She complained that the bird was acting aggressively toward one of her two cockatiels. The cockatiel, a female, was a favorite who'd been with Cynthia for many years. Apparently, the parrot was sweet on her other cockatiel, a male, and was trying to keep the female away from him. She liked the new bird, but it had become such a problem that she was hoping to find it a new home. Did I know anyone who might be interested in a female blue-crowned conure?

I was stupefied. I tried to give the idea a moment of sober evaluation, but it was merely a formality.

"Well, yeah," I told her. "As a matter of fact, I do know someone who'd be interested in a female blue-crowned conure."

Bucky

It took some convincing to get Cynthia to allow me to release the bird, Bucky, into the flock. I assured her that little could go wrong. I wouldn't even attempt a release unless I was certain that the two blue crowns were compatible. If they were, Connor would surely look out for her. And if by chance something did go wrong, I'd simply bring her back into the house—no problem. After thinking it over, she called to tell me that she liked the idea and that I could come get Bucky.

I was impressed by Bucky's size. She wasn't slender like other blue crowns I'd seen. She was hefty—not fat, just built. She didn't look like she'd have any trouble holding her own against the cherry heads. I told Cynthia that I intended to acclimate Bucky to nighttime temperatures first, so it would still be a few weeks until I released her. I'd give her plenty of notice. I was obliged to chat with her for awhile about Bucky's upcoming adventure, but I was impatient to get home. It was late in the afternoon, and the flock would soon be going to roost. I wanted to show Connor what I'd found for him.

Edna was in town again and staying in Maxine's house, so Dogen and I were staying down in the studio apartment. When I carried Bucky's cage through the door, Dogen was perched high on the rope gym and looking down upon us. I'd expected Dogen to be excited by the arrival of another parrot, but she showed no interest at all. When I set the cage down on the floor, Bucky began pacing energetically back and forth on her manzanita perch and screaming mightily. She had a pronounced breast that looked puffed up even when she wasn't strutting. I opened her cage door to put some food in her dish, and she was so charged that when she moved toward me, I flinched and stepped back. Bucky marched out into the room, and all I could do was stand and watch her. She intimidated me. Bucky flew up to where Dogen was perched and tried to establish dominance. In spite of being a much smaller bird, Dogen won the first round easily.

A group of parrots arrived in the garden, and I managed to herd Bucky back into her cage and carried her outside. Since I couldn't use the fire escape when Edna was in town, I'd started encouraging the parrots to come to a long balcony that was on Helen's level of the cottage, and to which I had easy access. I set Bucky's cage down and looked for Connor, but he wasn't in this group. Three cherry heads gathered around Bucky's cage and pecked at her from outside the bars. Bucky seemed oblivious to them. She continued to pace back and forth on her perch, shrieking out commands.

Bucky hadn't always been so robust. I never learned her full story, but the parts I heard were typical for many pet parrots. For some reason, one of Bucky's previous owners had given her away to friends. When she arrived at her new home, she was lavished with attention. But the novelty of owning a parrot eventually wore off, and the family began to neglect her. She became skinny and malnourished from a diet of seeds and water. Sometimes her water dish was forgotten and left bone dry. As time passed, Bucky was allowed out of her cage less and less often, so she started screaming. The son would yell at Bucky to shut up, and when she didn't, he'd throw a blanket over her cage. As her frustrations mounted, she started pulling out her feathers and biting her owners. A relative couldn't stand watching what was happening to her, so one day, when no one was around, he snuck into the house and rescued Bucky. He gave her to a friend who passed her on to Cynthia. Cynthia had a lot of experience with birds, and under her care Bucky stopped plucking and fattened up. Everything had been fine until the problem with the cockatiel cropped up.

Taking Bucky on had been a risky thing for me to do. Cynthia didn't want her back, so if I couldn't release Bucky, I was going to be responsible for both her and Dogen. And although I didn't know it, deliberately releasing a nonnative bird into the environment is illegal and something that technically I could have been prosecuted for. Still, even if I had known, I probably would have done it anyway. I loved Connor and I wanted him to have a mate. I knew it was childish, but I did have the faint hope that if I helped Connor, he'd be grateful to me and want to be my friend.

Connor was not entirely without companionship in those days. Shortly after Catherine's disappearance, an escaped budgie joined the flock. I named him Smitty. He was powder blue, with black and white stripes on his head and wings, and tiny black eyes. He was much smaller than the cherry heads, and his flight pattern was even more erratic than theirs; nevertheless, Smitty not only kept up with the flock, he often flew in the lead position. The parrots seldom paid any attention at all to the native birds, but they were invariably antagonistic toward other parrots. In the past, I'd seen another budgie, a white-fronted Amazon, and a canary-winged parakeet try to join the flock, and in each instance, the cherry heads had fought with the new bird. Typically, they were hostile toward Smitty. They'd threaten to bite him, but he was never intimidated. He'd open his tiny beak as wide as he could and return the threat. It wasn't bluster. He was ornery and quite willing to go beak to beak with them. Whenever one of the bigger birds got in his way, Smitty would bite his tail. He reminded me of the little guys who represent the Lollipop Guild in *The Wizard of Oz*. Connor wasn't actually friendly toward Smitty, but he was tolerant, so Smitty followed Connor everywhere he went.

Connor didn't show up that first day, so early the next morning I carried Bucky up to Helen's balcony again and waited. Bucky was quietly preening when the first group of parrots came to eat. This time Connor was with them, and when Bucky saw him she began screaming excitedly. The screams of another blue crown attracted Connor's attention, but like Dogen, he showed no special interest. He went to his usual spot four feet from her cage and ate seeds while calmly looking her over, expressionless. After Connor finished eating, he ambled over to the cage and climbed up on top of it, but he still didn't look particularly happy to see her. When the other birds flew away, Connor left with them. Before the group left the garden, though, he pulled away and landed at the top of a deodar cedar. Bucky called out to Connor in a shrill, desperate voice, and Connor perched in the tree preening and listening. Occasionally, he made a brief response to her calls. It went on like that for half an hour. I had a housecleaning job to get to, and since I couldn't leave Bucky outside while I was gone, I picked up her cage and started back toward the studio. As soon as he saw this, Connor flew down to the balcony railing and protested. I left ten minutes later, and he was still calling for her.

When I returned from my job, I put Bucky back outside right away. Minutes later, a large group of parrots flew into the garden. Connor was in this group, but so was another bird whose arrival, for the moment, interested me even more. It was early August, and for several days I'd been expecting to see the females coming off the nests. I was seeing my first one now, and it was a big surprise: Murphy. I'd been counting her among the dead. So she was Marlon's *mate*, not his sister. They'd paired up when both were less than a year old, and she had gone to nest before she was two. My understanding had been that they couldn't breed for another year yet. But maybe they were just going through the motions.

As he'd done earlier in the day, Connor ate first and then climbed on top of Bucky's cage. Every now and then one of the cherry heads would come over to inspect Bucky, and a scowling Connor would leap down and chase the bird away. When the group that Connor came with left the garden, Connor stayed behind. Curiously, he was still paying little overt attention to Bucky. He mostly preened and napped while perched on her cage. I don't know whether Bucky was wild caught or breeder-raised (in those days, few blue crowns her age were breeder-raised), but she seemed to know a few things about being a wild parrot. When other parrots approached from a distance, Bucky joined Connor in calling out to them and announcing their presence. Later, when a hawk flew overhead, Bucky fell silent and warily tracked its progress across the sky. Both behaviors are probably instinctual, but they made me feel a little more confident about releasing her. Although small flocks came and went throughout the rest of the day, Connor didn't join any of them, and he didn't leave to roost in Walton Square until dusk.

After Connor's departure, I brought Bucky inside and made another effort at getting acquainted with her. To pull off the release with confidence, I needed her trust. I'd told Cynthia that I was afraid of Bucky, and she said there was no need to be, that Bucky was quite tame. She told me that Bucky could speak—mostly "hello"—and although it took some doing, I finally got Bucky to say it. After a little more prompting, she mumbled a phrase that had the cadence and tone of a radio announcer, but I couldn't understand her. After that, she fell silent and wouldn't even say hello. I started working on getting her onto my hand, but she refused to do it. I sweet-talked her, pressed my finger against her legs, and came at her from several different angles, but she wouldn't step up. Dogen was perched nearby and watching. When Bucky continued to balk, Dogen began making a sound I'd never heard before. Suddenly, I realized she was saying, "Up, up." I was astounded. I'd deliberately stopped using the command weeks earlier, but Dogen remembered it. She never spoke again.

People often asked me if the parrots could talk. I thought it a peculiar question. Wild parrots don't talk, and, except for the African gray parrot, they don't even use their talent for mimicry. Intensely social creatures, they want to be full members of whatever community they find themselves in, so, as captive birds, they will learn human speech, but often only through drill—which isn't to imply that they don't understand what they're saying. There's good evidence that they do. Some parrot species are better talkers than others. The cherry-headed conure is said not to be a good talker, while the blue-crowned conure is only slightly better. But the ability to speak has been a curse for parrots. It's one of the reasons human beings have been so eager to possess them. And a parrot's failure to speak often results in the bird being neglected or abandoned by someone who wanted a talker.

If Connor's feelings for Bucky were ambiguous at first, they soon became clear: Bucky was his bird. He stopped flying with the flock and came to perch on Bucky's cage all day long, every day. Edna left town, so I moved back up to Maxine's house, where I started putting Bucky's cage out on the east balcony, along with a special food tray for Connor, so he wouldn't have to leave to forage. Smitty was spending all his time out there, too. He squeezed through the bars of Bucky's cage and scoured the cage bottom for scraps. Whenever Bucky was inside the house, the two blue crowns would call back and forth to each other. If Connor saw her through a window, he'd fly to that sill and stare in at her. When I had to leave the house for a job, instead of caging Bucky and Dogen, I started using the cottage studio as an aviary. It was so trashed that short of a complete renovation, I knew it could never be rented again. So I could leave them there uncaged and not have to worry about whether they were chewing the place up. Connor was aware of all our moves, and I often found him perched in the shrubbery surrounding the cottage, looking in through the windows. Bucky would scream deliriously, delighted at his persistence. Whenever Connor was absent, Bucky became anxious and went into an obsessive routine of walking down her perch, stepping up onto her water dish, turning around, and walking back to the other end of her perch again. She imitated Connor. If I handed Connor an apple slice, she'd eat the apple slices in her cage. If I gave Connor a sun-flower seed, Bucky moved to her seed dish. So Bucky loved Connor, and Connor loved Bucky.

I was becoming fond of Bucky myself. Because she was a new bird, I spent a lot of time with her—time that I used to spend with Dogen. Dogen didn't like it. In fact, she was quite jealous. I'd heard pet owners speak of their bird's jealousy, but I was still surprised and amused to see it myself. That it was jealousy was unmistakable. When-ever I gave Bucky attention, Dogen came over to get some, too. Bucky allowed me to cup my hands over her wings when I petted her, and Dogen always tried to make me stop. She bit my hand and tugged on my sleeve. Flock members would do the same to protect the others from my attempts at petting, but Dogen was not defending Bucky. After all, Dogen allowed me to pet her in the same way now. If, after giving Bucky attention, I went to lie down, Dogen would run to me, climb up on my chest, and want to be petted and scratched.

To prepare her for release, I began leaving Bucky outside at night. It was August and the weather was mild, so she handled it easily. The temperature wasn't really an issue, but I wanted to be as cautious and thorough as possible. I'd feel guilty if anything happened to her. The only real negative I saw was the possibility of injury, but I kept won-dering if there was something else I wasn't seeing. I called a woman who had some expertise in releasing birds and asked her for advice. I assumed that she'd be intrigued or amused by what I wanted to do, but she was dead set against it. Her concern wasn't for Bucky's safety as much as it was for the health of the native bird population. She told me that the native birds were already having a hard enough time, and that more competition could be a bad thing for them. She wasn't pe-dantic. She didn't have a problem with Dogen's release, since Dogen already came from the wild, but she didn't want me adding blue crowns to the mix. She never mentioned that it was illegal. She prob-ably assumed it wouldn't make any difference to me anyway. I told her I'd think it over. One part of me agreed with her, but my enthusiasm for putting Connor and Bucky together overwhelmed any other consideration. I still wondered if I was making a mistake, though.

The day for Bucky's release finally arrived. Cynthia wanted to be there when it happened, so I waited until she got off work. I knew that Bucky's flight muscles would have partially atrophied, so I thought it best to wait until late in the day anyway. I was concerned that if Bucky was exuberant about her freedom, and I released her too early in the day, she might exhaust herself. At 5:30 p.m., everything was ready: Cynthia, the flock, and Connor were all there, while Bucky paced back and forth restlessly on her perch. I was nervous, but eager to get it over with. I'd envisioned Bucky bursting out of her cage to join her beloved; but when I opened the door, she didn't move. The only activity came from the cherry heads, who, frightened by the opening of the door, fled to the lines. Connor remained on the fire escape and squawked at Bucky, but she wouldn't come out. A minute later, she made a timid step onto the bottom rung of the cage door, but then retreated to her perch. Connor kept squawking at her, so this time, timidly, she stepped all the way out. She was standing on the floor of the fire escape, looking all around. The flat expanse of the bay and the distant hills created a long horizon, and she seemed overwhelmed by the immensity of the world. Connor had grown impatient. He left the railing and flew around the corner of the house. Bucky hesitated a moment, and then took off after him. What I saw caused my heart to sink. Her butt end waggled so awkwardly that she seemed to be waddling in flight. Bucky managed to make it as far as a cluster of immense Monterey cypresses that grew a hundred feet to the east. Connor joined her there. A few cherry heads flew over to check out the new blue crown. They hassled her a little, but she held her own. All of a sudden, everybody—Bucky and Connor included—jumped out of the tree. I watched the entire flock fly north and then disappear around the hill. Cynthia was thrilled. She thought everything had gone marvelously. She hadn't noticed the struggle in Bucky's flight. I acted as though I was excited, too. But my secret feeling was that I'd made a big mistake.

∽∾∽

I got up early the next morning and took Dogen down to the dining room. We sat at the windows together and waited for Bucky and Connor to arrive. I was supposed to phone Cynthia with progress reports, but Dogen and I spent the entire morning at the window without seeing either bird. Finally, in the early afternoon, I caught sight of Bucky. She made a brief solo flight across the garden and into the Monterey cypress. Connor didn't seem to be with her. I went out on the fire escape and encouraged her to come eat, but she wouldn't respond. Connor didn't show up until late in the afternoon, and when he did, he was alone. An hour after Connor left, I caught another glimpse of Bucky flying across the garden. I couldn't understand why Connor was avoiding the house and why he wasn't with Bucky.

Early the next morning, Connor showed up on the fire escape. While he was eating, I heard Bucky squawking in the cypress, which seemed to have become her center of operations. Connor flew up to where she was perched, but he took off after a few minutes. At least she was still alive. Dogen and I stayed on the lookout for her all morning, and occasionally we'd catch a glimpse of her. Connor showed up every now and then, too, but never with Bucky. Nothing was going according to plan. I was anxious for Bucky now. I wanted to bring her back in, but she refused to come to the fire escape.

Shortly after noon the phone rang. I was taking a bath at the time, but something told me that I had better answer, so I jumped out of the tub and ran to get it. It was a neighbor, Louis. Something unusual had happened to him, and he wanted to know if I knew what was going on. A friend of his had gone out of town and asked him to water his garden while he was away. Louis was at the friend's house, just three blocks south of Greenwich, when he saw a parrot fly by. For no particular reason, he waved at it. The moment he did, the bird suddenly turned, made a beeline toward him, and landed in a nearby fig tree. Louis had some food in his hand and used it to make what he assumed would be a vain effort at luring the parrot down. He knew the parrots really were wild, so he was mildly astonished when the bird flew to his shoulder. She ate some of the food and then started nibbling on his ears. Charmed, Louis set the bird back in the tree and ran inside the house to get a camera. The parrot followed him into the house and started exploring. That was the point at which Louis called me. I told him not to let the bird back outside. He said to make it quick; he had a business appointment to get to. I threw on some clothes, grabbed the cage, and ran all the way. When Bucky saw her old cage, she hopped right in.

Paco and Company

So now I was responsible for two parrots. I felt confident that I'd be able to release Dogen once her flight feathers grew back, but I was going to have to find Bucky a new home. As with Dogen when she was ill, I pictured myself having to carry Bucky around the streets with me if I had to leave the estate before I found someone to take her. In that scenario, it was essential that Bucky be unable to fly, so I had her wings clipped. The man who did the clipping told me she was the biggest blue-crowned conure he'd ever seen.

Bucky and Dogen both liked to go outside, so every morning I put them out on the east balcony. Connor resumed spending his days perched atop Bucky's cage, and the budgie Smitty tagged along. Even though Smitty was a hand-raised bird who'd spent his entire life in the company of human beings, he was wary of me. He loved being free, so he kept his distance. Besides eating the food debris in Bucky's cage, he took advantage of Connor's tolerance, eating the crumbs that fell from Connor's beak. But the relationship went beyond scavenging. Both birds loved grapes, and since Smitty's beak was too small to get a grip on the skin to tear it open, Connor would hold his grape with his foot in midair and allow Smitty to chew on the exposed fruit.

I loved that I could hang out on the balcony without Connor being bothered by it. I made a game out of seeing how much normal activity I could get away with in his immediate presence. Sometimes I'd wait until Connor was sitting on top of the cage before I changed the water in Bucky's dish. I acted as casual as could be, but, like all the parrots, he recognized the difference between forced nonchalance and the real thing. When I was naturally relaxed, he didn't care what I did. When I was faking, he kept a close eye on me.

The year before, I'd had the dream in which the giant baby parrots bowled me over as they marched through my door. A year and a day later, I had another dream about the parrots. I came into the house from the fire escape and found five birds sitting around the dining room table. At first, I thought they were all babies, but as I got closer I saw that only one of them was—and one wasn't a parrot at all, but some kind of hairy mammal. Remembering that the first dream had presaged the arrival of the year's first fledglings, I kept an eye out for babies all day long. But I didn't see any. Nor did I see any on the next day, or the day after.

Four days later, I still hadn't seen a single baby. Concerned that something had gone wrong, I got up the next morning before sunrise and walked down to Walton Square. Although I knew the parrots roosted there, I still wasn't sure if it was where they nested. It's a lovely little square with a quirkiness that sets it apart from other parks in San Francisco. Covering a whole city block and enclosed by tall pines, the interior feels pastoral with its grassy hillocks, cherry trees, and weeping willows. Thirteen tall poplars grow in a circle around a boulder. The park's idiosyncrasy is in large part the result of three pieces of art scattered around the square. One is a bronze sculpture of the painter Georgia O'Keeffe and two dogs. Another is an obelisk surfaced with multicolored tiles depicting lobsters, seagulls, crabs, and a pine tree. A large fountain doubles as a piece of modern sculpture, its water flowing out of four bronze totem pole–like structures that rise out a jumble of concrete blocks.

When I arrived at Walton Square, I was hoping to find baby parrots hopping around the limbs of the pine trees. But I didn't see any. I didn't see any parrots at all. I'd made sure to come early enough that I couldn't possibly miss them leaving the roost. I asked a security guard if he'd seen them leave, and he told me that the flock hadn't been to the park in several weeks. I remembered bicycling past the square around the time he said they stopped coming. There was heavy street work going on. Maybe the jackhammers had frightened the parrots away, forcing them to abandon their nests. If so, it was a huge setback. In the last months, the flock had suffered many losses: Dogen was debilitated, and Catherine, Eric, Stella, Chomsky, and Mendelssohn had all died. (It was probably Mendelssohn's wing that the cat on the Filbert Steps dragged in.) There were only twenty-four birds now, two fewer than when the parrots first started coming to the fire escape. I left Walton Square with a black feeling. Resigned that there would be no babies that year, I feared I was witnessing the demise of the flock.

Later that day, the first fledgling of the year showed up. It was always like that with the parrots. As soon as I thought I understood something, they added a twist. Sometimes I felt as though they were playing practical jokes on me. He was a beautiful green baby whom I named Sebastian. The most remarkable thing about him was his parents: young Marlon and Murphy.

The year before, all the babies had fledged within a few days of each other, so I was prepared to see more. But a week passed without a single new baby materializing. I gave up then, and this time when I gave up, there still weren't any new babies. But there may have been another. A man told me he'd seen a cat get another parrot on the Filbert Steps. I grilled him, trying to determine whether the parrot had been a baby or an adult. He said the cat and the parrot had been in thick shrubbery, and it was too dark to see. Since no adults were missing, it must have been another baby.

For nearly a year I'd been borrowing cameras to photograph the parrots. I was so pleased with the results that every time I had a few extra bucks, I bought a new roll of film. I'd been especially eager for the fledge to get under way so that I could get some good photos of the babies. I'd taken some baby pictures of Mandela, but the camera and film I'd used were of such poor quality that the photos hadn't turned out well. I had access to better gear now, and I was eager to get some quality shots before I had to move. The babies were so playful that no still photograph could do them justice. So I was ecstatic when a neighbor offered to lend me his video camera.

I went out on the fire escape looking for something interesting to film when Marlon and Murphy's baby, Sebastian, landed on a line just fifteen feet away and began to put on a show. He was playing on two lines running parallel to each other. The lines were about six inches apart, one below the other and a little to the side. The top line was thick and taut, the lower line thin and slack. The shot begins with Sebastian hanging upside down from the top line by his left foot and stretching to grab the lower line with his beak. It takes some doing, but he finally anchors himself to both lines. He wiggles and rocks for a bit and then moves his free right foot toward the lower line. Once he grasps the line, Sebastian lets go of it with his beak so that he ends up doing a split. The lower line is too slack to allow him to hold the position, so he lets go of the slack line with his right foot and reaches for the top line so that he's hanging upside down by both feet. He raises his head, trying to chin himself up to perch. He fails, so he lowers his head and grabs onto the shaky lower line again with his beak. He hangs there for half a minute or so, chewing idly on the line. He raises his head again, and this time he manages to take hold of the top line with his beak. His feet then release the line so that now he's hanging onto it only by his beak. He claws at the air while his body does quarter turns back and forth, back and forth. Then, in a series of swift and graceful moves, he grabs the upper line with his right foot, turns upside down, grabs the lower line again with his beak and left foot, releases the upper line, and quickly moves his right foot to the lower line. He's perched—it's a perfect ten—but the line is shaky, and before he has a chance to fall, Sebastian flies out of frame.

One afternoon, just before the end of summer, the doorbell rang. I had so few visitors that hearing the doorbell was a novel experience. The man at the door looked familiar, but I couldn't place him. When he introduced himself as Jeffery Chinn, I remembered him. He was a guitar and lute player whose face I'd been seeing on posters ever since I arrived in San Francisco. Jeffery told me that the previous evening he and his girlfriend, Mary, had been walking through North Beach when they spotted a parrot hiding beneath a car. The bird couldn't fly, so they caught it and took it home. They put the parrot in a box with some food, but the bird wouldn't eat. Jeffery had seen me feeding the flock and hoped I could advise them. From his description, it sounded like a baby cherry head. I asked if I could come see it. He said, yes, of course. I was expecting to find Sebastian with some problem, but it wasn't. It was a new cherry-head baby. He was huddled in a corner of the cardboard box and looked dazed and exhausted. He still hadn't eaten because he was incapable of feeding himself. Jeffery and Mary had no idea what to do with him. Would I be willing to take him?

The baby had been saved by a soft-string guitar player, so I named him after one: Paco, for the flamenco guitarist Paco de Lucia. I was very curious to see who, if anyone, in the flock would claim him. I put Paco in a cage and carried him out to the fire escape. It was my first chance to get a good look at him. I couldn't see anything wrong with him. His feathers were beautiful—bright, fresh, and absolutely clean. His dark, shiny eyes had the innocence of a baby, and they were heavy with sleepiness. The beak is the one baby body part still underdeveloped, and Paco's was snub-nosed and nearly gray. On the side of his beak were the temporary flared notches that the parents touch to stimulate a feeding response. Except for an occasional low croak, Paco was silent. He seemed to have no awareness of me; he looked past me and seemed to be waiting for something. Paco would have been around eight weeks old then, and that's what he'd been doing all his life: waiting for his parents to return from somewhere.

It didn't take long for his father and mother to find and claim him. He belonged to Guy and Doll—Dogen's parents. The moment they spotted him, they flew to the cage and perched on top of it. Paco sprang to life. As Guy and Doll looked down on him, Paco climbed anxiously around inside the cage. Guy was chewing on the cage bars, trying to break them apart, when another cherry head flew over. Guy stopped work just long enough to chase the bird away. It was late in the day, and when dusk arrived Guy and Doll abandoned their attempt at rescuing their baby. As they flew away, Paco leaped from his perch to the cage bars and followed them with his eyes until they were gone.

I carried the cage inside and set it on the dining room table. He had no fear of me. When I opened the cage door and put my hand inside, he climbed right up onto my finger. I placed Paco on the floor, and he immediately began prowling around for a place to perch. I saw his problem then: His left wing was dragging a little. He hopped into the air a few times, but nothing happened. He couldn't flap the one wing, although it didn't seem broken. My hunch was that he'd strained it. Paco's eyes kept closing, so I put him on a portable T-stand and carried him up to the bedroom. I knew I had to get some food in him soon, but he was incapable of eating anything I had in the house. He needed mush. I drove over to Jamie Yorck's store and told him about Paco. As usual, I was broke, but Jamie came through for me once again. He gave me a can of baby bird formula and a plastic feeding syringe and wished me luck.

I was up before dawn and working on getting food into Paco. My first attempt didn't go too well. Reading the instructions on the can, I got the impression that a lot could go wrong. It was important to thoroughly sterilize the syringe before each feeding. There was danger if I overfed and danger if I underfed. I was supposed to stop when Paco's crop was full. I knew his crop was in between his mouth and his stomach, but I wasn't sure of its exact location or how to recognize that it was full. The formula was a mix of cornmeal and other ingredients that I made into a mush with hot water. I wasn't supposed to feed him until after the mush cooled down to 105 degrees. Colder than that wasn't good, and if it were hotter I could burn his crop. But I didn't have the right kind of thermometer, so I had to guess at the temperature. The first time I tried to suck up the mush with the syringe, I found that I'd made it too thick. I made a thinner version, but when I tried to squirt it down Paco's throat, he clamped his beak shut and refused to open it. Despite being such small creatures, parrots have extraordinarily strong jaw muscles, and I had to struggle to pry his beak open. He fought me so much while I was trying to pump the mush out of the syringe that I got more of it on him than in him. I looked over at Dogen and wondered if she might be willing to help.

I put all three birds in cages and carried them out to the east balcony. Bucky and Dogen were side by side in separate cages and Paco was in a cage on top of Dogen's. Connor and Smitty, who were like balcony sentinels, arrived just after sunrise. A few minutes later, Guy and Doll showed up. As they glided into the garden, they saw Paco in his cage, so they landed on the balcony railing. Guy and Doll called to Paco, who returned their call and began climbing anxiously around his cage again. Connor was angry about Guy and Doll being on the balcony. He flew to the top of the heap of cages and screamed at them to leave. Assuming that Connor was merely protecting real estate, I picked up Paco's cage, then carried it through the house and out onto the fire escape so that Guy and Doll could be alone with their baby. The family reunion had just gotten under way when Connor landed on the fire escape and started marching toward Paco's cage. Guy glared at Connor and gave him the parrot equivalent of "scram!" He lunged at the blue crown, but Connor eluded him. He refused to leave. Guy and Connor were both enraged now and screaming hysterically. It was early, so I was afraid they were going to wake the neighbors. Suddenly, they all stopped screaming and flew away in a panic. There must have been a hawk.

There was something in the altercation between Guy and Connor that fascinated me. I could tell that Connor wasn't merely defending his territory; he was laying claim to Paco. But it wasn't his claim on Paco, per se, that intrigued me so much. As I'd gotten to know the individual birds, I'd seen my intuitions about their personalities borne out in reality. In Connor's case, I'd sensed his resentment at being an outcast, and I'd often imagined him wanting his own flock. Connor's claim on Paco reinforced my sense that each bird had issues in its life and a distinct, discernible character. Over the next few days, Connor was unbending in his will to keep Guy and Doll away from their baby. He stayed on high alert all day long, clinging to the side of Paco's cage and issuing severe threats every time Guy and Doll approached. I thought Connor might calm down if I kept Paco inside the house for awhile. Even though they couldn't see Paco, Guy and Doll continued to call out to him. And Paco, who ignored the voices of the other parrots, always responded. When I put Paco back outside, Guy and Doll were still prevented from getting any closer than the balcony railing. Stopped cold by Connor's obsession, they looked at each other with bewilderment and then flew away.

As I grew more confident with the syringe, Paco became comfortable with me feeding him. He was bony and needed to be fed often, and I was beginning to enjoy it. I still hoped that Dogen would have the instinct to feed Paco, but so far she'd shown no interest in her baby brother.

When it wasn't being used, I kept the flock's seed bowl on the kitchen floor. In between flock feedings, Dogen often scuttled into the kitchen and searched through the scraps in the bowl for intact seeds. Paco was eventually going to have to learn to feed himself, so one evening, to get him started, I placed him on the bowl with Dogen. Paco watched Dogen carefully and then tried to imitate her by sweeping his beak back and forth through the empty shells, occasionally stopping to chew on a mouthful. There were very few whole sunflower seeds left in the bowl, but there were a few scattered around the kitchen floor, so Dogen hopped off the bowl and started eating those. Paco followed Dogen and tried to open one. He moved it all around inside his beak, but he couldn't figure out what to do with it. So he dropped the seed, walked over to Dogen, and began bobbing his head up and down. He puffed up his head feathers, lowered his wings, and bleated, all the while staring intently at Dogen. Dogen stared back for a moment and then turned and hustled out of the kitchen. When she disappeared around the corner, Paco became anxious and ran after her.

I saw that if Guy and Doll lost their bond with Paco before the wing healed, I wouldn't be able to release him. Paco wouldn't know the ways of the flock, and he'd need a teacher. The only solution I could see would be if I released Dogen and Paco together, and Dogen acted as Paco's teacher. For that to happen, they'd need to bond first. I put them together in a cage to see if I could get something going between them. Dogen took a drink of water, so Paco did, too. When I started to leave the room, Dogen jumped from the perch and clung to the bars, and so did Paco. Dogen was trying to tell me that she didn't want to be in the cage with Paco, so I brought both birds out and put one on each hand. Dogen started flapping her wings, so Paco did, too. The devotion was there from Paco's side, but Dogen was not reciprocating. The next day, I saw Paco standing near Dogen and bobbing his head. Dogen looked annoyed. Nevertheless, she reached out, grabbed Paco's beak, and jerked his head up and down a few times, but without actually regurgitating. Apparently, she just wanted to get Paco off her back. Paco didn't care that Dogen hadn't fed him. He squatted and extended his wings. He looked deliriously happy.

Guy and Doll came to the balcony every day for a full week trying to reclaim their baby. But Connor refused to allow them near Paco. One morning, after having failed to reach Paco, Guy and Doll flew up to one of the immense Monterey cypresses and perched next to a couple of parrots. I saw Doll bounce her head and then grab the beak of the bird perched next to her. I squinted to get a better look. Babies. Two of them.

Later that day, I was out on the fire escape feeding some birds when I spotted a contingent of six parrots flying toward the house. I knew at a glance that the arriving group contained more fledglings. They flew in a more exuberant and ungainly manner than the adults. The group landed on the lines above the Greenwich Steps, and I saw that it was Sonny and Lucia with four new offspring. The fledge was on; it was just late. Moments after they landed, the babies bolted from the lines and sped away on aimless paths. Sonny and Lucia had to chase after them. After they'd rounded up the babies, the whole family began flying around the garden in a long series of figure eights. I'd seen this before, but I hadn't realized what it was: Sonny and Lucia were giving their children lessons in formation flight. Over the next few days, the entire flock joined in. They were all flying around the garden and squawking even more boisterously than usual. They would circle screaming and then land in a tree, where they fell silent. A few seconds later, they all jumped from the tree and began circling the garden and screaming again. They often did the same thing when a hawk was in the area, but here the mood was ecstatic rather than fearful. They were rejoicing over their strength.

Eight babies were born that year. Marlon and Murphy had one, Sonny and Lucia had four, and Guy and Doll had three. Paco watched and listened to the flock's enthusiasm from inside the house, but he didn't seem anxious or sad about it. He was just as excited as the others, and although he couldn't fly, he'd run across the floor flapping his big wings and hopping a few inches into the air. It was hysterically funny, and since he seemed generally content, I allowed myself to laugh at him.

Paco accepted his situation with the innocence and trust of a baby, but Dogen sometimes seemed saddened by her confinement. There was something wistful about her. She spent hours perched quietly on the living room sills studying the garden and the sky. She was usually excited by the arrival of the flock, but sometimes she made quiet little calls that sounded sorrowful. A few times, I heard her make a sound that sounded like sobbing. Whenever I sensed her sadness, I would renew my vow to get her back into the flock. That didn't seem so far away now. She was molting; the clipped wing feathers were dropping out and being replaced by new ones. Although she couldn't climb yet, she could fly on the level. She still teetered when she walked across the floor—she'd lift her stiff legs high into the air as if she were climbing stairs—but her overall coordination had improved enormously. I knew I was going to miss her. We'd become close. We had a ritual that she expected every evening after dinner. She'd wait for me to lie down on the couch and then she'd climb up on my chest for a long evening of petting. She'd shut her eyes and lay her cheek on my chest as I stroked her body and scratched her neck. On the few occasions that I had visitors, they usually expressed surprise that a bird could be so affectionate. Most of them thought of birds as remote, unfeeling creatures.

I was obsessed with learning the flock's history, and as more people in the neighborhood learned about what I was doing, those who'd seen something interesting or knew some detail often got in touch with me, so that I gradually accumulated more and more pieces of the puzzle. One day, on my way down the hill, I ran into David Kennedy. David moved into North Beach around the same time I did, and he always paid close attention to everything that happened in the neighborhood. I'd talked with him many times about my confusion over how long the flock had been around. I still thought six years, which is what most people told me, but I didn't know how to deal with eyewitnesses who insisted on twenty. A lot of people told me things that were unreliable, but David knew parrots—he'd owned one—so when he told me he thought he'd figured it out, I listened.

"I'm pretty sure now that this flock has been here only six years. But there was another parrot flock that preceded them. They were a different species: canary-winged parakeets."

As soon as he said it, a whole set of details fell neatly into place:

Of course; there were *two* flocks of wild parrots in San Francisco. I'd never considered that possibility. It was strange enough that there was even one flock; two flocks had been unimaginable. I went home and looked through my notes and put in a few calls to some other sources. It all panned out. The wild parrots of Telegraph Hill that Armistead Maupin wrote about in *Tales of the City* were canary-winged parakeets. They'd once been regulars on the hill, but now they were in the Mission District. So the time that I was on my bike near Dolores Park and saw the silhouette of a parrot flying overhead, I'd seen one of the canary wings. I was surprised that this wasn't common knowledge among local birders.

One afternoon, I was on the fire escape feeding the flock when I noticed a woman standing on the Greenwich Steps watching me. She was unusually interested—she stayed for the duration—so at feeding's end, I went down to speak with her. Her name was Laurel Wroten. She told me that the parrots used to come to her bird feeder on Russian Hill. She'd observed them for several years until she moved away. I asked her for some details, but she couldn't remember much; it had been so long ago. In the beginning, there'd been two cherry heads, whom her husband named Victor and Inez. One year, they had babies, and after that the flock just kept growing. While Laurel and I were talking, the flock flew back into the garden. I asked her if she'd like to come up to the house and watch a feeding. She said she'd love to.

I opened the top half of the Dutch door that opened to the fire escape, and Laurel stood in the kitchen and watched the parrots as I fed them. She pointed to one of the birds on the bowl and asked me the name. I told her it was Erica. She couldn't be absolutely certain, but she had a feeling that this was her Inez. After the flock left, I showed her a photograph of the deceased Eric. She studied it for a little bit, and said, yes, that could be Victor. Like Eric and Erica, both Victor and Inez had been banded, but it wasn't the bands that made her think it was them. She just had a feeling. She remembered Connor, but she couldn't remember when he came into the flock. She thought it was fairly early on. I kept asking Laurel questions, but she couldn't recall many details. She said she used to keep a flock diary, and maybe the answers were in there. Oh, yeah, and she'd taken photographs, too. I was *stunned.* Did she still have everything? Yes. Could I borrow the diary? Yes. The photos? Yes.

It wasn't quite as detailed as I'd hoped, but Laurel's diary did provide me with solid information on the flock's beginnings. As I read it, I kept feeling as though I were reading excerpts from my own journal. Our observations and characterizations were nearly identical. Our personal experiences were the same, too, in that before she encountered the parrots, she'd had no interest in birds, but then the flock took over her life. She first started seeing Victor and Inez in March 1987. Then, in the summer of 1989, they had four babies, two of which died shortly after fledging. Victor and Inez and the two surviving babies were the four birds I'd seen first. In the late summer of 1990, Victor and Inez brought four more babies out of the nest. A few weeks later, Connor showed up. The photographs she had were taken right at this point in the flock's early history, and Connor is in them. Soon after that, a mitred conure joined the flock. Mitred conures were common in stores, so there isn't any reason to think that this was Oliver, but there aren't any photographs to say one way or another. It was this group of ten birds—with the possible inclusion of Catherine, who showed up at some point between late 1990 and early 1991— that I saw fly overhead on the morning of the big freeze. The next summer, in 1991, Victor and Inez had four more babies, so that when Laurel moved away from Russian Hill in early 1992 there were fourteen birds in the flock: Victor, Inez, their two babies from 1989, three of the four babies from 1990, all four of the 1991 babies, Connor and Catherine, and the mitred conure. The big question her diary raised for me had to do with banded birds. Laurel's diary accounted for only three: Victor, Inez, and Connor. But when I first saw the flock, there were at least six. When and how did the others arrive in the flock?

Not long after meeting Laurel, I talked to a woman whose brother used to put out seeds for the parrots. She thought he'd be happy to talk with me, and gave me his phone number. But Jim was reluctant to talk about the parrots. He doubted he could tell me anything of value: He'd fed them for just a few months; it was several years ago; he didn't remember much. Jim was a birder, and birders always made the clearest observations, so I persisted until he relented. We figured out that he'd been feeding the flock during the autumn and winter of 1992–1993, which filled some of the gap between Laurel's departure from the scene and my arrival. He said he'd once counted *thirty-five* parrots. I was so taken aback by the figure that I made him repeat it. Yes, thirty-five. Breeding wouldn't account for those numbers. Were any of the birds banded? He thought maybe a third of them were. He told me that later in the winter, the flock population dropped down to around half of what it had been. He remembered the decline as happening suddenly. That was all he remembered. He stopped feeding them shortly after that.

So at some point between Laurel's departure and my arrival there'd been a sudden increase in the flock population, and a lot of the new birds were banded. I can think of two explanations. One is a big accident—a box broke open, an aviary door was left ajar—and a lot of birds suddenly escaped. Or perhaps as the core group grew in size the flock's in-flight screams attracted all other individual escaped cherry heads in the northern waterfront area. Because of the catastrophic die-off, I lean toward the first idea. Although parrots can adjust to cold weather, the time of year that they enter the outdoors is an issue. If they escape in spring or summer, they have plenty of time to acclimate. But if a mass escape had taken place in the late fall or early winter, the abrupt change in temperature could have killed a lot of them.

Although the larger parrots can handle North American winters, the cold is fatal for escaped budgies. I wanted to get Smitty before the weather did, so in early autumn I started preparing a trap for him. But I was too late. He disappeared before I could spring it on him. After Smitty's demise, Connor was completely alone again and, for the first time since I'd laid eyes on him, looking unattractive. His head and neck were covered with a mass of ugly pinfeathers. When a new feather grows in, it's wrapped in a waxy sheath of keratin, and although the sheath will eventually wear away on its own, it's the task of a bird's mate to clean the pinfeathers growing in areas that a bird can't reach. They're itchy, so birds like to remove these sheaths as soon as possible. Bucky loved to preen Dogen, and I kept wishing there was some way I could hand Connor over to Bucky. One day, I realized that it wouldn't be difficult to accomplish that task. All I had to do was adapt my plan for trapping Smitty to Connor.

I'd been putting Connor's food on a plate. To execute my plan, I had to switch him to a smaller tray that fit through a cage door. When I was certain he recognized the tray as his, I started putting it inside an empty cage. He was comfortable with climbing into the cage to eat from it. I kept a good distance at first, then day by day I gradually drew nearer the cage. Although I was eager to get him, I did have some qualms about what I was doing. I had to tell myself over and over that I was doing this for Connor's benefit. And I promised to release him as soon as Bucky finished cleaning him up.

Finally, there was no reason to wait another day. Connor was in the cage eating, and I slowly walked toward him. It really was just a matter of closing the cage door, but my heart was racing as though the deed were fraught with complications. Finally, I pushed through my anxiety and shut Connor in. He had little reaction. He paused to look at the closed door, and then continued eating. I picked up the cage and carried it down to the studio where Bucky was waiting in her cage. I placed the two cages next to each other and opened the doors. They both stepped out calmly and then climbed on top of the cages and perched next to one another. Neither bird showed any emotion. Connor lowered his head and Bucky set to work.

Half an hour later, when Bucky took a break, Connor began to take stock of his situation. He seemed a little dubious about it all now. He took off on a hesitant, hovering flight around the room, looking for a way out. There was an eight-foot-long front window in the studio that I had covered with three sets of blinds. There was a gap between two of the blinds, and Connor tried to fly through it, smashing into the window. He wasn't hurt. He flew around a bit more, investigating the room, and then landed next to Bucky. They huddled together, cheek to cheek, and Bucky put her foot on top of Connor's. They looked like they were holding hands.

By the end of the next morning, Bucky had finished grooming Connor, who was his usual handsome self again. I'd promised to release him at that point, and the only way I could feel right about having deceived him was if I kept my word. But Bucky and Connor looked very happy together. I asked Connor if he wanted to go back outside. Just as I finished the question, he leaned his head against Bucky's breast. I saw no harm in taking that as a no.

I wanted to be certain that my motives were clean, so the next morning I decided to release Connor regardless of how well he and Bucky were getting along. He was welcome to return if that was his wish. To put him outside, I had to get him back into the cage first. Any other bird I would have chased down and captured with a towel, but I decided at least to offer Connor the easy way out. I put my finger next to his legs and he stepped right onto it. His response was so immediate and casual that I realized then he had to have been somebody's pet for a long time. He never would have done that out on the fire escape, though. I put him in the cage and carried him out to the balcony. When I opened the cage door, he was in no hurry to leave. He sat on the perch and looked around the garden. He took a drink of water and then climbed onto the bottom rung of the cage doorway. A minute later, he climbed up to the top of the cage, where he looked around a little more before leaping into the air. He flew around the house and landed on the fire escape. I ran back into the house and came out the fire escape door with a cup of seeds. He treated me the same as he had before I trapped him.

The experiment had gone so well that two days later I decided to set the trap again. Connor climbed into the cage without showing any concern. I closed the door and carried him inside to Bucky. He came out of the cage and perched next to her. They immediately resumed preening and cuddling. As I watched them, I started feeling my old desire to stroke the soft, fluffy feathers on the back of Connor's neck. It's a heavenly thing to be allowed to touch a bird. I walked over to where he and Bucky were perched and brought my hand down toward his back. I moved it very slowly and deliberately so that he could see what I was doing and not be afraid. But my hand coming down like that looked ominous to him. He flattened himself as though he thought he could avoid my hand by sinking into oblivion. But he didn't fly away, so I was able to pet him briefly.

I started up a routine with Connor where he would come into the house, stay for the night, and then go out again the next morning. Every time I set "the trap," he stepped right into it. He wanted to come inside; he was too intelligent not to understand what he was getting into. The arrangement worked well for both Connor and Bucky, and as their bond grew, Dogen and Paco were brought closer together, which was a welcome development given that Connor had succeeded in destroying the bond between Paco and his parents. Perhaps because he didn't have his parents to indulge him, Paco was learning to feed himself much more quickly than the babies out in the flock. He was on the formula for only one week. Once he'd learned to feed himself, he stopped the baby behaviors—puffing up his head feathers, bobbing his head, and making the begging sounds that I found so appealing. As the wing healed, I left him free to fly around the house. It was magical watching him test his wings. Paco *loved* to fly. He'd tear out of the living room, circle the dining room close against the walls, and then whip back into the living room, all in a flash.

By late October, the flock was flying as a single group again. It was the time of year in which I got my cleanest flock counts. The usual pattern was that a few babies died soon after fledging, and then the population stabilized, staying the same size throughout the winter. That year, two of the seven babies (eight were born, one of which was Paco) died, which left the flock population at twenty-nine. At a feeding in November, I noticed that five birds were absent. That was nothing extraordinary. It often happened that a small group got left behind at the previous feeding stop and then had to catch up with the flock. But I always paid attention to who wasn't there. A quick survey showed that the five missing birds were Sonny, Lucia, and their three surviving babies. Later, at a mid-afternoon feeding, Sonny and family were still gone. In the middle of the feeding, I spotted the five of them high up in the sky and zooming toward the garden. As they drew closer, I heard them announcing their arrival. The birds on the fire escape were getting edgy. Sonny's family landed in the deodar cedar, and four parrots flew out from the fire escape to meet them. Sonny had been kicked out of the flock again. When the four sentinels reached the deodar, a big fight broke out. The six adult birds were locked together in a tight bunch, going for each other's throats and eyes, screaming bloody murder. It was as intense as any dogfight. Sonny put up a strong defense, but he was overwhelmed. He and Lucia withdrew with their three babies.

I was keen to learn the identities of the enforcers. I expected that they would all be males, but upon their return to the fire escape I discovered that they were two couples: Scrapper and Scrapperella, and Henry and Mrs. Henry. I wasn't surprised to see Henry in this group—he seemed commanding, especially since Eric's death—but Scrapper's presence did surprise me. He was a quiet and small bird who usually minded his own business. I'd read that all bird flocks have pecking orders, so I'd been eager to learn this flock's. So far, though, I'd been unable to discern any hierarchy. If Scrapper was near the top, it was ironic given that he was literally henpecked. Scrapperella had plucked the area below his chin so many times that the feathers had stopped growing back. There were a lot of cases where a bird would do something that seemed to imply a strong standing, but it didn't bear out in the long run. For instance, Sonny had been the one bird Oliver couldn't intimidate, but it had done nothing to change Sonny's standing within the flock. Sonny had flown with Eric over the summer—and if there'd ever been a top bird, it was Eric—but the other birds were unimpressed. Nor had I ever seen Eric function in a clear leadership role. He'd never decided when it was time for the flock to leave the fire escape; that was done entirely by consensus. And although I wasn't sure of it, I thought I saw Eric lose a fight once. I'd also seen birds who were easily dominated have days when no one would dare cross them.

I might have been naive about it once, but I understood now that in the animal kingdom *wild* often does mean violent. One afternoon, I was feeding the birds on Helen's balcony when I heard a horrible scream. I looked up and saw, right in front of me and just out of reach, Marlon with his head caught between two telephone lines. He was strangling, and some of his flock mates were taking advantage of his defenselessness to peck at him. They were extremely excited and looked as though they intended to kill him. I clapped my hands and yelled at them to scare them away. I had no hope of saving Marlon. I assumed he was still going to strangle to death, but at least he wouldn't be pecked to death by his flock mates. But the moment the birds left the lower line, it lifted, and Marlon was freed. My anxiety had prevented me from seeing the actual situation. Marlon had evidently been hanging from the lower line when some parrots landed on the slack upper line. The weight of the birds brought the line below Marlon, and when a few of the birds flew away, the slack line rose just enough that it pinched Marlon's neck up against the line from which he was hanging. When the others saw that Marlon was in a vulnerable position, they attacked him.

Sonny's family kept themselves hidden for a few days after the fight. Then, just like before, Sonny and Lucia were gradually allowed to reintegrate into the flock. At first, Sonny was not permitted to come near the bowl or me. He was forced to wander the edge of the fire escape and hunt for stray seeds. He looked a little beat up, with a big scab above his cere. Lucia was not allowed on the bowl, either, but she was not stopped from approaching me. Although I'd had very little contact with her in the past, now she was coming to me every day for seeds. She'd perch on a ladder strut, lean forward, and give me desperate looks. She was irresistible, so I made a special effort to get seeds to her. Then, at the beginning of winter, just as Sonny's return to normalcy was almost complete, he suffered a hideous accident for which I was to blame.

On New Year's Eve, I was coming down the Filbert Steps when a couple stopped me and asked if I lived in the neighborhood. Roy and Courtney were birders who were looking for someone who knew something about the parrots. It turned out to be a serendipitous encounter for all three of us. Courtney said that earlier in the year she and Roy had observed some parrots climbing in and out of tree holes in a wooded area of the city. She asked if that was where the parrots nested. The location was plausible. I thought it could well be the answer to a question that had been puzzling me for years. I told them that come spring, I'd definitely check it out. As we talked, it came out that Roy was an arborist. I'd been wanting to learn the names of the different plants that I'd seen the parrots eating. He offered to teach me the names, and as we began a tour of the garden the flock arrived. They were on the lines above us, staring down at me and squawking impatiently, so I invited Roy and Courtney up to the house to watch a feeding. I had them stand in the kitchen at the fire escape door while I fed the birds. I was paying more attention to Roy and Courtney than the parrots, and at one point I felt something under my left foot. I looked down and saw a full set of tail feathers with no bird attached to them sticking out from under my boot heel. I was *horrified*. I looked up and saw a tailless Sonny flying awkwardly toward the deodar cedar. I thought he was going to die, and it was all my fault. Since all birds have a tail, I assumed they had an absolute need for one. I ended the feeding and hustled Roy and Courtney out of the house as politely as I could. I wanted to be alone with my worry and feelings of guilt over Sonny. Fortunately, he was alright. Although his flight was labored, he was still able to get around. When a feather is pulled out at its base, it starts to grow back immediately, so Sonny wasn't tailless for very long. But like schoolchildren, the parrots look down on flock members with deformities, so they had a new reason to taunt him.

⌒⌒⌒

Although Connor and Bucky seemed happy together, I still released Connor every few days so that he would know he was free to choose between the house and the wild. Occasionally, he spent the night with the flock, but more often he'd fly around the garden for half an hour or so and then want back in. Connor was still climbing into the cage and being carried back into the house. But he was so relaxed about getting onto my hand when we were inside the house that I began to wonder if he'd be willing to do it outside, too. The next time I released him and he returned to the balcony, I offered him my hand, and he climbed right on board.

It took me awhile to recognize it, but there was a striking difference in appearance between the outdoor Connor and the indoor Connor. Outside, he was always beautiful and vital; inside, he looked strangely plain and lifeless. Every time I released him, he immediately regained his beauty. I know it wasn't something I imagined; it's evident in the photographs I took of him inside and outside the house during that period. When he was inside, he sometimes acted decrepit. Occasionally, he had to struggle to pull himself up onto a perch, which I'd never seen happen outside. Connor was already an adult when he entered the flock six years earlier, and he was so familiar with houses and humans that he must have been a pet for several years before that. Conures don't live as long as some of the larger parrots. I've heard of pet conures living as long as thirty-five years, but that's extraordinary. Connor may have been old for a conure.

Like all living creatures, parrots become more sedate as they mature. Bucky was definitely an older bird—she was at least fifteen— and the two blue crowns did little other than preen, nap, and eat. Dogen was a year and a half now and not nearly as frisky as she was when I first got her. Unlike the stodgy adults, Paco was in near constant motion. He liked picking fights with Bucky, even baiting her at times. She'd get tired of him and lunge at him threateningly, but Bucky couldn't fly and Paco could, so he easily eluded the larger bird.

Paco was constantly trying to lure Dogen into play fights. Dogen resisted—she found the play tiresome—but Paco was so relentless that Dogen would have to fight him just to keep him at bay. The two pairs tended to ignore each other, and whenever there was a fight, the blue crowns usually won. But anytime Dogen and Paco could get Bucky or Connor two against one, they went for it. Parrots are partial to high perches, and the three fliers liked the high sills in the living room. Dogen's flight had improved to the point that she could gain altitude now, so she and Paco claimed the sills. Whenever Connor flew up to the sills, Dogen and Paco would harass him until he left, even when they weren't using them. Since Bucky couldn't fly, she was unable to come to Connor's side. One evening I had Bucky, Dogen, and Paco together in the bedroom—Connor was still down in the living room— when the two siblings ganged up on the blue crown. I thought Bucky could handle them, but they had her on the run. I knew that if I stopped the fight, they'd just start it up again a few minutes later, so I went down to get Connor. But Connor was no help to Bucky. He flew to the T-stand and perched. Still, all Bucky needed was to see him. Her pupils pinned and she puffed up her head and neck feathers so that she looked like a cobra. She strutted forward, confident and aggressive, and pounded the daylights out of Dogen and Paco.

In January, Connor started trembling. It was intermittent, and he didn't appear ill, but I decided to stop releasing him until the trembling stopped. The four birds and I spent the next weeks as constant companions, and I got to know their personalities intimately. Paco was a kid, still wild at heart; Connor was cooperative, but aloof; Bucky was a proud old queen; Dogen was gentle and affectionate. I seldom had visitors, and except for the occasional odd job, I almost never left the house. But I didn't see myself as friendless. The birds were my friends. While reading my diary one evening, I realized that my September dream had come true: There were four birds in the house, one of whom was a baby, along with a hairy mammal (my hair was almost down to my waist), and we were all sharing the table, figuratively and literally.

I'd been curious to know the gender of each of the four indoor birds. I'd read about a company that could determine the sex of a parrot from a blood sample. So I saved my money and ordered some kits. The test required that I cut off enough toenail to get it to bleed. It wasn't nearly as difficult an operation as I thought it would be, and it didn't seem to hurt the birds at all. I sent the blood off to the lab. One day, I came home and found the results in the mailbox. I tore open the envelope as I walked to the front door. Inside were four certificates, one for each bird. Just as I'd supposed, Paco was a male and Dogen was a female. Bucky and Connor? Both males.

year when the parrots put on their noisiest displays. By early November, everyone calmed down, and the flock remained cohesive and stable until February, when it began to splinter again.

The first splinter group I saw that February consisted of just two birds: Bo and Mandela. They weren't acting like typical breakaways, though. They were coming to the east balcony first thing every morning and spending their entire day there. For some reason, they'd taken a strong interest in Dogen and Paco. They perched on top of their cages and jousted with them through the bars. It was unusual enough that Bo and Mandela were coming to the balcony at all—the rest of the flock visited only the fire escape—but they stayed out there even when Dogen and Paco were inside the house. Sometimes I found Bo and Mandela clinging to the molding of the living room windows and looking inside for their two friends. Bo was especially tenacious. Whenever Mandela left to forage, Bo would be reluctant to join her. Since he was so intent on staying on the balcony, I started putting out food for him.

There was another unusual splinter group that February. Oliver, the mitred conure, had been accepted into the flock, and was now a member of a trio that included Gibson and Costanze, née Mozart. (I changed Mozart's name to Costanze, the real Mozart's wife, when I saw Gibson, a bird I believed was male, courting her.) It was the first time I'd ever seen a threesome. I thought it curious that Gibson and Costanze, a bona fide couple, had accepted Oliver so readily.

One morning, I was going about my usual morning chores—washing dishes, cleaning cages—when the phone rang. It was Edna calling to tell me that Maxine had fallen at the nursing home and broken her hip. Edna was flying to San Francisco the next day and wanted me to pick her up at the airport. Before hanging up, she told me it was quite likely that she'd be closing the house down on this trip. She hoped I'd found a new place to live.

I'd been dreading this moment for three years. It was like death: I knew it would come eventually, but I'd been living as though I could

A Walk on the Wild Side

I was beginning to recognize the details of the flock's yearly pattern of dispersal and reunion. The parrots flew as a single body from November until early February, when the first splintering occurred. Initially, it was slight—a small group cutting loose from the main body of the flock for part of the day—but the trend toward smaller, more numerous groups accelerated until it reached a peak at the beginning of summer, when the females laid their eggs. In late July and early August, after the eggs hatched, the females began flying with their mates again for part of the day. Throughout August, individual groupings increased steadily in size until just before the September fledge, when the flock dispersed again. Couples with offspring followed separate paths until late September or early October, when they brought the babies into the day-to-day life of the flock. This was the time of stay in the house forever. Now the end was near, and I fell into an unholy panic. I felt impelled to jettison everything I couldn't carry. What was I going to do with the birds? I could just turn Connor loose, but what about Bucky and the others? I'd been putting Dogen and Paco out on the fire escape at night to acclimate them for their eventual release, but I wasn't sure that Dogen was ready. She flew well enough around the house, but there were still a few stubby, clipped feathers—two or three, I thought—in the middle of her left wing that hadn't been replaced yet. She was sensitive about her wings, and every time I'd tried to examine them, she'd been less than cooperative. It was such a small gap, though, that I thought it wouldn't be a problem. There was one other consideration pushing me toward an immediate release: When Edna arrived, I'd have to move back down to the cottage studio, where it would be difficult to monitor Dogen's and Paco's conditions. I wanted to be in touch with them for at least their first day or two outside, and the only way I could do that was if I released them right away. It took me less than a minute to make up my mind.

I put Dogen and Paco in a cage and carried them outside. It was a cold and gloomy gray morning. Bo and Mandela were already out on the balcony railing, waiting. There wasn't time to be sentimental; I opened the cage door and stepped back. But Dogen and Paco wouldn't come out. In the past, whenever they were outside and I needed to open their cage door, I was always adamant that they not budge. They'd always obeyed me, and they were being good birds now, too. I had to reach into the cage and bring them out. As soon as they were clear of the cage door, Bo and Mandela flew toward them. Their approach intimidated Paco and Dogen, who flew to my shoulders for protection. I stood there waiting for them to fly away, but Bo and Mandela were too close. Dogen and Paco refused to move from my shoulders, so I put them back in the cage and carried them into the house.

An hour later, I decided to try again. This time when I opened the door, Paco and Dogen came right out. They flew straight up, around six feet, and hovered. Bo and Mandela flew toward them, so Dogen and Paco fluttered down to my head. Since they were still reluctant to take off, I started walking toward the door. Just as I was about to reenter the house, they jumped off and flew to the garden with Bo and Mandela in close pursuit. They looked slightly awkward, but I'd expected that. All four cherry heads landed in the deodar cedar, where Bo and Mandela chased Dogen and Paco around the limbs. They fled to another tree, and Bo and Mandela stayed right with them. Then all four cherry heads took off in the direction of Coit Tower, where I lost sight of them.

I had a lot of cleaning and packing to do, and as I worked I occasionally heard Dogen squawking higher up the hill. I was surprised that I could pick out her voice. I neither heard nor saw Paco. Late in the morning, when the flock came to eat, I scanned the crowd for my two ex-wards, but neither bird was present. After the flock left, I heard Dogen squawking in the distance again. I went back out on the fire escape and tried to locate her. She was somewhere near Coit Tower, but out of sight. Suddenly, Paco appeared. He was northeast of the tower, flying around and around in a big circle, screaming ecstatically.

Later in the day, the flock returned to eat, and this time Dogen was with them. I didn't recognize her at first, even though she was standing right in front of me on the railing. She looked a little tired, but I wasn't too concerned. I assumed it would take them several days to build their strength. When the feeding got under way, Dogen hopped up to her old position on my right wrist. As I was passing my hand around, Sebastian tried to pull out some of Dogen's head feathers, and she let him have it. She still knew how to fend for herself. When the flock made a quick bolt and return, Dogen took part. It looked like her return to the flock was going to be a simple affair.

At feeding's end, everybody left except for Dogen and Bo, who stayed behind to eat at the bowl together. When they finished, they flew up to the Monterey cypress and perched next to one another. Mandela had left with the flock, but she returned a few minutes later, looking for Bo. When Mandela saw that Dogen and Bo were perched side by side, a fight broke out between her and Dogen. Parrots have such strongly jealous natures that I would have been surprised if Mandela hadn't been angry at finding them together. It wasn't a major fight, and the three quickly made peace. Paco's continued absence was beginning to bother me. I kept thinking back to a conversation I'd had with an ornithologist a month earlier. I'd telephoned her seeking advice on Dogen and Paco's release, and she warned me that Paco might not have any "flock sense." Paco had put in a brief appearance during the previous feeding, once again flying high overhead in a big circle. His silhouette in flight—swift, stiff, shallow wing beats—looked silly. Add to that his noisy joy, and I had to laugh out loud. I stopped, though, when it occurred to me that the reason Paco was circling might be that he didn't know how to descend.

Dogen, Bo, and Mandela left the garden on their way to the evening roost, and as they left I got my first good look at Dogen's left wing. The gap was larger than I thought. Still, she was flying without any apparent problem. I went back into the house, sat down on the living room couch, and experienced a brief moment of calm. Bucky and Connor were asleep, and the city was quiet. I could feel a change in the atmosphere of the house. It felt strangely hollow.

If I'd had control of events, I would have waited until all of Dogen's clipped feathers had been replaced; I'd have made sure that she and Paco were completely acclimated; and I'd have checked the weather forecast. It turned out that I'd released them into the worst storm of the year. All night long there were heavy downpours and wind gusts that reached nearly fifty miles an hour. It was impossible to sleep. I kept picturing Dogen and Paco in the cold darkness getting drenched while clinging to a branch for dear life.

The next morning, as I was fixing breakfast, Bucky screamed out an alert. I ran to a window and saw three parrots streaking toward the fire escape. I went out to find Dogen, Bo, and Mandela perched on the fire escape railing. Dogen was soaking wet and looked exhausted, while Bo and Mandela had somehow managed to stay completely dry.

I was eager to get some food into Dogen, but she wasn't interested in eating. In spite of her apparent exhaustion, she was a little wired. She ignored me while waiting impatiently for Mandela and Bo to finish eating. Then all three birds jumped from the fire escape and continued on their way. Soon after they left, Bucky started screaming again. It sounded like another alert, so I ran outside to take a look. There I saw a lone parrot flying in a manic circle up near Coit Tower.

Later that morning, Dogen, Bo, and Mandela returned to the fire escape with a fourth bird in tow. It was Paco. He looked as though he hadn't suffered a bit from the weather. In fact, he seemed flooded with energy. Thinking he might like to eat from a familiar dish, I went back into the house and brought out his cage. But the moment Paco saw me with it, he fled the fire escape to perch on a line. I put the cage back inside the house and called to him, but he refused to come to me. I'd once thought that Paco would become the tamest of the birds in the house. I'd hand-fed him when he was a baby, which, according to the books, should have created a deep bond. But Paco had always maintained a slight distance and fear of me. He was still, at heart, a wild bird. As I was feeding the other three, the rest of the flock arrived. Paco still wouldn't come over. At the feeding's end, all four birds left with the flock. Fifty yards out, Dogen, Bo, and Mandela pulled away and went off on their own. Paco split from the flock, too, but rather than follow the other three, he again went his own way.

In bad weather, the flock usually came to me more often—sometimes as many as eight times a day—and this was one of those days. In the afternoon, Paco began to join in the feedings. At first, he wanted to be up on the seed cup I held in my left hand, but that was Mandela and Bo's place, and they refused to allow it. So Paco went to the railing and stood shoulder to shoulder with the others I was feeding there. He got into a few minor scrapes, but he handled himself remarkably well. When the flock bolted, Paco bolted, too, and this time he stayed with them.

Late that afternoon, I went to the airport to pick up Edna. On the drive back to the house, I steered the conversation toward empty pleasantries. I knew what was coming, and I didn't want to hear it. I much preferred leaving the property without any discussion of it whatsoever. Happily, Edna didn't bring up the subject. I parked the car and carried her luggage from Montgomery Street down the Filbert Steps to Darrell, and down Darrell to the house. She released me then, and I continued down to the cottage studio. Just as I was about to open the door, I saw something that stopped me in my tracks. A group of four parrots were flying around the garden in an endless series of loops and figure eights. They were flying extraordinarily fast, but that wasn't what startled me. It was that they weren't making any sound, which was so out of the ordinary as to be spooky. My first thought was that Dogen, Bo, and Mandela were giving Paco a lesson in formation flight, but that didn't ring true. Finally, one parrot emitted a squawk, and I recognized Oliver's voice. The group came to a stop on the lines, and I saw Mandela's sagging right wing. The other two were too far away to identify. After a brief rest, all four birds scrambled back into the air and resumed their incessant, silent looping.

I spent the night in the studio with Bucky and Connor. The weather was bad again, unusually cold, with snow falling on the Bay Area's highest hills. I knew enough now not to worry about the flock—they could take the cold—but I wasn't sure about Dogen and Paco. Early in the morning, I heard a single squawk and went outside to investigate. It was that same strange group of silently circling birds. I heard Oliver squawk once, and when they made a brief pit stop, I saw Mandela's sagging wing again. I still couldn't identify the other two, but I assumed that one of them had to be Bo.

Later that morning, I was out on my deck when I saw them again, but now there were six parrots in the group. They were still flying in complete silence, back and forth and around and around. In three years of daily observation, I'd never seen anything like it. Edna was spending the day at the hospital with Maxine, and she'd told me I could use the house if I wanted. So when the group broke out of their circle and flew to the fire escape, I ran up to see who they were. When

I opened the fire escape door, I found Gibson and Oliver chasing Bo around the fire escape floor with Dogen, Paco, and Mandela perched anxiously above them on the railing.

Gibson was doing the lion's share of the chasing; Oliver seemed to be acting in more of a supporting role. One of the most timid birds in the flock, Bo was not faring well at all. Each time Gibson caught up with him, he attacked Bo violently. I reached down and gently tried to break it up, but Gibson ignored me. I tried to bat him away then, but I couldn't scare him—which was bizarre. The birds had always had a hair-trigger reflex to fly away whenever I did anything brusque. I'd *never* been incapable of frightening them.

Still, I was able to create enough of a disruption that Bo escaped. He flew out toward the garden, but instead of looking for a place to hide, he wheeled around and came right back, landing on the seed cup in my hand. Gibson flew to the cup, too, and booted Bo off. After that, Gibson turned his attention to Mandela. He and Oliver chased her to a nearby set of lines, where she came to an abrupt stop. Mandela looked weary. Her bad wing was hanging lower than usual. She would have been easy pickings, but Gibson and Oliver didn't attack her. Then I understood what I was witnessing: Gibson was trying to steal Mandela away from Bo.

Throughout the fight, Paco and Dogen had been on the seed bowl trying to mind their own business. With Gibson momentarily distracted, Bo went to join them. I figured Bo's presence would attract Gibson, and I was intent on keeping Paco and Dogen out of harm's way, so I went over and sat down next to the bowl. Gibson came anyway. He kept trying to go around me, and I had to swat him. It was all so strange that I decided to get out of it for awhile and just watch what was happening. I went back to my usual spot at the other end of the fire escape, and Paco and Dogen came over to eat from my hand. Bo joined them, and this time Gibson allowed it. He and Oliver flew over to where Mandela was resting and perched on either side of her. When Mandela left the line to rejoin Bo, Gibson resumed his attacks. This time I got Dogen, Paco, Bo, and Mandela onto my arms, crossed my arms in front of me, and turned and faced the house. I was huddled as close to the wall as I could get, and Gibson *still* wouldn't quit. I was trying to shake him off my elbow when I heard a group from the flock approaching the fire escape. For some reason, their arrival restored order. Gibson and Oliver settled down and started eating. The feeding was a normal one, and when everybody was full, they all left.

A couple of hours later, the entire flock came in for a feeding. As she usually did, Mandela landed on the seed cup. Everything seemed to have returned to normal until Gibson landed next to her. He looked peaceful and as sweet as a parrot could be, but I was angry with him, so I knocked him off the cup. Gibson flew off looking for Bo, and when he found him the attacks were even more vicious than before. In the midst of all the chaos, Mandela landed on the railing right in front of me. Gibson saw and flew over, landing just a foot away from her. I blew my cork. I made a hard karate chop on the section of railing between them, which sent the entire flock back to the lines in a panic. A few minutes later, this mad scene with Gibson, Oliver, and Bo started up again. Gibson already had a mate, Costanze. Where was she? And why was Oliver involved? Bo was perched next to me on a ladder step, and when Gibson came after him, I started knocking him away again. This time Gibson gave me a hard bite on the arm. It *hurt*—enough so that I had to stop to massage the sore spot. While rubbing my arm, I started thinking that this was serious flock business, and maybe I should just stay out of it.

The parrots gradually filtered out of the garden with just Bo and Dogen staying behind. Maybe if Bo lost Mandela, he and Dogen would pair up. That didn't seem like such a bad thing. But I was beginning to have doubts about whether Dogen should remain free. She looked so tired. When she walked, she wobbled in a way that she hadn't done in months. Maybe her exhaustion was the result of the clipped feathers. Or maybe she had too much nerve damage and shouldn't ever have been released.

Early the next morning, Edna left town for an overnight visit to an old friend. She told me I could use the house while she was gone. I saw the group of six land on the fire escape, so I went up to see where things stood. Mandela was perched on a line near the fire escape, her wing drooping even lower than it had the day before. She looked worn out. Oliver and Gibson were perched near Mandela, shoulder to shoulder like two vultures, keeping her isolated from Bo, who was with Dogen and Paco on the fire escape. Each time Mandela tried to go to Bo, Gibson and Oliver flew over to keep them apart. I could see that Bo had been defeated. I had a small painting job to get to, and I was happy to go. I was sick of Gibson's ruthlessness.

When I got back home, I put my bike in the studio and walked up the path to the house. As I opened the door in the fence that surrounded the front patio, I heard a loud parrot squawk. It sounded as though the bird was very near me, which was puzzling. The parrots never came to the south side of the house. I looked up into the branches of the maple above me, but there was no parrot. I could hear the flock squawking on the north side of the house at the fire escape, so I decided I must have heard one of them squawk just as it flew overhead. I continued across the patio, and as I put the key into the front door I heard another loud, close squawk. The parrot was right next to my foot. It was Dogen. I opened the door, and she scampered into the house as fast as her stumbling little legs could carry her. She couldn't fly anymore. I heard a noise at a dining room window, looked up, and saw Paco clinging to a sill. I went out onto the balcony, and he flew to my head. I walked back into the house with Paco clinging to my hair. I put some seeds in a tray and set it on the floor for them. They were both famished.

The flock was calling for me, so I went outside. Bo and Mandela flew to the cup, and Gibson and Oliver began another attack on Bo. Although I'd resolved to stay out of the dispute, I simply couldn't do it. I couldn't stand the idea of Bo and Mandela being split apart. I started batting Gibson away again. He was relentless. But this time so was I. In our previous altercations, I'd restricted myself to acting defensively, but this time I went on offense. I was pissed off at Gibson. Our fight alarmed the flock. They'd never seen me do anything like that. They stopped eating and made low nervous squawks while I chased Gibson. Only Marlon seemed indifferent to what was going on. When Oliver saw that I was battling Gibson without restraint, he withdrew. Without Oliver's help, Gibson lost his steam. He made a few more halfhearted attacks, and then gave up on trying to steal Mandela. Just before the feeding ended, I offered Gibson a seed as a peace offering, and he took it.

After the flock left, I went back inside to check on Dogen and Paco. Paco was tired, but not as tired as Dogen. She was completely spent. I lay down on the living room floor and placed her on my chest. She closed her eyes, and I stroked her for nearly an hour. She would have stayed longer, but I had to get up and start packing.

Rage Against the Light

After a night's rest, Dogen was fine. I was curious to know whether she'd flown to the front door intentionally, or if she'd simply run out of gas while flying over the patio. If it was the former, she'd demonstrated a keen awareness of place and of my daily movements. Dogen had passed through that door only a few times and always in a cage, whereas I came and went through it constantly. Dogen had been very lucky. If she'd landed on the fire escape, I might not have realized that anything was wrong, and I would have discouraged her from coming inside. She'd been lucky, too, that Edna chose to go out of town that day. I think Edna found the parrots mildly annoying—she often referred to them as my "pigeons"—and if she'd been the one to find Dogen standing at the door, she probably would have shooed her away.

I'd been avoiding Edna as much as possible, but I couldn't put her off forever. One afternoon, she telephoned and asked me to come up to the house; she wanted to talk with me. After the obligatory cordialities, she got down to business: To pay for Maxine's care, she was going to have to put the house up for rent. I had to move. She asked what my plans were. My search for a new situation had been halfhearted at best. I knew that ultimately there was only one direction for me: I'd go wherever circumstance led me. It wasn't a happy decision. I was going through another round of frustration with the lack of development in my life, but I was afraid to break out on my own. My understanding was that if I quit my path, it would ruin me. There could be no other way. I couldn't tell this to Edna. She was in her seventies, a Christian from the Deep South, and she would not have understood. To be fair, except for a few old hippies, I don't think most people my own age would have understood, either. So I told her I had friends who were going to put me up until I could get started on this wonderful new project I had in the works. I was vague about the exact nature of the project, and she wasn't interested anyway. As she started going into the details of the property's new legal situation, my attention drifted to the parrots, who were calling to me from the fire escape. Oliver was clinging to the windowsill of the fire escape door, pressed right up against the glass, and staring inside. I thought about how I was going to have to spend time weaning them away from me, and it seemed a sad task. My attention drifted back to Edna just in time to hear the one piece of good news she had for me: She was returning to Louisiana for a few weeks, and when she came back to San Francisco she was going to need help moving Maxine's belongings out of the house. If I wanted, I was welcome to remain on the property for two more months.

Although I'd been feeding the birds four or five times a day, every day, for two and a half years, they were not, strictly speaking, dependent on me. There was plenty of food available to them. I'd seen or heard of them eating cotoneaster berries, toyon berries, blackberries, pyracantha, magnolia blossoms, cherry blossoms, coral tree blossoms, flowering eucalyptus, pine nuts, juniper berries, hawthorn berries, loquats, strawberry guavas, plums, apples, and pears. They recognized and made use of bird feeders, too. True, my handouts had made life easier for them. I think that if I'd done anything for them, it was giving them the opportunity to explore their territory on full bellies. So while not dependent, the parrots had come to rely on me, and my purpose in weaning them was to make the change as smooth as possible for them.

I began by feeding them every other day. Over time, some of the magic had gone out of what I was doing. There had even been occasions when a hawk was in the vicinity that I'd wished for the hawk to come closer so that the flock would go away. But now that it was ending, I cherished the time I had left with them. It was spring, the season when the biggest changes took place within the flock. Oliver and Gibson were an exclusive pair now. What a strange end to that story. Oliver had to be a female, so I changed her name to Olive. Erica, the flock matriarch, had found a new mate, a bird I called Russell. Marlon's red head feathers had bloomed outrageously; only one bird in the flock had more red. Sometimes it seemed that the more red on the head, the more dominant the bird. But this wasn't the case for Marlon. He picked a lot of fights, but he nearly always lost them.

One day, Marlon and Murphy and another adult pair showed up on the fire escape on what was supposed to be a weaning day. I was working in the kitchen, and they saw me, so I moved to another room. The two couples waited for me a long time, and eventually a fight broke out. The noise was so intense that I came out of hiding and ran to the window to see what was going on. They were psychogobbling fiercely and striking each other with their beaks. Rather than break it up, I decided to watch them. It wasn't nearly as violent as it sounded; it was just light pecking and beak banging accompanied by horrible screams. The fight ended when Marlon and his male opponent got tangled up in each other's talons and tumbled to the fire escape floor. They all flew away then. After that, I hung a sheet over the fire escape door on weaning days. It was still awkward for me: Although they couldn't see in, I could see them in silhouette lined up on the railing for hours at a time. It was hard to refuse them.

I still hadn't figured out what to do with the birds in the house. I hated doing it to them, but since my future was unclear, I felt I had no alternative but to clip Dogen and Paco. It was Paco's first clipping, and it changed him. He'd always been feistier than everybody else, but after the clipping he was much more cooperative. With Dogen and Paco unable to fly, Connor became the master of the high living room windowsills, and he exacted retribution on the two cherry heads for past abuses. He was especially hostile toward Dogen, which was strange considering that Paco was the one who'd given him the most trouble. Sometimes Connor got so nasty with Dogen that I had to intervene.

I was considering keeping the two blue crowns together, but there was an unexpected complication: Cracks were beginning to form in their relationship. The problem was Bucky's chronic possessiveness. Connor liked to go out every now and then for a flight around the neighborhood. On rare occasions, he spent the night out with the flock, but he always returned the next morning. Bucky didn't want Connor going out at all. Whenever I reached into their cage to get Connor, Bucky would bite my hand and then pin Connor up against the cage wall and bite him and preen him, bite him and preen him. His meaning was intuitively clear: "Don't go, I love you." It was a neurotic, clinging kind of love that I think only a caged bird could have. Sometimes Connor chose to stay in the cage with Bucky, but other times he scrambled to get up on my hand. As the weather warmed up, Connor began spending longer periods of time outside.

Edna's nephew, Joe, often came to San Francisco on business, and whenever he was in town he stayed at the house. One time, I mentioned to him that I was thinking of writing a book about the parrots. He said that if I was going to write a book, I'd need a computer, and offered to send me his old one. I didn't know anything at all about computers—how they worked or what they did—and I couldn't understand why anybody would need one to write a book. I never really expected to see it—it seemed like an awfully expensive thing to give away—but one afternoon a deliveryman brought it to the door. Joe had sent me the works: computer, monitor, and printer. I had no idea what to do with the thing, so I went down to the library and got some books. Once I had the basics down, I started typing in all my handwritten notes and diaries.

It was an effort to keep my attention on the machine. The day of my departure was just weeks away now, and I still had nowhere to go. In North Beach, I'd been through this kind of insecurity many times, but it had been eight years since I'd last had to endure it. I'd grown accustomed to the security of the property and my caretaker role within it. Now I was reduced to waiting for that unforeseen event that would come riding magically to my rescue. I know that's completely alien to the modern way of life, where an individual cuts a path of his own choosing. But it's at the core of the ancient way of following the Spirit. The deal is that you do the work of cultivating the inner self, and the Spirit sees to your needs. To my mind, the natural next step for me was to have a mate and find work that could support us. And I still wanted to move to the country. In fact, I craved such a move, especially after having experienced what I believed was a moment of great insight.

One day, I recalled that the first time I ever came to San Francisco I stayed in an apartment just a few doors down from Maxine's house. Darrell Place is an obscure, block-long path, and I thought the odds of that happening by chance were extremely slim. I put that coincidence together with the fact that when I sat on the living room couch I could see, miles away, the tall bell tower on the Berkeley campus, where I'd worked as a street singer when I first moved to the Bay Area. I took it as a sign from the universe that I'd come full circle, that it really was time for me to leave San Francisco. I loved this interpretation so much that I started demanding that it be real. I kept telling myself that I'd paid my dues, and if the universe were just, everything would happen exactly as I wished. But my time in the house was almost up, and I hadn't yet seen any signal that it was really going to happen. I was growing uneasy—and a little mad.

I took breaks from the computer to feed the flock or to visit with Bo and Mandela. Bo was still obsessed with Dogen and Paco, and Mandela was sticking by him. On one occasion when the flock flew away and Bo remained behind, I went outside to be with him. Together, we watched the flock head north. As the parrots neared Fisherman's Wharf, which is at least a quarter mile away, they wheeled around and started coming back toward us, but then they turned again and resumed their original heading. At a point far from the house, I saw a single parrot break loose from the flock and circle back. She flew all the way to the house and landed on the fire escape railing right next to Bo. It was Mandela, of course. Somehow she'd realized in the midst of all the in-flight chaos that Bo had not come with her. I thought it remarkable that she was able to separate from the pull of the flock. The instant Mandela landed, she and Bo bit each other's beaks, which made a funny, squeaky, crunching sound. I'd seen the parrots do this many times. It was clearly a form of greeting.

Bo, Mandela, and Connor, when he was free, all laid claim to the balcony. Sometimes they got into fights over it. Bo and Mandela would pin their eyes and spread their wings—fighting position—while Connor puffed up with rage. Bo, with Mandela's backing, could usually outmuscle Connor, who would go to hide behind Bucky's cage. An inadvertent result of weaning was that some of the parrots started coming around to the balcony to see what I was up to. Sonny and Lucia were among those who came, and they got into fights with Mandela and Bo. Their rivalry was especially interesting given that Sonny and Lucia were Mandela's parents. I saw no clear evidence that any of them recognized it. They didn't seem any closer than other pairs in the flock. Babies stayed in close contact with their parents until the following breeding season, at which point the relationship seemed to end. Still, I doubt that it was a matter of anybody forgetting. As I would learn, they have excellent memories.

I wasn't all that sad about saying good-bye. I felt that I needed to get on with my life. But while one side of me looked at the parrots as a diversion, there was another side that wondered if the flock and I had been destined to meet. I did feel a real connection to them. I saw them as my friends, and, to a degree, the feeling was mutual. One morning, the flock arrived at a moment when I was too involved with the computer to feed them. I carried the bowl out, set it down, and went straight back to work. A few minutes later, I had a change of heart and went back outside. There was a crowd on the bowl, but as soon as I came out with my cup, they all left the bowl and came to me.

After nearly a month in Shreveport, Edna returned to San Francisco. The night before she arrived, I moved Dogen, Paco, Connor, Bucky, the computer, and all my possessions back down to the cottage studio. Since Connor wasn't accustomed to coming and going from the studio, I stopped releasing him. I hadn't decided yet what to do about him and Bucky. I was still inclined to keep them together, but there were several arguments against it—not the least of which was the continually growing trouble in their relationship. In recent weeks, whenever Connor spent the night outside with the flock, Bucky would push Paco aside and perch next to Dogen. Now Bucky sometimes went to Dogen even when Connor was in the house.

Edna allowed me to come up to the house to continue the weaning process, and I cut them back to once every three days. One day, my old downstairs neighbor, Harvey, moved out, and I finally learned why I'd had no further trouble with him. It seems he'd fallen quite a few months behind in his rent, so he'd been in no position to complain. The new tenant, Dick Lane, told me he was interested in feeding the parrots. I told Dick which seeds the parrots preferred, and he bought a big bag of raw grays plus a feeder. The feeder hung from an arm that extended out from the building. It was just below the east balcony, so Bo and Mandela were the first to discover it. Soon the others began coming to it as well.

The end was getting closer and closer. Edna found buyers for the kitchen equipment, the furniture, the artwork, and the books. Finally, nothing was left except for the junk that nobody wanted and the bed she'd been sleeping in. I'd been helping her out a little, but the main thing she wanted from me was a final cleanup: vacuuming, dusting, washing, and so on. I had three weeks in which to complete it. After that, a management company was going to take over the property, and I would have to leave. Edna wished me luck and returned to Louisiana.

I moved back into the house for those last weeks. It felt hollow and gloomy now, but it was better than the studio, which was cold, damp, and moldy. My first day back up at the house, I released Connor. When he showed up at the fire escape a few hours later, he was unusually wary of me. I put Bucky, Dogen, and Paco out on the east balcony, and Bo and Mandela immediately resumed their daylong vigils. This time Connor refused to join the others there; he would come only to the fire escape. Whenever I tried to get him onto my hand, he flew away. Although Bucky had taken up with Dogen again, I assumed that he still preferred Connor. I wondered if Connor was avoiding the balcony because of Bo and Mandela. Then Connor disappeared entirely, and I didn't see him again for six days. When he returned, he came in a group. He was still acting aloof. During the feeding, I saw an unusual event: Scrapper and Scrapperella got into a big hassle. Couples often bickered, but this was more intense than that; it looked more like a real fight.

When the flock left, Connor stayed behind to eat some more. I had to understand what was going on between him and Bucky, so I did something that was against all my rules: I snuck my hand over Connor's back and snatched him. He struggled to free himself, but gently, as though he were concerned that he might hurt me. I carried him into the house and put him into the cage with Bucky. Bucky immediately flew into a rage, assaulting Connor with all his strength. He was extraordinarily vicious and would not relax his attack. It was as if Bucky were saying, "You *bastard*! How dare you abandon me! I never want to see you again." Connor made no effort to defend himself. He cowered in a corner of the cage while Bucky continued his assault, so I reached in and pulled Connor out. I didn't fully understand why, but it was clear that Bucky and Connor's relationship was finished. I carried Connor out to the balcony and set him free.

The less often I fed the flock, the less often they came to me. They have no time for sentimentality. They can't store food, so their first concern every day has to be the search for it. They liked Dick's feeder, and the number of parrots using it increased daily.

Both the flock and I were having to find new arrangements, but I hadn't seen a hint of a direction yet, and my anxiety and frustrations were growing. I felt as though I was being forcibly held down by a ghoul while year after year my youth was stripped away from me. While others my age had been falling in love, traveling, and having adventures, I'd been sitting on my butt in a closet. While they'd studied and moved on to careers, I'd read books about God and cleaned toilets for a living. I saw myself as getting old and going nowhere, and I was bitter about it. I didn't doubt the existence of God, or the Spirit, or cosmic consciousness—whatever you want to call it—but I was beginning to believe that it was utterly indifferent to my happiness.

My last task in the house was to give the fire escape a thorough cleaning. Before starting, I fed the parrots one last time. It was close to the breeding season, so the flock had dispersed. Nevertheless, I got lucky: An unusually large group came to eat. I had the chance to say good-bye to most of my favorites. All my original hand feeders— Noah, Marlon, Murphy, Scrapper, and Connor—were there. It was an extraordinarily long feeding that I finally had to end myself. As I closed the door on them, I felt little emotion. I was too preoccupied with my own cares. After they left, I went back out and swept the fire escape, hosed it down, and scrubbed off the accumulated layers of bird shit.

The property management company was coming out the next day and there had been no unexpected, magical turn of events to save me. There was only one place in the world that I could see to go: the cottage studio down below. It was in such horrible condition that I knew they wouldn't be renting it. Helen's emphysema had gotten much worse, and she desperately wanted my help. She was happy to conceal my presence on the floor beneath her. The only thing I'd have to worry about was the property managers snooping around the cottage.

Although the way was clear for me to return to the studio, I was furious about having to go back down there. Since I first landed on the street, each of my living situations had been a slight improvement over the one that had preceded it. This time I was in retreat, and I'd never been forced to go backward before. I felt I'd been betrayed by a mean-spirited God. Just before moving out of the house, in a spasm of rage, I tore up all my spiritual books and threw them into the trash. I vowed that I would never again have anything to do with religion.

Tupelo

The cottage studio was small, and this time I was sharing it with three birds. When I originally moved in eight years earlier, I was coming from a place that was infinitely worse, so I'd happily accepted the room's deficiencies. But after three years of living in luxury, all I could see now was how dank and dismal it was. Even though I'd had to stay there whenever Edna was in town, I hadn't done a major cleaning in years. It was cobwebby, and the bathroom walls had grown mold again. At night, I could hear rats scampering across the ceiling, scattering debris as they ran. The only nice thing about living there was that it put me right in the garden. But I couldn't allow myself much time to enjoy the scenery; I had work to do.

I was determined to free myself from the frustration of being an odd jobber. The only thing I could see to do was to write a book

about the parrots. I felt it was an unusual story that was worth telling. Writing fit all my criteria for work: It was something I liked to
do, and it was creative. As for my old fears about the fate of writers,
I was *already* destitute, and having survived the street, I was no longer
afraid of going insane or becoming an alcoholic. I found some milk
crates and an old door and improvised a desk. I'd written short stories
and I'd written songs, but I had no idea how one went about writing an entire book. My usual method would have been to buy some
books on how to write a book, but I didn't see myself as having the
time for that. I didn't delay even a single day; I just sat down and
started writing.

I was so focused on my work that I had little time for Dogen,
Paco, and Bucky. I didn't want to keep them locked up all day, so I
encouraged them to use the rope gym. Whenever they were hungry,
they jumped to the floor and went to their cages. I bought a long bird
ladder so they could climb back up to the ropes when they were done
eating. After eight years of having secure housing, I'd accumulated a
lot of stuff, and living with three birds in such cramped quarters was
messy. I had to spread newspapers underneath the lengths of rope to
catch their droppings, and I was continually tracking empty seed hulls
across the carpet. At the end of the day, I was so spent from writing
that I seldom had the will to clean up. A neighbor told me it looked
like I was living in a giant birdcage. To add to the effect, the sliding
glass windows were double-paned, and sandwiched between the
panes were decorative grills that looked like the bars of a cage. The
three birds and I were living so intimately that sometimes we got on
each other's nerves. Paco had developed an obsession with sneaking
up on me when I had my shoes off and biting my toes. I found it
amusing only the first couple of times. Parrots, like most birds, go to
sleep when the sun sets, but my activity was keeping them awake. As
it got late, I could see the annoyance in their eyes. The moment I
turned out the light, they always threw up a little cheer.

The parrots were still coming to the garden and to Dick's feeder,
but I was such a hermit that we seldom saw each other. Dogen, Paco,

and Bucky paid close attention to the flock's comings and goings. I was impressed by their awareness of events outside. They often made the low cawing sound that the flock used to warn of hawks. They made it even when I had the blinds down and they couldn't see anything. Every time I went out to check, I would find a hawk soaring high overhead. Maybe they heard the native birds' warning sounds, or maybe they heard the hawks themselves. I still doubted that their concern was legitimate. But that changed one afternoon while I was taking a break from my work. I was standing with my back to the north window and holding Bucky when all three parrots jumped to the floor in a panic. Simultaneously, I heard something bang hard against the glass just behind me. I wheeled around in time to glimpse the tail of a hawk as it disappeared into a nearby tree.

One morning, I was at the computer when Dogen, Paco, and Bucky broke out into a fit of excited screaming. I turned to my right, and there at the east window, perched in a fuchsia, were Bo and Mandela. I was absorbed in my work, so I turned away from them. Later, I glanced over again, and they'd gone. The next day, though, they were back in the fuchsia and staring inside. I ignored them, so Bo flew around to the front of the studio. There was a lot of ivy attached to the cottage, and a long stretch of it grew across the top of the north window. Bo landed on one of the vines, hung upside down, and stared in at us. Then he started fluttering from vine to vine like he was Tarzan. It amused me, but I still refused to acknowledge him, so he rejoined Mandela in the fuchsia. There were some parrots up at Dick's feeder who'd become curious about what Bo was doing. Two flew down to the fuchsia, and then they were joined by the others. Before long, Olive, Gibson, Sonny, Lucia, Scrapper, Scrapperella, Pushkin, and Jones were all perched outside my window and staring in at me. I refused to respond to them, but they wouldn't leave. After awhile, I started feeling hypocritical. I mean, there I was, working on a book about my supposedly deep-seated love for these birds while simultaneously shunning them. I got up, put some seeds in a cup, and opened the sliding window. While I fed the first group, others arrived.

It had been weeks since I'd last fed them, and I was feeling happy—until I saw something that made my heart sink: A juvenile was flying erratically and having trouble landing on the fuchsia. Her symptoms were identical to those of Dogen, Martha, Stella, and Chomsky.

The birds I fed came again the next day, and they continued to come every day thereafter. When I was at the computer, I'd often feel them gathering behind me in the fuchsia. They'd wait silently and patiently until I got up to feed them. Then all hell would break loose. The feedings at the window were unusually competitive. I couldn't reach the birds on the farthest limbs, so they were all fighting each other to get up on my arms. I kept seeing that sick juvenile fluttering around the edges of the group. I couldn't tell who she was. She was getting worse every day, but there was nothing I could do to help her.

A month after I moved into the studio, Maxine passed away at the nursing home. It happened before the property managers were able to find anyone to rent the house. Under the terms of the will, Edna was to turn the property over to several designated charities, who were intent on selling. Helen heard that an appraiser was coming out to look at the property. San Francisco's soaring rents were making tenants anxious whenever the building they lived in changed hands. Helen was as afraid of losing her home as she was of losing my help. She said she'd give me a warning if she found out exactly when the appraiser was coming. It wouldn't have made any difference, though. It was impossible for me to conceal my presence. All my belongings were there, not to mention the birds, and I didn't have any place to hide it all. All I could do was to keep writing and wait for the knock on the door.

I was at my desk when the knock came. I sighed and steeled myself for a hostile interrogation, but it wasn't the appraiser; it was Terry, a neighbor who lived in the compound of old cabins and shacks next door. Terry was excited and out of breath. He started telling me that he and his girlfriend, Jackie, had been eating lunch on their deck when one of the parrots crash-landed right next to their table. Jackie had picked it up, but the bird struggled loose and flew away. He pointed to the bird, who was now at the top of a tall incense cedar and under attack from three other parrots.

I ran down Greenwich to get a closer look. The bird was crawling down the trunk, trying to escape her attackers, when she lost her grip. She fell twenty feet and landed in some ivy that was working its way up the cedar's trunk. The three parrots came down to where she'd landed and resumed their attack. They were merciless. The sick bird lost her grip again and fell into some bushes at the base of the tree. There were feral cats in the garden, and I didn't want them getting her. I sprinted back into the studio and grabbed a towel. Then I ran back down Greenwich, jumped over the railing, and struggled down the slope. The woman who tended the garden had died the year before, and everything was so overgrown that I had difficulty picking my way through the tangle of weeds and blackberry vines. When I reached the tree, I found the parrot hanging upside down from the limb of a low shrub. When she saw me, she panicked and dropped into the nasturtium ground cover. I threw the towel over the spot where she'd fallen and dug around until I had her. I wrapped her in the towel and carried her up the slope and home.

It was the same sick juvenile I'd seen out the window. She was in pitiful condition—even worse than Dogen had been. Her feet were all balled up so she couldn't walk. She kept falling onto her back, where she kicked her legs like a beetle trying to right itself. I had to push her to get her onto her belly. Like Dogen when she first got sick, the bird's head hung to the side, and the only way she could keep it upright was to rest the tip of her beak on the floor. But she had so little control over her neck that even this was difficult for her. There was a telltale patch of bare skin on her throat where the three attacking parrots had torn out the feathers. Nearly all weakened birds had a similar mark. I tried to figure out who she was. I knew she was one of four surviving juveniles—birds that had been born the previous summer—but I hadn't been close to any of them. And in the weeks since I left the house they'd all developed more red head feathers, so I'd lost track of the changes in their appearance. She looked a lot like Sonny, so she might have been his offspring, Georgia or Matthew. Since I couldn't be certain, I gave her a new name. There was something exceptionally sweet about her, so I named her Tupelo after the Van Morrison song "Tupelo Honey."

Tupelo was so skinny that the keel-shaped bone in her chest stuck out. I handed her a seed, and although she was able to open it, it took her a long time. When she finally stripped off the hull, she dropped the kernel and didn't have enough control over her neck to pick it up. I was going to have to feed her. I dug through some boxes and found the syringe and baby bird formula that I'd used to feed Paco. She was so ill that I felt I had to get her to a vet. The neighborhood grocery, Speedy's, served as the de facto community center. One window was reserved for neighborhood messages, and I taped up a plea for donations. Within an hour, a customer had left a $100 bill with the store owners.

The veterinarian who examined Dogen had suspected toxins, but this one believed that Tupelo's problem was viral. She said it wasn't psittacosis ("parrot fever") or Newcastle disease, both notorious bird killers. She thought that the most likely candidate was something called pigeon paramyxovirus, a disease that attacks the nervous system. But that was only an educated guess. Without running expensive tests, she couldn't say for sure. I asked her why only the juveniles were coming down with it and why it broke out in the spring. She said the virus was always present, but it could be that in the spring the immunities the babies received from their parents began to fade, while their own immune systems were still insufficiently developed. She said there wasn't any medicine that would help, that the only thing I could do was give Tupelo rest. She estimated Tupelo's chances for recovery at fifty-fifty.

Tupelo immediately began taking up large blocks of my time. Besides having to feed her several times a day, I was giving her heat lamp treatments, so I had to monitor the temperature constantly. With rest, she stabilized to a point where she stopped flipping over onto her back. She still couldn't walk, though. She learned to motor across the floor by pushing with her legs and scooting around on her chest. For greater speed, she'd flap her wings as she pushed. Between working on the book and taking care of Tupelo, I had less and less time for the other three birds. Dogen and Paco disliked the new member of the household. When she wasn't under the heat lamp, I left Tupelo free to wander the room. But I had to keep a constant eye on Paco or he chased her. One time he caught her when I was outside and bit her feet until they bled. When I came back in and found Tupelo on the floor bleeding, I was furious with Paco. To give him a taste of his own medicine, I chased Paco around the room until he was so exhausted that he couldn't move. He was cowering on the floor and waiting for me to deliver the fatal blow. I bent down and picked him and told him how angry he'd made me. But I didn't yell at him, and I kissed him when I was done. My pursuit of Paco had been so intense that Dogen had gotten swept up in it a couple of times. Afterward, Dogen came to me and seemed concerned that our relationship had been ruptured. She looked at me with friendly but worried eyes; she wanted to make sure that everything was still alright, that I still loved her and Paco.

The flock was beginning to take up my time again, too. I couldn't resist them. The birds I'd fed were bringing others to the window, and the crowds grew daily. To feed the parrots perched on the fuchsia's outermost branches, I had to hold onto the frame of the sliding window and lean out. The feedings were tremendously exciting to the cherry heads inside the house. Paco and Dogen would psychogobble and squeal helplessly for the duration. Tupelo would crawl out of her cage and scoot across the floor to my feet. Some days she was so happy about the flock's presence that she'd scoot and flap in circles around the room while sounding her weak little squawks.

Other than the brief moments of joy inspired by the flock's arrival, Tupelo's life inside the house was a gloomy one. Parrots are impulsive and compulsive, and it didn't matter how much I punished Paco; he couldn't restrain himself from attacking Tupelo. So Tupelo was reluctant to venture out of her cage much, and spent most of her day inside of it, asleep. Wanting to alleviate her boredom, I started carrying her outside for walks. She'd grown up among branches, leaves, flowers, wind, and sun, and I thought it might be comforting for her to revisit them. She loved going outside. She'd lie absolutely still in my hand and bask in the warmth of the sun. I walked her all around the garden, stopping in front of various flowers and holding her up to them so she could look. The parrots are blossom eaters, so they must make distinctions between types of flowers. I'd never seen the parrots eat them, but Tupelo seemed most interested in the fuchsias. She would stare at them intently for as long as I cared to hold her up to them. Maybe she saw their beauty. Who knows?

The appraiser came and went, and it turned out not to be a problem for me. He was an outside consultant and had no idea who was supposed to be on the premises and who wasn't. Nor did he care. His only concerns were the condition of the buildings and the views. I was relieved to have dodged that bullet, but the tension of the situation was wearing on me.

One day, I was feeling down in the dumps and decided to take Bucky outside for a walk. I still don't know exactly why I did it. For some vague, half-conscious reason, I thought it might make me feel better. Bucky's flight feathers had started to grow back, but he hadn't been flying in the studio at all. I assumed he couldn't fly. I was out on the Greenwich Steps with Bucky on my shoulder when I suddenly asked myself what the hell I was doing. I started back toward the cottage, and just before I got to the door Bucky jumped off my shoulder and flew away. He landed in a pepper tree that arched over the Greenwich Steps, and then took off again, disappearing behind a nearby apartment building. I wanted to kick myself. I immediately began to scour the neighborhood, asking all the people I encountered if they'd seen a parrot with a blue head. I walked up and down the hill's staircases until I was too exhausted to continue. I called Cynthia, the woman who gave me Bucky, and told her what had happened. She was furious with me—as I knew she would be.

A couple of days later, I met someone who knew what had happened to Bucky. A security guard at the bottom of the hill had been making his rounds when he came upon a blue-headed parrot lying unconscious on the sidewalk. Apparently, Bucky had flown into a window and knocked himself out. There was another blue-headed parrot on a tree limb just above Bucky who was calling down to him as if to encourage Bucky to get up and fly away. The guard was worried that Bucky would die from the cold, so he took him home to San Anselmo, a small town twenty miles north of San Francisco. Shortly after he brought Bucky inside, the blue crown escaped again, flying right out the front door. He hadn't seen Bucky since, but he said his neighbors had. I called Cynthia and told her what I'd learned. She came over immediately and we drove up to San Anselmo. We carried Paco and Dogen around the streets in a cage as bait, looked everywhere, talked to everyone, but we didn't find him. Cynthia was still angry with me and chewed me out for the duration of the trip. I felt bad about what I'd done, but as far as she was concerned I couldn't feel bad enough.

Tupelo and I kept getting closer. As I'd done with Dogen, I'd put her on my chest and pet and scratch her neck. She loved it. She'd lift her wings to make sure I got the area underneath. Her eyes looked so unfocused that I assumed she was completely disoriented, but over time it became clear that she knew the shape of the room and where I was at all times. Dogen had survived her illness, so I didn't see any reason why Tupelo couldn't survive hers. I monitored her progress constantly. If she squeezed my finger with a toe, I'd see in that the return of her ability to perch. If she held her head up, even for an instant, I saw her regaining control of her neck. On her bad days, I worried like a mother.

I used to have an involuntary negative reaction to handicapped children. It wasn't something I liked in myself, but I always wondered how parents could handle the burden of caring for a child for the rest of their lives. With Tupelo, I got an inkling of how little the infirmities matter. You don't even see them. Tupelo's feathers were tattered, broken, and caked with shit (which was difficult for me to clean off), her head listed constantly to the side, and she had crippled, balled-up feet. But she was my baby, and I loved her as she was. I slept on a futon on the floor. My usual nighttime routine was to get into bed and read. As soon as I was under the covers, Tupelo would crawl out of her cage and push herself across the floor to be with me. I'd put her under the covers and let her snuggle up against me until I was finished reading. I'd put her back in the cage then, but she always made complaining noises. She couldn't sleep with me—I could have crushed her—so I started wrapping her in a towel and putting her on the floor right next to my pillow, which satisfied her. The studio came with a portable, oil-filled electric heater, the kind that looks like an old-fashioned radiator, and sometimes she slept near it. She respected the heater—she always stayed at least a foot away from it—so I allowed it.

Contrary to what I would have expected, the flock suffered few losses in fall and winter; most deaths occurred in spring and summer. During the flock's May to mid-August dispersion, it was difficult to determine who was alive and who wasn't. I often became anxious about some of my favorites. Marlon had been at the side window for the first feedings I gave there, but he'd since vanished. But there had always been males who made themselves scarce during the breeding season. When Bo started showing up without Mandela, it was reasonable to assume that Mandela had gone to nest. Then, about a week after she would have laid her eggs, Mandela showed up without Bo. The females always stay in the nest until the eggs hatch. If Bo was spelling her, it was the first time I'd seen that. Mandela didn't come around again for several weeks, and Bo resumed coming to me for food. Late one afternoon, I was standing at the side window when I noticed three parrots up on the lines. One was by himself, and the other two were together. The pair launched an attack on the solitary parrot, who flew down to the fuchsia to escape them. It was Bo. He had a chunk of feathers missing just above one eye ring, a sign that he'd been in a serious fight. When I opened the window to hand him some seeds, the pair flew down, chased Bo away, and took his place. It was Pushkin and Mandela. Pushkin had a big tear in the flesh of his eye ring. Bo came back to the fuchsia, and another fight broke out. Pushkin and Mandela were acting as a team against Bo. All my efforts at keeping Bo and Mandela together had been completely futile. After a bit more fighting, Pushkin seemed inclined to let Bo eat, but Mandela was adamant about keeping Bo away. She took up the fight all by herself. Bo was nothing to her now.

One day while I was writing, I felt someone staring at the back of my head. I turned around and saw Connor perched quietly in the fuchsia. Since moving back to the cottage, I'd seldom seen him. On the few occasions I had, he was usually alone. It seemed as though he intersected with the flock only occasionally. I got up to see if he'd let me feed him, and he acted as if everything was fine. He didn't look very good, though. His head and neck were turning into a mass of pinfeathers again. As I handed him the seeds, I thought over a strange truth: When I first started watching the flock, Connor had enchanted me, and I'd longed to get close to him. But once I had the opportunity, I didn't take advantage of it. I'd paid very little attention to Connor when he was in the house. In part, I think I felt Connor's preference that I keep some distance. But that doesn't explain it fully. In a way, it reminded me of the man who falls madly in love with a beautiful woman, but once he has her loses interest.

In late July, I began to receive visits from birds I hadn't seen in many weeks. As always, the flock was giving me new puzzles to contemplate. One of the reappearing birds was Olive. Her haggard appearance was typical of a female coming off the nest. I didn't know whether it was possible for a cherry head and a mitred conure to interbreed, nor did anyone I asked know. There was another parrot who had some tarlike material stuck to her chest feathers. I'd seen this before in nesting females—the tar was tree pitch—but this bird was without a mate. When I first saw her, the only other bird in the vicinity was Bo. I had a feeling that the pitch-covered bird was Murphy.

But if so, where was Marlon? And Mandela had disappeared again. She'd paired up with Pushkin late in the breeding season, but I wondered if she'd gone to nest anyway.

. One day, I met a woman who told me she'd recently seen two parrots crawling in and out of a hole in a Canary Island date palm. I'd known the general location of the nests since the incident on New Year's Eve when I met the two birders and stepped on Sonny's tail. But the park had so many trees that finding a nest would have been like picking a needle out of a haystack. The woman was able to describe the tree's exact location, so I decided to go and check it out.

As if by appointment, when I arrived on my bike the pair was sitting side by side in a six-inch hole near the top of the twenty-foot-tall palm. I'd borrowed a pair of binoculars, and identifying the pair was easy: It was Mandela and Pushkin. The area they were sitting in was directly beneath the green palm fronds, the stubby field of ends where the old fronds had broken off. It looked like an old corncob. Their nest hole was right in the middle of the cob, where a frond end had either rotted and fallen from the tree or had been dug out. A chunk of an old frond end was lying on the ground, so I picked it up to see what it was like. It was brittle and weak, easy work for a parrot's beak. From where I was standing, the hole looked shallow, but it must have had some depth, since whenever Mandela and Pushkin went inside, they completely disappeared. They were going in and out of the nest hole constantly. Sometimes they went in one hole and out another, so they must have dug out a tunnel. I was hearing other parrots calling out to one another, so I went off to look for more nests, but I couldn't find any. I returned to Mandela and Pushkin's palm, took a few photographs, and got back on my bike. As I was leaving, I decided that the nesting location was one secret of the flock that should remain so. I just call it the Republic of El Coto.

A parrot's beak grows continually and has to be worn down through chewing. Because Tupelo didn't have the strength to chew, she'd developed an elongated lower beak. I didn't want to be constantly asking

Jamie Yorck for favors, and there was another San Francisco bird store that clipped wings and filed toenails for free. I hoped they could file down Tupelo's beak, but because she was so ill, I called first to make sure that it was alright to bring her over. The store owner wasn't in yet, but an employee told me he didn't see any problem with it.

The free clippings were popular, and when Tupelo and I arrived there was a line out the door. When the people standing around waiting with their pretty pollys saw Tupelo—her neck twisting and craning uncontrollably, and her eyes bulging and twitching—they pulled away and gave me nervous looks. One woman finally asked me about Tupelo's condition, so I told her the story. Suddenly Tupelo became a bit of a celebrity: one of the legendary wild parrots of Telegraph Hill!

Our turn finally came, but before I could even begin to explain what I wanted, the store owner started shaking his head. "Oh, no. No, no. I'm sorry. I can't work on this bird. She's too sick."

I understood. If Tupelo was shedding a virus and it got on the owner's tools and then infected other birds, it would have been disastrous. That was the reason I'd called in the first place: to be certain that it was alright to bring her. There'd been a misunderstanding between his employee and me. I turned around and carried Tupelo back to the bus for the ride home. The incident had put me in a dark mood. She didn't really need to be caged, so I took her out and set her on my lap. I stroked her, and she snuggled against my belly. I started thinking about all the rejections Tupelo had received. The flock had rejected her, Dogen and Paco were constantly attacking her, and now this man refused to work on her. I felt sad for her. I was the only friend she had. I remembered a day when I took Tupelo out for a walk and got into a conversation with two tourists who were on their way up to Coit Tower. Just before they left, one of the women told me she'd been watching Tupelo, and that throughout the conversation the young bird had been staring up at me with big, devoted eyes.

The time for the fledge was approaching, and as more and more of the birds came to me to eat, I started finding out who was dead and who was alive. Marlon was among the missing. I'd first suspected he was dead several weeks earlier, but now I was sure of it. Although Marlon and I had had little contact in the last year, he was still one of my favorites. Murphy, Marlon's mate, had paired up with Bo. I hadn't been certain of her identity when her chest feathers were matted with tree pitch, so I gave her a new name—Sticky Chest—and the name stuck. Another bird among the missing was Dogen's sibling and Pushkin's old mate, Jones. Pushkin must have taken Mandela away from Bo after Jones died. Mandela was the last of the females to come off the nest. Maybe she was going to be a mother now. I was still very curious to see if she'd be more permissive than the others in allowing me contact with her babies.

Of all the changes, the biggest surprise was that Scrapper and Scrapperella had gotten divorced. I'd never seen that before. I searched my diary and found an entry that described an intense fight between the two shortly before the breakup. This wasn't an instance of one bird abandoning the other for somebody else. Both birds were single now. I couldn't help but imagine that they'd quarreled over Scrapperella's obsessive feather plucking. She'd kept promising to quit, but couldn't. So Scrapper left her.

As the flock flew in larger groups, the number of birds perched in the fuchsia at any given feeding had grown to the point that their weight was causing the branches to bend down toward the ground. I worried about the neighborhood cats getting one of them. It was difficult to be on the lookout for cats when I was so busy refereeing the fighting among the birds eating from my hand. But the new setup had been awkward from the start, so one day I decided to move the feedings to my front deck.

The deck was a rectangle twelve feet long and six feet wide. Because the cottage was built on a slope, the deck was three feet above the Greenwich Steps, which made it seem like a stage. It had fallen into a state of ruin. Some of the underlying support beams had rotted through so that one corner was tilting down toward the staircase. Some floorboards were so soft that I had to cover them with sheets of plywood in order not to step through them. All but one of the posts for the surrounding two-foot-high railing had crumbled from dry rot. The railing was being held up mostly by the ivy growing up and over it, and by the limbs of a mirror plant, a large shrub with small shiny leaves. I put a seed dish on the ivy-covered corner post and waited for the flock to come down to eat. They were nervous about landing so close to the ground, but they overcame whatever qualms they had. Only about a dozen parrots could fit on the dish at any one time; everybody else perched on the railing and either took seeds from me or waited for a space to open on the dish. It was just like old times.

One morning in early September, I was standing on the deck chatting with Lee, a neighbor, when I saw a group of nine parrots flying toward the garden. I could hear that one of them was Olive. I'd developed a sixth sense when it came to the parrots, and I knew right away that there was something out of the ordinary in this group: The first babies had arrived, two of them. It always pleased me to see new babies, but when the two landed on a nearby power line, my pleasure turned to astonishment. One of the babies had a small red patch on its forehead. This never happened with baby cherry heads, but it was typical of baby mitred conures. The babies belonged to Olive and Gibson. They were *hybrids!* I was bouncing from the excitement of it. Lee asked what the hell was going on, and I explained it to him in the most joyous terms. He looked at me blankly, shrugged his shoulders, and continued on his way.

Two days later, the flock came up with another surprise: two more babies, and they both belonged to Bo and Sticky Chest. As near as I could tell, Bo had lost Mandela to Pushkin in the week just before the females usually laid their eggs, so I was amazed that Bo had been able to find a new mate and get her into a nest within such a short window of opportunity. Bo was a first-time parent as well as one of the weakest males in the flock, so maybe his success was a good omen for the flock as a whole.

Two days later, Sam and Kristine showed up with two babies. In the previous two years, at least one set of parents had brought out four babies. All I needed was to see one group like that, and I'd be content. A few mornings later, when a large group landed on the power lines outside the cottage, I ran outside to count babies. There were ten, the minimum I'd hoped for.

As the flock grew more and more boisterous, it set off Dogen and Paco, who, with eyes pinned, would shriek and psychogobble madly at the flock's arrival and continue for the duration of its stay. Some days they'd go on for nearly an hour. It was like living inside of a continuously ringing bell. Late one afternoon, while they were perched on the ropes and screaming deliriously, I noticed that Tupelo was sitting on the floor silently and staring up at them. I had the sense that she was admiring Dogen and Paco for their ability to perch and wail like that. It was as though it didn't matter to Tupelo that they were mean to her; she had a good-hearted admiration for them as healthy and strong parrots. There are people who will shake their heads and say that I'm merely projecting my own feelings onto her. Maybe so, but that's what passed through my mind as I looked at her.

That evening, as usual, I crawled into bed with a book. Soon after I started reading, I became peripherally aware of Tupelo scooting across the floor toward me. Without taking my eyes off the page, I reached over and picked her up. The moment I had her in my hand I felt a strange sensation pass through me. It was a combination of happiness and gratitude that seemed to be coming from Tupelo. It was as if she were saying, "Oh, thank you, thank you. I'm so happy you did that." It wasn't the words, but the feeling the words represent. "That's odd," I thought to myself. "I wonder what that was." It was a fleeting sensation, gone as soon as I noticed it, and I went back to reading with Tupelo tucked up against my belly. I read until I was too sleepy to concentrate. Just before turning out the light, I picked Tupelo up to put her on the floor. The moment she was in my hand I felt another emotion pass through me. This time it was a feeling of deep disappointment mixed with resignation, and again, it seemed to come from Tupelo. I was distracted at the moment it happened—my thoughts were still with the book—and because the feeling was spontaneous and didn't linger, I sort of scratched my head, forgot about it, and went to sleep.

When I woke up the next morning, I started thinking about what had happened the night before. I didn't know what it was, but it had left me with a spooky feeling. I wanted to see Tupelo, so I turned over expecting to find her in her usual spot in front of the heater. She wasn't there. I got out of bed and started searching for her. She wasn't in her cage or under the table or behind any chairs. I couldn't find her anywhere. That was impossible. Then I spotted her. Her tail was sticking out from beneath the heater. Horrified, I ran over, lifted the heater, and pulled her out. Her eyes were hard and dry and split with small cracks. My first thought was that she was dead, but then she exhaled. I was so relieved! I didn't care that she was blind now. I'd take care of her. Then I realized that the exhalation had just been the heated air rushing out of her body.

Although I understood that she was dead, I felt a strange disconnect from the fact. My mind was racing too fast to take it in. I tried to force myself to calm down so that I could come to terms with what had happened. One has to be an adult about death, I told myself. Death happens, and Tupelo was dead. I was just going to have to accept it. I carried her body over to where Dogen and Paco were perched on their ropes and showed them her body. They had no reaction. They seemed not to care. I couldn't stand to have her corpse in the house for any length of time at all. I found a shovel and dug a hole right outside the door and buried her. While standing over her grave, I started to feel a touch of misery. I thought back to something that had been happening to Tupelo all that week. She'd been shivering. It wasn't major, so I hadn't worried about it too much. But the shivering had never really stopped. I wondered whether she'd died because she got stuck underneath the heater, or whether she was already dying and had sought the heat because of it. I remembered again the strange events of the previous evening. It made me think Tupelo had been feeling the cold of death coming on and that she'd wanted me to comfort her. She'd been grateful when I picked her up, and disappointed when I put her back on the floor. She knew that was the routine, so she'd accepted it, but with regret.

As I stood there thinking about all these things, a neighbor walked by and asked me what I was doing with the shovel. I started to explain, but as I did, all the feelings I had for Tupelo welled up out of me. I broke down into tears and couldn't continue.

I'd never lost someone I loved dearly to death. But now I'd lost Tupelo, and I was devastated. For the next three days, every time I tried to talk to someone, I'd break down again. I kept wishing that I'd known she was dying. I could have been there for her, I could have been holding her. I longed to tell Tupelo, one last time, how much I loved her.

I know there are people who will think it childish for a grown man to be so distraught over the death of a bird. But I'd put a lot of worry and care into Tupelo, and she had looked to me for protection and sustenance. It created a bond between us that was just as real as any that connects two human beings. Tupelo's death forced me to acknowledge something. People who knew I was feeding the parrots would say things to me like, "You're really deep into this thing. You must really love those birds." Despite years of trying to overcome a middle-class upbringing, I still worried that people would consider me eccentric. So I always played down my interest. I'd say, "Oh, it's just a hobby, really, a curiosity." I'd gotten a couple of tags that I detested. One was the "parrot man," the other was the "birdman of Telegraph Hill." I never let people call me those names. Sometimes I'd refer to the thousands of pages of notes I'd made and imply that I was doing scientific research. But the notes had always been of secondary importance. It was my day-to-day friendships with the birds that mattered most to me. To continue to minimize my love for them after all the misery I'd gone through over Tupelo felt horribly cheap. I was doing what I was doing because I loved them. I promised myself that in the future, I'd be honest about it.

Back out in the World

Dogen had been jealous of all the attention I'd given Tupelo, and now that Tupelo was gone, she reclaimed me. Whenever I lay down on the futon, she'd run across the floor, climb up on my chest, and want to be petted and scratched. She reciprocated by preening the hairs of my face. She was especially fond of cleaning my lashes, which brought her beak so close to the surface of my eye that it made me uneasy. But she was attentive and precise, so I relaxed and let her do it.

Paco continued to keep his distance. He tolerated me, but the only friendship he wanted was Dogen's. He was still reluctant to let me pet him. Whenever he saw my hand coming down toward his back, he ran away. I started saying the word *pet* first, and once he'd learned the meaning of the word he relaxed somewhat and let me touch him. But he never completely lost the skittish, high-strung nature of a wild bird. I felt that if I could figure out a way to get him a teacher, he still had it in him to be a member of the flock.

Not that the flock was in dire need of new members. The breeding season had been a phenomenal success—greater than I'd dreamed possible. Seventeen babies fledged that year. I'd never seen more than three pairs breed successfully, but this time at least seven pairs had babies. Maybe the parrots were discovering more and more suitable nest holes as they became intimate with the landscape. The flock population now stood at forty-one. There were so many that I had trouble keeping everyone's identity straight. Adding to the difficulty was that I couldn't hang out with them after feedings. They disliked being close to the ground, as they were now on the studio deck, so they always flew back to the trees and the power lines as soon as they were finished eating.

Because they were unique, I was especially attracted to the two hybrid babies. Of the two, my favorite was the one with the red splotch on his forehead. It reminded me of a painter's palette, so I named him Picasso. He had the length of his mitred conure mother and the bulk of his cherry-headed conure father, so even as a baby he was the largest bird in the flock. Once Picasso overcame his initial clumsiness, he started throwing his weight around, overpowering even some of the adults. He began taking seeds from me as soon as he was capable of opening them, and he quickly laid claim to my right wrist as his own personal perch. Picasso and his mother, Olive, would land together right in front of me on the railing, and when my palm came around to them, Picasso would raise a stiffened right leg, which was his signal to me that he wanted on my hand.

Except for being slightly larger and having a whiter eye ring, the other hybrid looked like a normal cherry-head fledgling. I named him Blake. A friend had told me about the poem by William Blake that says, "A robin red breast in a cage / puts all heaven in a rage," and I wanted to honor the poet for saying that. Blake was even friendlier than Picasso, but I never got to know him very well. Just three weeks after I first saw him, he disappeared. It always happened that one or two babies died shortly after fledging, but we also lost an adult that autumn: Lucia, Sonny's mate. I don't know what happened. The last time I saw her, she looked fine. For Sonny, Lucia's death could not have been more untimely. She left him with four babies to raise, and until they were weaned, he was going to have to feed them all by himself. Sonny was still unpopular with the rest of the flock, and whenever he approached the seed dish, they chased him away. He looked so beleaguered that I went out of my way to get seeds to him. He'd always been somewhat aloof from me, but his need was so extreme that he sought me out now. Sonny had become much more timid than the hoodlum I'd known in the beginning. He still had occasional spells of orneriness, but the flock always ganged up on him at the first sign of trouble. At one feeding, they hassled him so much that he retreated with all four babies to the mirror plant that grew just outside my door. The entire family was perched in a row, shoulder to shoulder, their feathers puffed out because of the cold. They looked like little refugees from a war.

As it got deeper into fall, the flock settled down. There was still the usual squabbling, but the intense screaming and fighting had stopped. The new feeding situation on the deck took on a regular shape. I'd found a larger seed dish that could accommodate fifteen parrots. Just behind them, on the ivy stretching over the railing's corner post, stood a second tier of parrots waiting for a place to open up. Sonny and his children were always on the railing to my right, and on the railing in front of me was another line of birds that usually included Olive. A new favorite, Miles, one of Bo and Sticky Chest's babies, perched on my right shoulder and took seeds from my lips. The rim of the seed cup still belonged to Mandela, who shared it with her new mate, Pushkin. I often brought Dogen and Paco outside in a cage, and Bo and Gibson, no longer mortal enemies, would perch side by side on top of the cage and take seeds from me. Some birds waited on the telephone lines for an opening on the dish. The moment a bird spotted one, she'd jump off the lines in free fall like a high diver, wait-ing until the last moment to spread her wings to brake her speed.

Connor was traveling with the flock again. At first, he tried to join the birds on the front railing, but it was too competitive there, so he made a claim on a stubby fuchsia branch that stuck up through the ivy surrounding the dish. From there, he would wait for a place on the dish to open up. I often walked over to hand him seeds and try to get in a few surreptitious strokes. The flock molted right after the fledge, and Connor had so many pinfeathers hanging down the back of his neck that they looked like dreadlocks. Two of his tail feathers were still wrapped in their sheaths, and when he flew they dangled like two chopsticks. It got to the point again that I couldn't stand looking at him. So one day I walked over to pet him, and as my hand slid over his back, I grabbed him and took him into the house.

Dogen and Paco were up in arms over Connor's return. Their flight feathers were coming back in, and they chased him so relent-lessly that I was forced to intervene. When I had Connor in my hand, I noticed that he was much more bony than he'd been in the house. It was true of every parrot I ever had in my care. Wild birds are lean. Once Connor adjusted to being back inside, I wrapped him in a towel so he couldn't bite me and began the tedious task of picking off the feather sheaths. It took me two days to get him looking good again. I released him as soon as I was done.

When I was feeding the parrots up at Maxine's house, I'd largely been hidden from public view. But now I was on a platform just three feet above and one foot away from the Greenwich Steps. I was now having to give what were, in effect, shows. I'd been a hermit for so long that it was a big change for me to be out in the open and meeting people again. While the neighborhood people knew about the birds, most San Franciscans and out-of-town tourists were still unaware that the city was home to flocks of wild parrots. It was fun to watch the sur-prised looks on the faces of passersby. I got to see people at their most beautiful. Instead of the hip aloofness that's so common nowadays, I saw open-mouthed astonishment and eyes filled with wonder. Most passersby assumed the flock was mine, and they would invariably ask me how it was that I could allow my pets to fly free. I had to answer the same questions over and over again, day after day. I seldom minded, though. I'd once been totally mystified by the parrots myself, and I enjoyed telling people what I'd learned. People appreciated that I took the time to talk with them. Some gave me donations to buy seeds.

One evening, I was lying on the futon reading when I saw Dogen waddling purposefully across the floor toward me. She grabbed onto my shirt with her beak and pulled herself up onto my belly and then marched up to my heart, where she stopped. I cocked my head so I could focus. Dogen was looking me straight in the eye. Her gaze was neutral, but pointed. It was as if she were sizing me up, trying to decide whether I was okay. I didn't know how to respond. Finally, I got so unnerved by the steadiness of her gaze that I had to break eye contact. When I did, she jumped off my chest and went back to play-ing with Paco. It was a highly embarrassing moment for me. I'd been developing elaborate theories about interspecies communication, and I'd often hoped to delve deeper with one of the birds. Suddenly, I'd been presented with the opportunity, and I'd blown it. Later that night, I was thinking over what had happened, and it occurred to me that a look of intelligence *is* intelligence. I was certain that Dogen had been doing what I thought: She'd been sizing me up. But if that were so, why didn't that kind of thing happen more often? I think that like human beings, Dogen spent her days rushing around her world, cov-ering all the bases that needed to be covered. Only at rare moments in a life do things come together cleanly enough to be so solid and clear. That was one of Dogen's moments, and I felt some shame at having missed the chance to be there with her. Just as I had that thought, Dogen came over and perched on my shoulder. She didn't hold it against me. She loved me anyway.

∾◠◡∽

Shortly after New Year's, representatives from the management company and the charities that now owned the property began showing up with increasing frequency as they prepared to put the estate up for sale. Somehow it never occurred to anybody they sent out that I wasn't supposed to be there. My string of luck had to run out eventually, and whenever I heard a knock, I was reluctant to open the door unless I was expecting someone. One time I went to answer, though, and it turned out to be one of the best things that ever happened to me.

The woman at the door was small and trim with gray hair. I knew her by sight as Adah Bakalinsky. Adah had written a popular guidebook to stairway walks in San Francisco that I'd been seeing on friends' shelves for years. She was active in teaching about San Francisco's natural world, and she often brought tour groups down the Greenwich Steps. Adah had come to my door to ask if I had any slides of the parrots. When I told her I did, she asked if she could arrange for me to give some slide shows. I had to think that one over. When I was a singer, I'd had to deal with stage fright at every performance. I'd never been on a stage without having had a drink first. That I'd been a recluse for so long made the idea of getting up in public all the more distasteful. But there was a great deal of misinformation going around about the parrots, and I liked the idea of having an opportunity to set things straight. So after some hemming and hawing and a little prodding from Adah, I gave her the go-ahead.

Within two days, she'd set up a show at the North Beach library. The date stared at me for weeks while I put together something that I hoped would be informative, yet not too boring. By the day of the show, I was so nervous that I got sick. I felt even worse when I saw the crowd that showed up. The week before, an article I'd written about the parrots was published in the Sunday paper, and it was quite popular, generating a lot of mail. The article and the neighborhood's curiosity about the mysterious parrots brought so many people to the library that a lot of them had to be turned away. There was no microphone, so I had to raise my voice to be heard. I kept fading, but the audience loved the presentation anyway. There was constant laughter, even in places that I hadn't expected it. It was all for aspects of the parrots that I personally found funny or charming, but that I didn't think the audience would catch. But the parrots' humorous spirit came across even in photographs. After the show was over, quite a few people came up to tell me how much they loved what I was doing. They thrust money into my hands and asked me to buy more seeds. It was a little overwhelming. The success of the article and the slide show pleased me, but there was an awkward consequence: My squat in the cottage was no longer much of a secret. Thousands of people knew about me now.

In February, it finally happened: A couple made an offer on the property, and the charities accepted. When Helen passed on the news, I shrugged my shoulders. It depressed me, but there was nothing I could do. I got a message that the new owners, Tom and Denise, wanted to have a meeting with me. Even if they offered to let me stay on as a renter, I couldn't have afforded it. I was making around $250 a month, which in San Francisco wasn't enough for a room in a skid-row hotel. The day before the meeting was supposed to happen, Tom got called out of town on business, so I got a short reprieve. After he returned, I bumped into Tom and Denise on the street. I was anxious throughout the encounter, but all they did was ask a few questions about the parrots. They didn't say anything about another meeting. I ran into them several more times over the next few weeks, but they still didn't broach the subject of my squat. In order to be at least somewhat useful to them, I started filling them in on the idiosyncrasies of their new home. We continued to see each other in passing, and it was always the same: We discussed everything under the sun—except for the fact that I was paying no rent.

Eventually, however, they were going to resolve whatever issue was preventing them from sending me on my way, and as spring approached I started thinking hard about releasing Dogen and Paco again. I'd read about a method called *soft release,* whereby you release a bird, bring it back in, and release it again, gradually increasing the time that the bird is free. While I couldn't count on Dogen and Paco cooperating with the plan, it seemed the way to go. Besides worrying about having the extra baggage of two birds, I couldn't get away from the idea that a bird *should* be free.

There was another less idealistic reason for my wanting to turn them loose: Paco was becoming a handful. As he got older, he became more and more excited about the flock. He loved being outside in his cage during the feedings. Sometimes I had to leave him and Dogen inside, so Paco started chewing a view hole in the bamboo blinds covering the long front window. The window was so big and the studio so small that the blinds were the only thing preventing me from being on constant public display. I had to interrupt many a feeding to go over and pound on the window to make Paco stop. Paco's excitement over the flock was also inciting Dogen, and the noise inside the studio was reaching unbearable levels.

Besides being noisy and manic, parrots are obsessive. Dogen and Paco had developed an odd little enthusiasm that was part of the nightly household routine. The moment they saw me heading to the studio's tiny bathroom to brush my teeth, they'd stop whatever they were doing and zoom over and land on my head, where they'd begin an intense round of play fighting. While I stood in front of the mirror brushing, they'd be crawling around my head and shoulders trying to bite each other and screaming in my ears. I have no idea what the appeal was. I got so accustomed to it that while they were fighting I'd be brushing and thinking about something entirely different, as if they weren't even there.

I called an ornithologist for advice on the release. He told me I should wait until May. The expanse of bay that the Golden Gate Bridge crosses is part of a major hawk migration route. It's least active in May and June, and Dogen and Paco would be most vulnerable to hawks during their first weeks outside because they'd have little endurance. But it wasn't just the migrating hawks that posed a danger; San Francisco has a large resident hawk population as well.

One afternoon, I was walking up Sansome, a street that runs along the base of Telegraph Hill's east cliff, when I heard the parrots making alarm calls. I scanned the cliffs, looking for them, but they were out of sight. Two blocks north, a red-tailed hawk came soaring out from the area of the Greenwich Steps. He was being chased by a mob of angry blackbirds. They were all around a hundred feet up and flying straight down the Sansome Street corridor. The hawk veered west toward a grove of eucalyptus trees on the cliff directly above me, which flushed the parrots out of their hiding place. They left the grove screaming and flew up above the hawk, circled out over Levi's Plaza, and back into the Greenwich gardens. In the meantime, the blackbirds continued their pursuit of the hawk. I'd been watching the flock dodge this very same hawk for several days. Knowing exactly what was going on up above while all the people around me were oblivious to it made me feel as though I were in on a secret. Gary Snyder is right: You can find nature anywhere, even in a big city like San Francisco.

Even though I complained sometimes and wanted to end my time with the parrots, I still loved being with the flock. Magic is as important as food and shelter, and the parrots were bringing me magic at a time in my life when I couldn't find it anywhere else. It happened in different ways. One time, I was invited to a wedding reception at a restaurant just up the hill from where I lived. The gathering was held on a patio on the building's roof, from which there was a spectacular view of the gardens. In the distance, I could see the parrots waiting on the lines in front of my place. Eventually, they became impatient and took off. They flew south, away from the restaurant, and then arced high and wheeled around, heading back north again. They were coming directly toward the wedding party—all thirty-eight birds. At first, the screaming was remote, but as the flock drew nearer it got louder and louder. Most of the wedding guests were only peripherally aware of the commotion until the parrots were directly overhead, just fifteen feet above us. By then, the sound was so overwhelming that it cut short every conversation. The bride and groom and all their guests stood frozen in awe, champagne glasses in hand. After the flock had passed, there was a moment of stunned silence. Then everybody broke into applause. It felt like the marriage had just been blessed.

The day after the wedding, I saw Connor and Sonny perched three feet from one another on the same telephone line. Every now and then Connor took a few side steps toward Sonny and then stopped. He kept inching closer and closer. Connor, who was usually quiet, had been exceptionally noisy the last few weeks. I assumed he was calling out for a mate. Now he seemed to be making overtures to Sonny. But Sonny wasn't interested. When Connor got to within a foot of him, Sonny made a violent lunge that backed Connor off. A few days later, I was watching Sonny preen on a branch when, in the background, I saw Connor descending from the sky at full speed and heading directly toward Sonny. He slammed into Sonny so hard that he knocked him off the branch. It wasn't the first time I'd seen a parrot deliberately crash into another at full speed. It usually happened between two birds who had some kind of rivalry going. I had to wonder if Connor was getting revenge on Sonny for having rejected him.

Free as a Bird

It had been more than a year since I last released Dogen and Paco, and as May approached, I was eager to try again. I had anxieties—there were things that could go wrong—but the hawks had cleared out and both birds had a full set of flight feathers. If it was ever going to happen, now was the time. All I needed was some good weather.

One morning in early May, I opened the door and found the perfect day: clear and warm, with only a light breeze. I put Dogen and Paco in their cage and carried them out to the deck. I'd been expecting to deal with some heavy emotion, so I was surprised to find myself feeling quite matter-of-fact about it. When I opened the cage door, Paco came right out and climbed to the top of the cage. But Dogen refused to leave her perch. Suddenly, a dog ran down the Greenwich Steps and frightened Paco, who bolted away. I didn't want him on his own, even for a moment, so I reached into the cage and brought Dogen out. The moment she was clear of the cage she flew off to join Paco. As with the previous release, she flew a short way up the hill and perched on a tree limb, while Paco flew in enthusiastic circles high overhead, screaming happily. I was happy, too, but a little nervous. Once they were both out of sight, I went back inside. It was the first moment since taking in Dogen two years earlier that I didn't have a bird living with me.

I didn't see Dogen and Paco again until late in the day, when the flock arrived for a feeding. I saw Paco first. He was under attack from another parrot as he attempted an awkward landing on the limb of a coral tree. He kept flying up and down like a yo-yo, trying to hit the limb. Seconds later, Dogen flew in. She, too, was being chased. Paco finally managed to perch, so I called to him, patting my arm to indicate that he should fly to me. He came immediately, and I quickly stuck him back inside the cage. Under relentless pursuit, Dogen landed right next to me on a branch of the mirror plant. She was exhausted; her eyes were closed and her feathers were all puffed up. I offered her my hand and she got right on. I put her in the cage with Paco and carried them back inside the studio. Within a few hours, both birds were rested and acting normally. I was quite pleased with the way things had gone. I wasn't certain I'd release them again, but their willingness to get back in their cages made it more likely. The only difficulties I saw were their lack of endurance and the flock's response to them as outsiders rather than as fellow cherry heads.

A week later, on a whim, I turned Dogen and Paco loose again. This time both birds immediately understood what I was doing, scrambling out of the cage the instant I opened the door. They were gone in a flash, delighted to be free. An hour later, I spotted them in the garden at the top of a large cotoneaster bush eating berries. I'd hoped to see something like that. The cotoneaster has the kind of small red berry that most people would never consider eating but wild birds love. The berries didn't resemble anything I'd fed them in the house, and while Dogen knew from experience that they were food, I wondered if Paco would have known had Dogen not been there to show him.

This time the two birds confined themselves to the garden area, perhaps to avoid the flock. Throughout the morning and early afternoon, each time I stepped outside I'd catch a glimpse of them. I saw Paco more often than Dogen. Some "tough-minded" scientists insist that birds get no special pleasure out of flying, but Paco was clearly having the time of his life. I'd become quite familiar with the variety of sounds that the cherry heads make, and his enthusiasm was unmistakable.

Toward late afternoon, I saw the two of them racing low through the garden, being chased by a small group from the flock. When Dogen and Paco saw me, they made a beeline to the deck and landed on top of their cage. I quickly got them onto my hands and put them inside before the birds from the flock could get to them. This time neither Dogen nor Paco seemed the least bit tired. On the contrary, they both looked energetic and upbeat. Maybe they felt they'd outfoxed their pursuers.

Continuing their soft release, I gave Dogen and Paco just one day of rest before putting them out again. Both were eager to go. I sat in a chair on the deck and watched them fly from the deodar cedar to the Monterey cypress to the cotoneaster, stopping to eat at each tree. In Paco's previous outings his landings had been clumsy, but he was beginning to master them now. They both looked like perfect wild birds. I was so pleased with them that I started feeling giddy. I clapped my hands and cheered them on, singing, "I love it! I love it!"

I was inside when I heard the flock arrive. I went out to feed, but the parrots were eating loquats and in no hurry for seeds, so I stood on the deck and waited for them to finish. Parrots are notoriously wasteful with food; they usually take just a bite or two from a piece of fruit, drop it, and then grab another. While I was watching the flock in the loquat, Dogen and Paco flew into the garden. They landed on the rim of the seed dish and began to eat. I expected that they'd get chased away from the dish once the birds in the loquat spotted them.

But when one of the parrots came to the deck railing, Dogen and Paco jumped off the dish, ran down the railing, and kicked him off. Others came for seeds, and each time the same thing happened. Dogen and Paco wouldn't allow any of them on the dish. I was surprised they got away with it. Dogen and Paco were in a highly excited state. Their eyes were pinned and they were doing the display, turning in unison, holding their wings away from their sides, and looking demented. I'd always kept my hands away from any parrot in a frenzy, but I was curious to see if Dogen and Paco were too far gone to recognize me. I walked over to the dish and cautiously offered each of them a finger. Both climbed up without hesitation. I kissed their heads and set them back down. The fights with the flock continued, and Dogen and Paco won each round. It was reassuring to see them holding their own, but it made me wonder whether their time indoors had created an unbridgeable gulf between them and the wild parrots. Yet when the flock left the garden, Dogen and Paco took off with them, and they didn't return to the cottage to sleep that night.

I'd already made plans to spend the next morning at the flock's nesting grounds, and when Dogen and Paco didn't show up I decided that they'd looked strong enough, so I didn't need to hang around waiting for them. But just as I was locking the door, they whipped across the deck and landed right behind me in the mirror plant. Both of them were wired, rushing—just like real wild birds. They were eager to go inside, so I opened the door and let them in. They flew straight to their cages and devoured the food in their dishes. Although they both seemed to be in high spirits, I thought to be safe I should leave them inside until I got back. But when I opened the door to leave, they were frantic to go back out. They headed west up the hill and disappeared. I picked up my bike, carried it down the 105 steps to the bottom of the hill, and rode off to the Republic of El Coto, my code name for the flock's nesting site.

When I arrived, I could hear parrots scattered all across the grounds. I made my way to the tree where I'd seen Pushkin and Mandela the year before. They'd failed to breed, but I found them again in the same tree, busily gnawing on the nest hole entrance. Although it was still too early for Mandela to lay her eggs, I hadn't seen either bird in recent weeks. Maybe they were having to defend their nest from interlopers and were unwilling to stray far from the tree because of it. I wanted to find some other nests, but there were so many trees that I had no idea where to begin looking. I heard a parrot squawking in a nearby palm. I'd brought binoculars, and as I tried to locate the bird I heard a voice behind me.

"Whatcha lookin' at?"

I turned around to find a burly, middle-aged man with graying crew-cut hair. He looked sort of like a truck driver.

"I'm looking for parrot nests."

My voice inadvertently came out sounding a little snotty, and since most people were still unaware of the city's parrots, I expected him to look at me as though I were being a smart-ass. Instead, he nodded and said, "Follow me. I'll show you some."

As he led me across the park grounds, we introduced ourselves. He not only looked like a truck driver, he had the name: Mack. He questioned me about my interest in the parrots, and I told him what I'd been doing. His own interest was more than casual. It turned out that Mack was a serious birder who spent part of each summer in the Sierra Nevada helping researchers band wild birds. Locally, he liked to bird-watch in El Coto, and he knew the locations of the nests of many different species. He pointed out one work in progress: the nest of a red-shouldered hawk. He told me the hawk's nest was unusual for El Coto, that the ravens seldom allowed one to get that far along.

We walked under the limbs of an enormous eucalyptus, and Mack stopped and pointed to a four-inch-wide hole in a thick bough thirty feet above our heads. It was a parrot nest, he said. The hole had formed when the wood rotted out where a branch broke off many years before. I looked through the binoculars, and a bright red head popped out of the darkness of the hole. The parrot pulled herself up onto the lip of the nest-hole entrance and tilted her head to one side, casting a concerned and curious eyeball down upon us. It was Erica. Mack seemed impressed that I was able to recognize an individual bird. He led me over to a nearby palm that grew up behind an old shed. It was a massive palm, at least thirty feet tall, and there were two parrots picking their way across its field of old, broken-off frond ends. They looked like rock climbers. Once I'd made the identification—Olive, the mitred conure, and her mate, Gibson—Mack and I walked to a far corner of the park, where he showed me another Canary Island date palm with a nest. Again, the occupants were home, and although I couldn't identify them at the time, I figured out later that they were probably Dogen and Paco's parents, Guy and Doll. It's quite possible that Dogen and Paco were born in that tree.

Those were all the parrot nests that Mack knew about. I thanked him for taking the time to show them to me. He said few birders knew anything about the parrots, and he was glad someone was studying them. He meant it, which set him apart from most of the elite birders I'd met. Rank-and-file birders usually loved the parrots, but those with the long life lists were often dismissive of them. At first, I assumed it was solely the parrots' status as nonnatives. When my slide show was included in a series on local natural history, one regular attendee had been angry enough to boycott my presentation. But I don't think being nonnative is the only reason for their low status. Because parrots have been kept as pets, I think it stigmatizes them in the eyes of some birders. It's as if they could never be authentic wild birds.

After Mack left, I got on my bike and headed back to Telegraph Hill. Along the way, I decided to make a pit stop at Fort Mason and see what was going on. As I came up the main road, I heard Connor's distinctive shriek. He was perched in a magnolia near some old officers' housing. Straddling the bike, I pulled the binoculars out of my backpack. As I adjusted the focus, I heard a woman holler, *"They're parrots!"*

I turned around and hollered back, "Yeah, I know. I'm studying them."

She walked toward me, her face all lit up. "Are you the guy who wrote the article in the Sunday paper a few months ago?"

"Yeah. That was me."

"Oh!" she exclaimed. "I've been wanting to meet you."

She introduced herself as Peggy Ensminger. She and her husband, Scott, had been living at the fort for three years. Scott was a career navy man, and the Ensmingers were the last military family still stationed at Fort Mason. Peggy told me that when they first moved in, she used to see the parrots from a distance, but had no idea what they were. From the racket they made, she guessed they were some kind of California crow. Scott built a multilevel bird feeder in their backyard, and Peggy began putting out seeds. A few weeks later, she attracted her first "California crow."

As she was telling me her story, a small group from the flock arrived at her feeder. We watched them eat and exchanged our names for the individual birds. She said the first bird to start using the feeder was "Blue Head"—Connor, of course. She called Scrapperella "Grandpa" because of the exposed, scraggly white down feathers on her breast. A bird whom I called Monk was called Jimmy by her; he was named after Jimmy Durante, because he'd damaged his beak. I asked what she called Sonny, but she'd never singled him out. So that she could remember him next time, I pointed out the band on his leg and the eroded area down the middle of his beak. She said Connor was her favorite. Whenever he showed up and the feeder was empty, he'd demand in a high shrill voice that she come outside and fill the thing up. She loved that she could fill the feeder without him flying away. We had identical impressions of Connor's personality, both seeing him essentially as a regal curmudgeon. She said that in the beginning, Connor was the only parrot to come to her feeder, but that gradually the other birds had followed his lead. At first, she fed them only in the morning, but one afternoon Connor showed up demanding more seeds, and she'd been feeding them twice a day ever since.

Since the parrots spent so much time at Fort Mason, I saw that it would be helpful to my study if she and I stayed in contact. Peggy told me that if I liked, she'd keep notes on what she saw and call me if anything extraordinary happened. So that we'd speak a common language, she agreed to learn my names for the birds.

Late that afternoon, Dogen and Paco showed up at the door wanting to come inside. They were hungry and a little tired, but otherwise they looked fine. After they'd eaten, I offered to let them back out, but they chose to spend the night inside. The next morning, though, they were impatient for me to open the door again. They were still in control of landing rights at the seed dish, which amused me. After all, Dogen was one of the smallest parrots in the flock, and Paco had been domestic since the day he fledged. Paco was militant in his relations with the flock. He especially had it in for the hybrid, Picasso, and although Picasso regularly beat up on many of the adult parrots, he couldn't handle Paco. Occasionally, Paco picked a fight with a bird he couldn't beat, and he'd fly to my shoulder for protection. It was interesting to me that many of the adults who overpowered Paco were birds that Picasso dominated easily.

I'd been seeing this kind of thing ever since I first started identifying individuals. It had completely frustrated my search for a pecking order. One day, I read a science article that ridiculed those who insist that all bird flocks have pecking orders. I found the article illuminating. Of course! *There was no pecking order.* Unconsciously, I already knew it. I'd kept looking for one only because the biologists I'd read insisted that there had to be one. It surprised me to discover dissension within the scientific world. I'd assumed that scientists knew everything when it came to animals.

Parrot society is complex, but I don't think it's so different from ours. It's a community made up of pairs and individuals. Mated birds squabble with one another and with other couples. Certain individuals have it in for each other. Most couples are in it for the long term, but some get divorced. Although the flock functions as a single community, nobody makes decisions for the community as a whole. When a parrot thinks it's time to leave a foraging spot, he starts up a conversation about it. If the flock leaves, it's a community decision. Often, some birds will dissent from the general consensus and stay put. Whenever I was feeding a solitary parrot and the flock flew by, the parrot I was feeding would call out to let the others know where she was, and that food was available. This was true even of weaker birds who would have benefited personally by concealing their location from the rest of the flock. It sounds almost . . . altruistic.

As the weeks passed, and Paco and Dogen's endurance grew, they stopped coming inside to spend the night. We didn't stop being friends, though. They still allowed me to pet and kiss them, and they still came in to see what was cooking. Occasionally, they took a nap, but that was the longest they were ever inside. Everything was working out just as I'd hoped. Dogen was demonstrating the ways of the wild parrot to Paco, who followed her everywhere. Then, a month after I released them, everything changed.

I was pushing my bike up the Greenwich Steps on my way back from a job when I saw parrots napping in the loquat. I put my bike away and brought out the seed dish. As soon as I set it down, Paco flew out of the tree and landed on the dish rim. He was alone, which was slightly unusual. Moments later, Connor came out of the loquat and joined Paco. Then Sonny came. The moment Sonny landed, a fight broke out between him and Paco. Paco briefly had the upper hand, but Sonny overpowered him, so Paco flew to my shoulder. It had been an unusually intense fight, and Paco was panting hard. When the fight ended, Dogen flew out of the loquat and joined the others on the dish. She perched next to Sonny, and the two of them broke out into the display. Their pupils contracted to tiny pinpoints, and they held their wings away from their sides while turning like dervishes in slow, menacing circles. Three more parrots came out of the loquat and landed on the dish, but Sonny didn't want them there. When he attacked them, Dogen backed him up. I could not have been more dismayed. Sonny and my Dogen were a pair! My immediate reaction was to start thinking up ways of putting an end to the relationship. The idea of them being together was intolerable to me. Anybody but

Sonny! I rationalized my opposition as concern for Paco. I didn't think he'd had enough teaching to make it on his own, and for Paco's sake I considered bringing the two back inside until the bond between Sonny and Dogen had been broken.

After the initial shock wore off, and I'd seen them together for a few days, I had to admit that Dogen and Sonny were actually quite an attractive pairing. It wasn't anything that I could put my finger on; they just looked right side by side. I was relieved that Dogen hadn't changed her attitude toward me; she was as friendly as ever. Sonny, though, was bothered by me handling Dogen and flew away every time I picked her up. Like Connor, he was a very serious bird whom I never saw act playfully. He must have been old. His eyes looked ancient, with what appeared to be cracks in the iris. Whenever Dogen came into the studio to eat, Sonny waited outside until Dogen finished. I loved Dogen's visits so much that in good weather I kept the door open so she could come and go at will. It was a pleasant surprise whenever I looked up and found her perched next to my desk.

Unlike Dogen, Paco was coming in less and less often. Occasionally, he tried to tag along with Sonny and Dogen, but they wouldn't allow it. Although he was alone and seemed somewhat adrift, he wasn't having any trouble making a go of it. But now that Paco no longer had Dogen's backing, he was losing most altercations at the dish, and he was having to come to me for protection more often.

Summer was approaching, and I waited to see if Sonny would take Dogen to nest. It didn't happen. They'd paired up late enough in the spring that Sonny had probably lost the hole that he and Lucia used to nest in. I was still eager to see if a mother who was especially friendly toward me would allow or encourage her babies to approach me more closely than other mothers did. Since Dogen wasn't going to nest, it fell to Mandela to be the test. I saw her for the last time just days before the first of summer, which is my best guess for the time they actually lay their eggs. I didn't expect to be seeing her again for several weeks. I wished her success.

That year I'd already seen two parrots die from the illness that struck the juveniles every spring, and now I was seeing a third sick bird: Ginsberg. I didn't want to get involved, but it was impossible to ignore her. Late one afternoon, I was standing near the dish when Ginsberg made a botched landing right in front of me. Impulsively, I grabbed her and ran with her to the door, quickly tossing her inside before she could bloody my fingers. For someone eager to be free of all burdens, it was a crazy move, but I was helpless to do otherwise.

Ginsberg deteriorated quickly. Her condition got to be as bad as Tupelo's. Although I was unencumbered by any other birds, I didn't give her the best of care. I was distracted by my own problems, and the novelty of having wild parrots in the house was long gone. One day, thinking that the lack of attention might be contributing to her decline, I picked her up and tried to give her some affection. She was stronger than I thought and managed to jump out of my hands. She landed on the floor and started scooting toward the open door. I hadn't clipped her wings, and I was terrified she might fly away. So I sprinted after Ginsberg, pouncing on her just as she reached the welcome mat. She was in my hands, squirming and biting, while just a few feet away a scrub jay, who had witnessed the whole thing from the mirror plant, started screaming bloody murder. The jay was chastising me vehemently and would not stop. I liked to think of myself as a friend to all the birds, and feeling the desire to defend myself against his unjust accusations, I gave him imploring looks. But he kept glaring and screeching at me. Finally, in a snit, I wheeled around and took Ginsberg back inside, slamming the door.

Neither veterinarian that I'd gone to had been able to help, but it was clear to me that if I didn't do something for Ginsberg soon, she was going to die. Jamie recommended another vet whose office was thirty miles away in Marin County. To get there, I had to catch a special intercounty bus. I had to meet the bus at the intersection of Union and Van Ness Avenue. Van Ness, the crosstown route for Highway 101, is six lanes wide and carries a constant stream of cars, trucks, motorcycles, and buses. Standing at the bus stop beside all that speed, noise, and poisoned air, I felt inconsequential. I couldn't help but focus on the difference between the beauty of the wild bird in the cage I was holding and the urban mess all around me. There was a big junky patchwork of cable hanging overhead that powered the buses over the cracked, littered pavement. Across the street were the metal and plastic of a smelly filling station and the tacky garishness of a liquor store. Behind me stood a wall of anonymous-looking apartment buildings that seemed devoid of community. Wild nature is never so ugly—it's never ugly at all, really—but modern cities almost always are. Even in San Francisco, which is considered beautiful, much of the city is awash with cheap, thoughtless development. It's so common now that most of us don't even see it or question it anymore.

The new vet thought that a diagnosis of pigeon paramyxovirus made the most sense, but he couldn't be certain. He agreed with Tupelo's vet that the only thing I could do was give Ginsberg rest. He must have seen the disappointment in my face, for he seemed to have second thoughts. He left the examination room and came back with a bottle of what he said was an experimental mushroom extract. I took it, grateful that he was willing at least to try something.

When Ginsberg and I returned home, there was a large box on my porch. Attached to the box was a note from a man who worked at the bottom of the hill and often came up the stairs on his lunch breaks to watch me feed. He'd found a parrot on the ground at Walton Square, and since the wild bird rescue center told him they couldn't take nonnative birds, he'd brought it to me. I opened the box and found yet another sick juvenile. The bird had the usual symptoms: instability and head tilt. I reached into the box to examine him, and he gave me a hard bite. He was furious about being in captivity and remained so for weeks. He was so angry that I named him Yosemite, after the cartoon character Yosemite Sam.

The mushroom extract didn't seem to do any good. I was sick of watching birds die, so I started reading about avian viruses. In what was probably a simplistic understanding of what I'd read, I started giving the sick birds megadoses of vitamins, hoping that this would boost their immune systems. Because many of the sick birds had developed symptoms that seemed respiratory, I also started giving them an over-the-counter bird tetracycline. Several vets had told me the medicine was useless, but Jamie recommended it, so I tried it. I also put them out in the sun as much as possible. One afternoon, I was sitting out on the deck reading while Yosemite and Ginsberg huddled next to each other in the corner of their cage. Connor flew into the garden, so I went inside and brought out the dish for him. I set the dish down and went back to my book. But Connor refused to eat. Instead, he paced back and forth along the deck railing, squawking relentlessly. Like the scrub jay who'd chastised me for grabbing Ginsberg, Connor was glaring at me, shaming me again for putting birds in cages. This time I was adamant about not feeling guilt. I ignored Connor's scolding. But I thought it interesting that the only birds concerned with the plight of the two sick cherry heads were a scrub jay and a blue-crowned conure. The flock had shown little interest.

Paco had stopped coming into the studio entirely by this time. I often saw him perched alone on the lines making calls that sounded like complaints. When he came to the deck, he was often hostile toward me. Sometimes Dogen acted funny, too, as if it was strange for her not to be with Paco. One day, Paco showed up in the company of another parrot with whom he seemed to be on friendly terms. I didn't recognize her—I was losing track of the identities of birds that I didn't know well—so I gave her a new name: Amarou. Over the next few days, Paco and Amarou continued to show up together. She was a good-looking cherry head, with a large red cap. With Amarou's backing, Paco quickly regained his ruffian status. They were both tough—a tough little team. Before I knew it, they were kicking ass all around the garden.

Fleeting Happiness

While Paco was becoming increasingly distant and wild, Dogen had lost none of her friendliness. She still came inside to visit, and though her interest was primarily in what I was cooking, she often stuck around even when there was nothing on the stove. Sometimes she perched on my shoulder while I worked at my desk. The biggest change I saw in her was how high-strung she'd become. Like most wild birds, she was in a near-constant hurry, avoiding hawks and keeping pace with her hunger.

On warm days, I liked to take my meals out on the deck. I ate everything from the same black bowl, a bowl that Dogen and I had shared many times. Whenever Dogen and Sonny were flying past the cottage and she spotted me with the bowl, she would abruptly change course and fly to the deck. I was usually unaware of her until the moment she landed on my lap. It amused and charmed me to have a bird flutter down from the sky to join me for my meals. One morning, Dogen and I were outside sharing my breakfast, and as I looked at her standing happily at the bowl, clumps of oatmeal attached to her beak, I suddenly realized that my old wish had been fulfilled: I had a close friendship with a wild parrot who came to visit me. It hadn't happened the way I'd imagined—it never would have happened at all if she hadn't been a patient of mine—but there she was.

One day in mid-July, I was outside reading when a small group of parrots arrived and flew straight into the loquat. I went inside to get the seed dish and set it down on the railing. One by one they began streaming out of the tree to eat. As I was walking back to my chair, I saw a bird make a landing on the railing that was so uncoordinated it alarmed me. It was Sonny. He bobbed and weaved clumsily across the ivy surrounding the seed dish. When he tried to pull himself up onto the rim, the others harassed him. Dogen had to kick everybody off the dish so that Sonny could eat unmolested.

After the feeding ended, I went back inside, made some notes about Sonny's condition, and started fixing my lunch. A few minutes later, I saw that Dogen was in the fuchsia at the side window. She was excited and trying to get my attention. She'd seen that I was fixing pasta, her favorite of my dishes, so I opened the window and let her in. Dogen remembered the entire procedure. She knew to be patient while the noodles boiled, but she had difficulty restraining herself when I drained them. I had to push her away from the bowl repeatedly while mixing the noodles and tomato sauce. Finally, it was ready, and we shared the bowl. We were both pasta lovers, and we ate quickly in serious silence. Once I'd had my fill, I put the bowl on the floor and let her clean it.

About that time, Connor showed up in the fuchsia. He stared inside, looking unusually inquisitive. He'd never come into the house through the window, and when I went to see if he wanted to give it a try, he flew around to the front of the house and landed in the mirror plant. I went to the open door and offered him seeds, but he ignored them. Standing near him, I realized that he was staring at Dogen. He started up the loud squawking he made whenever he was adamant about something. Dogen flew out the door, and Connor followed close behind. It was a peculiar vignette. It made me wonder if Connor was courting Dogen. Was Sonny dying? And did Connor know it? Dogen and Connor were my two favorite birds in the flock, and the idea of them pairing up appealed to me immensely. But it seemed implausible. When they lived together in the house, they'd never gotten along at all. I often had to remind myself that I understood only a fraction of what the parrots were doing, and I decided that in this case I was seeing what I wanted to see. There had to be some other explanation.

Within a few days, it became apparent that unless I brought him inside, Sonny was not going to survive his illness. He looked old and depressed. When he perched, his wings sagged as though he were exhausted, and he was getting clumsier by the day. But I had qualms about taking in any more sick birds. If he was simply dying of old age, I was inclined to let him die a free bird. But it was sad watching him go into decline. He'd always been so proud. Even when pushed to the fringe and obliged to act meek, Sonny had maintained a glimmer of impenitence. Dogen was still loyal to Sonny, coming to his defense whenever the other parrots attacked him. But someone was trying to drive a wedge between the two birds. It took awhile to convince myself of it, but I saw that Connor really was courting Dogen. He followed her and Sonny everywhere they went. Sonny was too ill to travel very much, so Dogen spent much of her day foraging without him. But Connor always accompanied her. She wouldn't let Connor get too close, though. Whenever he tried, she lunged at him to back him off.

Not long after Sonny fell ill, another juvenile got sick. One morning, Paco and Amarou were chasing a parrot around the garden. I thought it was the sick juvenile until the bird made a desperate crash landing in the seed dish, and I saw it was Sonny. He had a bare patch on the left side of his face where another parrot had pulled out his feathers. Impulsively, I tried to grab him, but his reflexes were still sharp enough that he got away. He flew to the top of the incense cedar, where Paco and Amarou continued their pursuit. They were screaming and psychogobbling hysterically while hacking at Sonny with their beaks. Like a fighter plane shot from the sky, Sonny fell from the tree in a slow tailspin and plunged into the same patch of ground that Tupelo had the year before. I ran down Greenwich and jumped over the railing and into the garden. It was even more over-grown now, and Sonny was in a section thick with ferns, blackberry vines, and a row of tall, tightly packed ginger stalks. I had to work my way down the garden's steepest slope, where it grew up along the edge of an old quarry cliff. When I got near the trunk of the incense cedar, I stepped into a bog. I tried to push forward, but couldn't get my footing. I kept slipping in the mud and getting my pant legs caught on blackberry thorns. I searched for Sonny until I felt it was a waste of time to continue. I hoped that he'd get some rest and crawl out before a cat got him. As I worked my way back up the slope, I saw Paco and Amarou up on the power lines. They were screaming and psychogob-bling and biting each other's beaks as if celebrating their victory over Sonny.

A little later in the day, the sick juvenile showed up alone to eat. Paco and Amarou were still in the garden, and when they spotted him wobbling weakly on the rim of the dish, they flew down and knocked him onto the Greenwich Steps. The sick bird landed on his feet, but he was too disoriented to fly away. I jumped down after him, which sent him scampering into the garden. For the second time that day, I leaped over the railing and took off after a sick parrot. He was clumsy on foot, but I was hamstrung by blackberry bushes again. I found a corridor of thornless vines and tried to power through them, but I pulled a thigh muscle. It hurt like hell, so I gave up on the sick juve-nile and limped back to Greenwich. Once again, Paco and Amarou were up on the lines celebrating. I felt a twinge of contempt for Paco.

It was a dismal moment. My muscles ached, and my lungs were burning. I was sick of seeing dying birds. Sonny's fall had been particularly distressing. I was nursing my leg when a neighbor, Veronica, passed by. She asked how things were going, and I started complaining about Sonny and the sick juvenile and how all the dying birds were getting to me. I expected to hear some expression of sympathy, but she just made a face. Veronica was unusual for an American in that she'd been raised as a Buddhist, specifically a Mahayana Buddhist, and she regarded my frustration as unenlightened.

"Come on, Mark. You should be used to this by now. What business is it of yours anyway to take care of these birds? I think you're being a little naive. In Mahayana Buddhism, you don't get attached to life and death. It's all part of the natural order."

I liked Veronica, but she was argumentative at times, and although I knew to expect it from her, I felt defensive. No one had ever criticized what I was doing.

"Well, there is such a thing as stewardship," I told her. "I think we have a responsibility to help nature out." It was a conventional answer, and there was no conviction in my voice. Veronica took full advantage and pressed forward.

"Oh, Mark. That really reeks of vanity. That's *so* egotistical. How do we know what nature wants? How do you know Sonny didn't want to die alone in the garden?"

I hadn't asked for this. I was exhausted and feeling low, and suddenly I was having to justify myself. As I searched my brain for some appropriate philosophical response, I remembered the vow of the bodhisattva.

"Sentient beings are numberless; I vow to save them all."

"What do we mean by *save*?" she countered.

I thought it was a terrible answer. She was just being difficult. Nevertheless, I felt stymied and vulnerable. She had me doubting what I was doing. Why *was* I so upset about the natural order? I *should* be used to the birds dying. She was right. But did that mean I should stop caring for them? I couldn't agree. I remembered Tupelo's wish to be comforted as she died. But I was too wasted to talk seriously about what I was doing. All I wanted was to go inside and lie down. I started talking to her about Buddhism in general, thinking she might lighten up on me if she knew I'd studied it. She wasn't impressed, though. She went on talking about her own Mahayana Buddhist beliefs.

"Practice is all that matters. I've been sitting since I was a little girl. All you should do is sit and not expect anything. Not even enlightenment. That's what Mahayana Buddhism says. The desire for enlightenment is no different than the desire for a TV."

I'd heard that before, and I didn't disagree really, but she wanted an argument from me, and I let myself get sucked in.

"Yeah, but you'd have to want enlightenment or you'd never practice."

She gave me a look as though I were nothing but a rank amateur. Since I couldn't say anything substantive or clever—I was only going to fall into one trap after another—I waited for a lull in the conversation and made my getaway. As I left, I got in the last word, although it was kind of punk. "You're not a Mahayana Buddhist, Veronica. You're a hard-ass Buddhist."

She laughed. Still, if I'd had it together, I would have said this:

"Not to hurt or humble the animals is our first duty to them, but to stop there is not enough. We have a higher mission, to be of service to them whenever they require it. If you have men who will exclude any of God's creatures from the shelter of compassion and pity, you will have men who will deal likewise with their fellow man." —SAINT FRANCIS

In late July, as the females started coming off the nests, I kept an eye out for Mandela. I hadn't seen Pushkin in weeks. When he finally did show, he was alone, and he had a problem that made me worry about Mandela: All of Pushkin's tail feathers were missing. New ones were growing in, but all at once. That was unusual for two reasons: It was too early in the year for a molt, and in a normal molt, feathers are replaced one by one. They only grow back in a single bunch when they've been pulled out all at once. The only thing I could imagine doing that was a human hand. Maybe someone had gotten close enough to grab Pushkin and Mandela, but only Pushkin had escaped.

People often asked me if the parrots have any predators. I usually said, "Hawks and cats." But I think the biggest danger they face is the desire of human beings to own them and to make money from them. Occasionally, someone would ask if I'd catch a parrot and sell it to him—a question that I found extraordinarily obtuse.

One day, I was feeding the flock when a man came walking out from the side lot east of the studio. The instant I saw him I had an intuition that he was a danger to the flock. I'd developed an uncanny sense for that kind of thing. He'd never seen the parrots before, and he was standing on the Greenwich Steps staring up in amazement, saying over and over how he was "blown away" by them. After asking me the usual questions about what they were and how they got here, he started talking about trying to catch one.

"Well, that wouldn't be too cool," I told him in as friendly a tone of voice as I could muster.

He looked at me as though I were insane. "But they'd be worth *money.*"

"Well, not really. The pet stores only want breeder-raised birds nowadays. If you couldn't show some kind of breeding record, they probably wouldn't have anything to do with it."

"Oh, I could sell them somewhere. I'm sure somebody would buy one."

"Besides," I said, "they only come to me, nobody else. It'd be really hard to catch one. They're quick."

"I don't know about that. I'm a pretty ingenious guy," he assured me.

He started scoping out the gardens, trying to figure out how it might be done. It hadn't occurred to him yet that I wanted to dissuade him. I looked him over, trying to decide whether he was a real threat. He looked like he might be homeless. Although his clothes were clean, his shoes had almost completely fallen apart. He seemed a little crazy around the edges, but I couldn't tell whether he was just a homeless crazy who talked big, or if he was more sinister than that. I made one more effort at friendly dissuasion.

"This flock is a rare and beautiful thing. You don't often get to see something like this. People here love them wild and free. They ought to be left that way."

Suddenly it dawned on him that I was trying to talk him out of it. He looked me straight in the eye and said in a soft but surly voice that dared me to oppose him, "Maybe you're talking to the wrong person."

The parrots must have felt the tension, for in that frozen moment they all left, panic-stricken. I knew that if I continued to challenge him, his ego would feel obliged to go after them. So without saying a word, I turned around and reentered the cottage. Every few minutes, I peeked through the blinds to see if he was still there. He cased the garden for another half hour before leaving. I worried about the flock's safety for more than a week, constantly checking to see that everybody was still accounted for, until I finally felt that the danger had passed.

I never saw Mandela again. I prefer to think that someone grabbed her rather than that she died. While I don't believe hand-reared birds should be released—they would not survive—I have a big problem with people who think they have a right to put a healthy wild bird in a cage. Birds cherish their freedom just as much as human beings do. The sick parrots that I brought inside always screamed in terror and despair at the moment of capture. Each time a parrot is taken out of the wild, a family—the members of which feel real affection for one another—gets broken up. The wild bird trade has treated parrots with a capriciousness that has ended up as cruelty. The parrots have gotten it from both ends. First, importers took them out of their wild, natural homes and shipped them to the United States and other countries where some escaped. Then, when the parrots followed their natural instinct to breed, environmentalists and wildlife managers called for their destruction. The introduction of nonnative species has created ecological problems, but to punish nature is absurd—especially given that humans created the problem.

ᐤᐤᐤ

After Sonny's fall from the incense cedar, Dogen stopped coming around to the cottage. I called Peggy Ensminger to find out whether Dogen was at Fort Mason. She said that Dogen was showing up at her feeder every day, but she hadn't seen Sonny; Connor was still tailing Dogen, and Dogen still refused to allow him near her. I wanted to see for myself, so I got on my bike and rode the mile to Fort Mason. I brought a camera with me. There was an enormous blackberry patch near Peggy's house, and the parrots had been showing up with blackberry stains on their beaks lately. I hoped to document the parrots eating the berries.

When I arrived at the fort, I didn't hear or see any parrots at all. I walked around the grounds, taking light readings and looking for a good vantage point from which to shoot, all the while keeping an eye out for Dogen. As I passed the edge of the blackberry patch, I heard a low croaking sound. I turned and saw a cherry head perched on a vine just four feet away. It was Sonny. The old coot was still alive. He looked exhausted—his eyes were half closed—and he was a mess. His beak and the feathers surrounding it were stained a dark purple from the berry juice. I took a few photographs, and as I was shooting, Dogen swooped down and landed next to him. She must have seen me, but she completely ignored me. All her attention was on Sonny. She sidled up to him and began to groom him. Dogen was sticking by her mate, comforting him to the end. I took a few more shots and left them alone.

I walked over to Peggy's to say hello, and we got into a conversation about the flock. While we were trading notes, some parrots came to Peggy's feeder. Many people had asked me whether the birds recognized me away from the Greenwich Steps. I was curious myself, but I'd never had the opportunity to find out. Peggy suggested that I try feeding them. She went inside her house and brought out a cup filled with sunflower seeds. We were standing about twenty feet away from the birds, and I approached them slowly. The feeder was a six-foot-high tower built from PVC pipe, with two seed trays, one above the other. As I drew near, the parrots watched me uneasily, as though I were a cat. One of them jumped off the feeder, and I thought they were all going to fly away, but the bird flew straight to me and landed on the cup. It was Dogen. I wasn't sure whether that proved anything, so I continued inching my way forward until I was standing right next to the feeder. Not one left. I slowly extended my hand toward the lower of the two trays, and after a moment's consideration, one of them took a seed. Then another did. But only those two were willing to eat from my hand, which made the test feel inconclusive. Still, I have little reason to doubt that they recognized me. That they weren't alarmed when I was standing next to them was proof enough. I think they were a little flummoxed at seeing me somewhere else, though. What are *you* doing *here*?

Four days later, I saw Sonny and Dogen in the Greenwich Steps garden again. They were still being tailed by Connor. Dogen came to my shoulder to eat, and Sonny headed for the dish. But Sonny's clumsiness had gotten so bad that he was having serious problems with approaches and landings. He kept having to circle out and come back to try again. When he finally succeeded in landing, Connor and Amarou chased him away. Dogen stayed out of it this time. At one point, Sonny fell to the ground, but I made no effort to grab him. He looked tormented, and I didn't want to add to it. The next time he approached the dish, I batted Connor, Paco, and Amarou away. It was strange to find myself siding with Sonny against Connor. Sonny was too unsteady to perch on the rim, so he stood in the middle of the dish among the seeds. His eyes were unfocused and glassy. The other parrots were scattered across the garden foraging in the trees, and they started making the low cawing sound that indicated there was a hawk in the vicinity. I saw it—a Cooper's hawk. It came close, so everybody bolted except for Sonny, who remained in the center of the dish, too weary to move. I did consider trying to catch him, but I couldn't bring myself to do it. He stayed in the dish for over an hour as if in a trance, reaching down occasionally to pick up a seed. Then two cherry heads passing overhead caught his attention, and he lurched out of the dish and took off after them.

As Sonny got weaker, Connor became more aggressive, even assuming the duties of Dogen's mate. Whenever another parrot hassled Dogen, Connor rushed to her defense. One afternoon, while working at my desk, I heard a big ruckus out in the loquat tree. I ran to the door and saw Connor chasing Sonny around the outer branches. They kept disappearing and reappearing, in and out of the foliage, until Sonny finally emerged from the loquat and flew up to the incense cedar. Connor came out of the loquat looking for Sonny, but he'd lost track of him. Visibly annoyed, Connor flew to a power line and eyeballed the garden, searching for his rival, but Sonny had given him the slip.

All through August, Sonny continued to deteriorate. But he refused to die. Dogen maintained her loyalty, and I was firmly in Sonny's corner as well. The two cherry heads were spending most of their time at Fort Mason, so I rarely saw them, but whenever they were at the cottage, I protected Sonny as much as I could. Peggy continued to phone reports over to me. She told me Sonny was seldom on her feeder, that more often he was in a nearby bush, waiting for an opportunity to eat, but nobody would allow him to land. She said he was looking progressively worse. In mid-September, she called to tell me that she'd seen some parrots attack Sonny while he was perched in the camellia next to her feeder, and that Sonny had put up virtually no resistance.

The next morning, I heard squawking outside my door that sounded like Dogen. I poked my head out the door and spotted her and Connor on the lines above the deck. When Connor saw me, he started shrieking for the dish. I brought it out and stood next to it, waiting for them to come down to eat. They wouldn't leave the lines, though, so I retreated to the doorway, and only then did they go to the dish. There seemed to have been a change in their relationship. Dogen was allowing Connor to perch quite close to her now. I felt funny keeping my distance, so I went to greet Dogen. She let me approach, but she ate without looking at me. It seemed best to leave them alone, so I went back to the doorway. After they'd finished eating, they flew back up and perched on the same line, but thirty feet apart. Dogen started up a mournful squawking that had a vaguely ritualistic air to it. As ·she moaned, she puffed up her feathers and moved her neck and head around in strange gyrations. Occasionally, she'd stop her sorrowful squawking, walk a few feet toward Connor, stop, and then start moaning again. Each time she moved toward him, Connor would back away, but only an inch or two. The gap between them kept narrowing until they were only a foot apart. Just then a bunch of parrots flew into the garden, and Connor and Dogen jumped off the line and vanished into the loquat.

I didn't see Connor and Dogen again for three days. One afternoon, I was out on the deck eating when Dogen landed on my shoulder. She was friendly, but in a hurry. We shared my bowl, and then she flew over to the plum tree that grew next to the loquat. Seconds later, Connor landed on a nearby branch. Each bird did a few minutes of solitary preening, and then Dogen hopped over to Connor's branch, where they began to preen each other. When they were finished, Connor fed her. My two favorite birds had become a pair.

But what happened to Sonny? I hadn't talked to Peggy in several days, so I called to ask if he was still around. Peggy said she hadn't seen him since the day he'd been attacked in the camellia. That was probably the last day of his life. I checked my diary and saw that Dogen had allowed Connor to approach her the next day. So she'd remained loyal to Sonny to the very end.

Connor and Dogen started coming by the cottage every day. They were seldom with the flock, though. The fledge was over, and the flock was beginning to regroup, but Dogen and Connor flew a separate course. They seemed to start the day in Walton Square with the others, but during the flock's morning flyby of the garden, Dogen and Connor pulled away and came to me to eat. Dogen had not been inside the studio in quite some time, and the first time she entered, she got a big surprise: I had seven parrots living with me now. Dogen still maintained a claim on the studio, and she chased the new birds around the room. Having established her authority, she flew to the highest perch and surveyed her realm. What were all these parrots doing in her house? It was a reasonable question, and it had a sad answer.

It had been a horrendous year for the juveniles. Although the previous breeding season had been an outstanding success, it resulted in there being more babies liable to catch the virus—or whatever it was. Over the spring and summer, at least nine came down with it. Of the seven birds living with me, some I'd picked off the railing, some had been brought to me, and one I'd had to track down. Sophie had fallen out of a tree at Washington Square. A homeless woman found her, put Sophie in a bag, and went around the neighborhood trying to sell her. A shop owner who'd seen my slide show called to tell me what the homeless woman was doing. I ran all around North Beach searching for the woman, finally finding her back in Washington Square. I explained to her that Sophie was very sick, and that if she didn't hand her over, Sophie was going to die. The homeless woman said okay, but she needed some money. We haggled for a few minutes, and she gave me the bird. She cost me twenty bucks.

Having seven sick parrots to care for was overwhelming me. I didn't have enough cage space for all of them, so I was forced to let them roam the studio. They cruised the floor clumsily, constantly changing direction and running into each other, like little bumper cars. I was hustling from dawn to dusk, trying to feed, medicate, and clean up after the sick birds at the same time that I was feeding the flock, working on my notes, running errands for Helen, and doing my odd jobs. I couldn't feed the sick birds the sunflower seeds that I fed the flock—it was an insufficient diet—but I didn't have enough money to buy the food they needed.

One day, I remembered the first dream I'd had about the parrots, the one where I was overwhelmed by a large troop of baby birds. At the time I had the dream, I was impressed that it had predicted by just a few hours the arrival of the year's first babies. Now it seemed to have been predicting events happening three years later. The babies catching this disease were overwhelming me, and I was having trouble staying on my feet. Things finally got so bad that I had to make a public appeal for help. I put out a little newsletter and asked for donations. The neighborhood came through. I was able to buy new cages and stock up on proper parrot food. The only advantage to having so many sick birds was that I didn't have the difficult chore of cleaning their feathers; there were enough relatively healthy birds in the house to keep everyone's feathers in decent shape.

Throughout the fall, Dogen and Connor were inseparable. But as winter approached, Dogen started coming inside alone to visit. Most visits were brief—to say hello, to see what I was eating—but this was an El Niño year, one of the heaviest, and she sometimes spent rainy nights inside with me. Connor would call to her, demanding that she come back out, but if the rain was strong, she refused. In the morning, Connor would be out front calling to her again. I'd open the door, and she'd rejoin him. One morning, well after the time we usually heard his call, I put Dogen on my shoulder, and she and I went out to look for Connor. When I opened the door, the morning light was breaking through the remnants of towering clouds. The air was cold and crystal clear, and the patches of sky between the clouds were a deep dark blue. Connor was there, in silhouette, waiting patiently up on the power lines, a row of pelicans flying over the bay behind him. Dogen left my shoulder and flew to join her mate.

I loved to see them perched side by side. The red of her head and blue of his created an aura that was pleasurable to look at. Unlike Sonny, Connor wasn't bothered by me petting and kissing Dogen. Sometimes I kissed him too, and he didn't flinch. At flock feedings, Dogen came to the seed cup, and Connor joined her there a couple of times—something he'd never done before. For the first time, I saw Connor do the display, where two birds flash their eyes and turn in circles in unison. He'd always seemed somewhat discontented when he was with both Catherine and Bucky, but with Dogen he looked the best I'd ever seen him. Their happiness wasn't to last long, though.

〜〜〜〜

Dogen and Paco still had enough of a relationship going that they could share the seed cup. But Paco and Amarou were so well suited to one another that Paco no longer had any real need for Dogen. I was happy with Paco's progress as a wild parrot. I once saw him do something that impressed me. He was perched on the seed cup when the flock abruptly bolted from the garden. Paco hesitated to leave with them. The flock was heading due north toward Fisherman's Wharf, and after some deliberation, Paco decided to chase after them. But instead of heading north, he flew east. A few moments after he left the cup, the flock turned and began heading southeast. They joined up perfectly at a distant point, and he continued on with them. I'd seen absolutely nothing to indicate that they were going to turn, but somehow Paco had anticipated the flock's ultimate direction.

I was completely used to the parrots, but sometimes there were funny situations that would remind me how unique their presence is. The cottage was constantly falling apart, and the section of deck I stood on to feed had developed some dangerous soft spots. So, on a cold and blustery Christmas Eve, I put on gloves and a heavy jacket and went outside to make repairs. While I was working, a group of tourists came up the Greenwich Steps, and as they drew near the cottage, the entire flock of thirty-seven parrots flew into the garden. They landed en masse in the plum tree directly across from the cottage, where they began to bicker loudly. The tourists were completely confounded and talked in loud, astonished voices about the strange green-and-red birds. I kept working and offered no explanations. It seemed like such a fine joke. Christmas conures.

The garden was deteriorating as much as the cottage. The mirror plant next to my deck had been killed by the uncontrolled growth of ivy. It was a good thing for the parrots, though. They'd always had difficulty finding places to perch during feedings, and now that its branches were bare, the hand feeders were using the mirror plant as a large perch.

El Niño brought so much rain that my ceiling began to leak. Then the bottom of the hot-water heater rusted out and flooded the area behind the walls. It was an awkward situation for me. Although we'd never discussed it, my landlords had obviously decided to let me stay. They were already paying my garbage and utilities, and I didn't want to sound as though I were complaining about the water heater. Still, it seemed like the kind of thing they ought to know about. So I told them, adding that I was quite willing to forgo hot water. But they insisted on replacing it. It seemed that no matter what happened, I came up smelling like a rose.

San Francisco was getting hit by heavier and heavier storms. Dogen continued to come inside during the worst of them, and Connor continued to protest. One afternoon, his shrieks were so persistent that I walked Dogen to the door and encouraged her to rejoin her frustrated mate. It was already raining hard, but soon after I opened the door the rain became a massive downpour. In response to the squall, the flock started up a manic scream. Dogen sat on my shoulder screaming, the sick birds indoors were screaming, and the sound of the rain was so percussive it sounded as though it was screaming, too. The sheet of falling rain and mist was so thick that the only thing I could distinguish in the garden was a remote blur of lavender magnolia blossoms. When the rain finally eased up, Dogen flew to the lines. Connor urged her to fly away with him, but she wouldn't leave, so he took off in a huff. I stood in the doorway, watching her think it over. Connor had stopped somewhere in the distance and was calling to her again. Abruptly, she left the line and chased after him.

Late one afternoon in early February, Dogen came inside for a visit. It wasn't raining, but the weather report was predicting an especially intense storm. I figured she knew what was coming and had decided to wait it out with me. We shared dinner, and then she perched on top of one of the sick birds' cages. During our meal, she was unusually subdued, so I gave her a thorough examination. I couldn't find anything wrong with her. I started thinking about how I wouldn't be with the parrots forever, that one day I'd have to leave, and Dogen's life would end in some way that I wouldn't know about. I decided to give her some special attention. We spent a lot of time together that night. She was so beautiful to me. She was a small cherry head with wistful eyes, a cheerful demeanor, and a desire to please me. I stroked her head and scratched her neck, and reminded myself again how much I loved her. There was no one on earth to whom I was closer. But I'd had no regrets about having let her go. I was happy that she'd been able to return to the flock and have a mate and be a normal wild parrot as she was born to be. I felt that I'd saved her life.

The next morning, Dogen was her usual bright self again. I made some oatmeal and we hung out a little longer, waiting for the flock's morning flyby. There was one strange thing about her overnight stay. I'd assumed that she'd come inside to escape a storm, but the storm never hit. It had rained, but lightly, at a level she was usually quite willing to endure. When we heard the flock, she was on the floor eating oatmeal. I opened the door, and she abandoned the bowl. She flew under the rope gym and out the door to join Connor. It was the last time I ever saw her.

Later that morning, I spotted a hawk perched near the top of the incense cedar. For several days, neighbors had been telling me about an enormous raptor who'd been perching in that tree. People were so impressed by its size that I was getting phone calls about it. I was curious to see it—the descriptions made me think it might be an eagle, something I'd never seen before—but the bird was never around when I was home. The hawk I saw now wasn't that large. I couldn't tell what species it was, so I went inside and got the binoculars. But I had a poor angle on the hawk, so I went next door and climbed the tall wooden staircase of an old, abandoned cottage. As near as I could tell, it was a red-shouldered hawk, which was common. Maybe this wasn't the same bird everyone had been seeing. I started back down the wet, mossy staircase when suddenly my feet flew out from under me. I went up in the air and came down hard on my right shoulder blade. The moment I hit the ground, I knew I'd done some serious damage. I made my way back to the studio and stripped off all my clothing. I knew heat was wrong for it, but I couldn't stand the pain. I got into the shower and soaked my shoulder. Then I lay down on the couch, feeling feverish. My arm was locked in one position across my belly, which made me worry that I'd broken something.

A few hours later, the flock arrived to eat, but I couldn't go out. With my good arm, I pushed myself up to look out the side window. Connor was in the fuchsia, just two feet away. I'd seen him in the fuchsia at other times, but he didn't go there often. For some reason, it felt like a bad omen to me. I got up on my knees and started looking for Dogen, but I didn't see her anywhere. It was raining hard now, so I thought maybe she was in a tree waiting for it to stop. Couples didn't spend every minute of the day together, so I didn't have any good reason to be concerned, but something told me that Dogen was gone.

Although my neighbor Dick was a doctor, I was reluctant to ask him for an examination that I couldn't pay for. But I was starting to have visions of my shoulder not setting properly and becoming a lifelong disability. So I called. He came down and checked me out. He didn't tell me what was wrong, but he assured me I'd be okay. He handed me some pills and told me to get some rest.

I was too busy as a one-armed caregiver to the sick parrots in the house to dwell much on Dogen's absence. In spite of the ache in my shoulder and my stiff arm, I started feeding the flock again. I kept a constant eye out for Dogen, but she was gone. I've often wondered if that hawk got her. I've read that a hawk will single out a particular bird and follow it for hours. If that hawk had targeted Dogen, it might explain why she'd been so subdued that evening. Maybe she knew her time was up. Connor had no obvious reaction to being alone again. I've often wondered if he saw what happened to Dogen.

After handing that first seed to Noah, I formed the goal of having a close friendship with a single wild bird. I'd reached my goal with Dogen. She'd been the heart of my experience with the flock. Now that she was gone, something went out of it for me. There was nothing left to reach for. It was time for the story to move to its end.

Snyder

A couple of weeks after Dogen's disappearance, I received a phone call from a woman who lived in the large condominium complex at the bottom of the hill. She told me that one of the parrots had smashed into a window at full speed and was seriously injured. Would I come get him? I didn't hesitate. I ran straight down the Greenwich Steps and into the condo association's lobby. The concierge told me to wait and left through a side door, returning a minute later with a shoe box containing the injured parrot. It was Snyder, one of Olive and Gibson's hybrid offspring from the previous summer. He was on his back, barely conscious, with his eyes swollen shut, and wheezing from the blood in his nostrils. His condition demanded immediate attention— he sounded like he was drowning—so I thanked the concierge and raced back up the Greenwich Steps with Snyder in the box.

I didn't have time to get him to a vet, and with no idea what else to do, I laid Snyder next to the heater, hoping it would dry the blood out of his nostrils. It seemed to do the trick. The next morning he was well enough that I was able to set him on a dowel. He was unable to do anything more than perch there, though. He was silent and had no appetite. One eye was still swollen shut, and he had a big bruise on his beak. I'd seen those bruises before. Like a lot of birds, the parrots often flew into windows. Sometimes they survived, sometimes they didn't. It looked like Snyder was going to be one of the lucky ones.

The next day he began to eat, and his bad eye opened a little, but he was still groggy. On the third day, he seemed more alert, so I put him in a cage and took him outside for a visit with his family. His father, Gibson, and his sister, Wendell, perched on the cage and watched over him, while Olive, who knew cages, kept her distance. Snyder was aware of their presence, and for the first time he showed alarm at being behind bars. He started chewing on them, trying to figure out a way to escape. By the fourth day, the eye was almost completely open, and he seemed vigorous enough that I decided it was safe to release him.

Two days after I let Snyder go, I was out on the Greenwich Steps brooding over my life again when I saw someone who made my heart jump. It was Gary Snyder. He was a good fifty yards away, but I recognized him instantly. My first impulse was to run into the cottage and avoid him. I held him in such high esteem that I was afraid of speaking with him. But some part of me couldn't allow the opportunity to pass. I moved off the steps and waited for him to get close, my anxiety rising with every one of his footsteps. As soon as he was within earshot, I blew it and started babbling.

"Hi! I know who you are. It's . . . *amazing* to see you here. I'm doing this thing, that, um, you're kind of responsible for. See, I, I, used to read you a lot and, uh . . . Ohh, I'm nervous . . ."

He looked slightly annoyed, but he was patient with me. He's known to thousands of people all around the world, and I'm sure I wasn't the first stuttering fool he'd ever encountered. But I think Gary Snyder has worked at not having his head turned by fame. To be bowled over by someone's fame is boyish, and I respected him, so I got hold of myself and started talking to him as I would to anyone else. I figured he'd be interested to learn that there were wild parrots on the hill, so I told him.

"Yes, I know," he said. "Someone else told me about them. I've come up here looking for them."

I introduced myself as the authority on the flock. He started asking me questions then, and I answered them. It was a funny position to be in. I told him that if he waited around just a little bit, they were likely to show up soon. I had no idea when they were coming, but I was comfortable now, and I wanted to keep the conversation going.

While we waited, I told him how much his work had meant to me, that he'd actually affected the course of my life.

"Before I read you, I never knew what any of the birds or the trees or the flowers were called. Now I'm learning their names."

He smiled and nodded. "It's only polite," he said.

He asked if I'd been in contact with any trained ornithologists. I told him that I'd talked to a few, but they'd shown very little interest. I expressed my reservations about scientists in general, and he assured me that there were good ones. He knew some good ones personally.

Suddenly, the flock arrived. I went inside to get the dish and my seed cup. It was a normal feeding with parrots on the branches of the mirror plant taking seeds from my hand, while others perched on my shoulders and on the rim of the seed cup. As he watched, I gave him a running commentary on what was happening. They weren't pets, I explained, but wild birds that I'd tamed to me.

"Semi-tamed," he said, correcting me.

I nodded in agreement.

It turned out to be a brief feeding. Only minutes after it began, the flock stopped eating and began to make their cawing sound while staring up at the sky with their heads cocked to the side. Suddenly, they let out a huge scream and bolted in unison out of the gardens.

"Why did they do that?" he asked.

"There's probably a hawk in the area." I knew there had to be one, but Snyder is a very precise man, so I was reluctant to go out on a limb.

We talked a little longer, and then he gave me his card and told me that if anything interesting happened to let him know. And then he left.

Just before he showed up, I'd been in a funk. I went back into the studio feeling *high*. A few minutes later, I heard an intense fluttering of wings out on the deck. I ran outside just in time to catch a glimpse of a Cooper's hawk disappearing behind the coral tree. There were clumps of mourning dove feathers everywhere. An attack right on the deck. Unusual.

I'd been so excited about meeting Gary Snyder that I'd completely forgotten to tell him that just two days earlier I'd released a bird named after him. I had to wonder if there was a larger synchronicity at work with his visit. Over the years, I'd discovered a number of parallels in our lives. Snyder had grown up in Portland, Oregon, which is right across the Columbia River from my hometown of Vancouver, Washington. As a boy, I'd been fascinated by the two snowcapped mountains on the Vancouver horizon—Mount Saint Helens and Mount Hood—and he'd climbed both peaks. Around the time I was born, he left for San Francisco, moving into a place on Telegraph Hill that was just three blocks from the Greenwich Steps. We'd both lived in Seattle. He'd worked on a trail crew in the Gifford Pinchot National Forest, the place I'd loved hiking through when I was a boy. He'd lived in an obscure corner of Marin County in a shack that Jack Kerouac wrote about in *The Dharma Bums*. It turned out that I'd bicycled past the shack's location many times. And there was, of course, his interest in Eastern religions. It was as if he'd cut a trail that I'd followed a large part of. None of it was a deliberate following until I got into the birds. So he was one of my natural teachers. I felt as though I'd just been through some kind of graduation ceremony. Maybe my time with the parrots really was at an end.

Back in the fifties, Snyder began work on a book-length poem entitled *Mountains and Rivers Without End*. Over the years, he'd published excerpts, but it had taken him forty years to complete the project. Its publication two years earlier had been a major event within the literary world. At any other time in my life, I would have gotten it the day it came out, but I'd been so occupied with the flock that I still hadn't read it. I walked over the hill to City Lights Bookstore, bought a copy, and took it out on the sidewalk, where I opened to a page at random. My eyes fell on a translation of something called "Painted Rice Cakes," by the Zen master Dogen.

> *An ancient Buddha said "A painted rice cake does not satisfy hunger." Dogen comments:*
> *"There are few who have even seen this 'painting of a rice cake' and none of them has thoroughly understood it.*
> *"The paints for painting rice-cakes are the same as those used for painting mountains and waters.*
> *"If you say the painting is not real, then the material phenomenal world is not real, the Dharma is not real.*
> *"Unsurpassed enlightenment is a painting. The entire phenomenal universe and the empty sky are nothing but a painting.*
> *"Since this is so, there is no remedy for satisfying hunger than a painted rice cake. Without painted hunger you never become a true person."*

I had no idea what he was talking about.

Act Naturally

As her emphysema worsened, my upstairs neighbor, Helen, had a harder and harder time managing the ups and downs of the Greenwich Steps. She was having episodes of dementia, and eventually her condition deteriorated to the point that a relative had to start looking for a nursing home. She'd lived alone in the cottage for nearly forty years, and the idea of moving terrified her. She and I were about as different as two people can be, and we did have a few unfriendly political discussions, but we depended on each other, which created a mutual respect. She told her niece that I was "a communist, but a nice one." I felt bad for Helen when they came to get her and her belongings. She died soon after leaving the hill.

After Helen moved, my landlords, Tom and Denise, invited me up to the house for some frank talk. Helen had been content to live in the shambles of the cottage, and they hadn't wanted to make her leave. But now that her unit was vacant, they felt they had no choice but to renovate the building. That meant jacking it up and putting in a foundation as well as replacing the plumbing, wiring, and virtually every board. It would be impossible for me to live there while the work was being done. I had to find a new place. They were apologetic, as though they were taking some kind of liberty in removing me. But it was fine with me. I was tired of clinging to temporary quarters. I wanted a solution. They told me it would still be several months before work began, and I was welcome to stay until then.

Along with everything else, there were changes in my bird household. I'd been able to release one of them back into the flock. Another had died from her illness. One day, I put everybody outside, and Sophie and her cage mate, Chauncey, picked the lock and escaped. Chauncey didn't last long, but Sophie hung on. Although she was small and unstable from the damage to her nervous system, she was strong-willed. She managed to maintain a place in the flock through sheer feistiness.

For awhile, I was down to just three birds—Ginsberg, Anditson, and Yosemite. Then I was adopted by a fourth: Mingus. One day, I was out doing a feeding when I saw a cherry head desperately tearing off and eating flowers. When he came to the deck, I discovered that he was a new bird. He was a wild-caught cherry head who was so comfortable with me that he'd obviously been a pet for many years. I doubt Mingus was an escapee; I think somebody got rid of him. When Mingus saw what I was all about, he started coming inside and refused to leave. It wasn't hard to understand why his previous owner had dumped him. Mingus was even meaner than Sonny. He constantly attacked the other birds and bit me several times, too. He had a severe limp, the result of a broken pelvis that hadn't healed properly, and his right leg hung when he flew. I think the bad leg was the reason he rejected freedom: It was too much work for him. I tried to get rid of him once. I took him on a bus to Fort Mason—over a mile away—and released him, but he nearly beat me home. One afternoon while playing my guitar, I looked up to find Mingus moving his head in perfect time to the music. He alternated between swinging his head back and forth like a metronome and bopping it up and down like a hipster. I gave up trying to keep him out after that. He'd won me over. He did his dance almost every time I played.

Because the flock feedings were happening in public, I seldom got the chance to be alone with the birds anymore. As more and more people heard about what I was doing, I started attracting small crowds. I had regulars who brought friends. I even got phone calls from people wanting to make an appointment to watch a feeding. One day, I received such a call from a woman named Loretta who'd seen my slide show and wanted to bring her cousin Maria. Loretta said that I'd been around North Beach long enough that I'd probably recognize her cousin. She described her to me, and, in fact, I did know her. Maria was one of the Italian women from the bakery where I used to get free bags of food. I told Loretta that I'd be honored if Maria came, and although I'd never talked about that part of my life with anyone, I explained why.

The flock seldom came when they were "supposed to," and in spring I couldn't always count on them showing up in large numbers. But on the day of Maria's visit, they were on time and in full force. The only bird missing was Connor. I wanted it to be a special occasion for Maria, and the parrots obliged me by being especially animated. Instead of leaving after eating, they flew from tree to tree, hung upside down, and yakked like maniacs. I stood on the deck and watched Maria from the corner of my eye. She was smiling broadly, and had the look of childlike wonder I'd seen the parrots bring to so many people's eyes. I doubt that she remembered me as the dust-covered boy who used to come to her for bread. She knew me from years later when she ran a café that I used as a place to tutor Italian. I'd always been grateful to the women of the bakery, and I was happy that I could give one of them something in return.

Connor's absence wasn't unusual. He was growing more and more remote from both the flock and me. I'd continued to bring him inside to clean him up whenever I thought he needed it, but he didn't like it. After one such abduction-and-cleaning, he stopped allowing me to touch him. Sometimes he even flew away when I approached. I didn't make an issue out of it; I let him be.

With the arrival of spring, I began to lose some favorites. Amarou was the first to disappear that year. I don't know what happened to her. Paco teamed up with Connor for awhile after that. It was an odd pairing that didn't last long; Paco vanished that summer, too. As with Amarou, I never saw any sign of illness or injury. One day, he was gone. Most wild birds have relatively brief lives, and I'd become so inured to their disappearances that my reaction, even to the passing of birds that I loved dearly, was often little more than a note in my journal.

There was one thing that didn't happen that summer, and it was a tremendous relief to me: Not a single juvenile came down with the virus. Maybe they were developing an immunity to whatever was killing them. One result was that when the babies fledged that summer the flock's population was much higher than it had ever been. The previous breeding season had been only moderately successful— nine fledglings—but this was the best ever. At least nineteen babies fledged. One day, I got a clean count of fifty-two parrots. The first time I saw the flock fly overhead in one group at full strength, the sight and sound thrilled me so much that I broke out into a spontaneous little dance. I laughed, clapped my hands, and shouted out loud. I always told people that I didn't believe I was responsible for the flock's growth, but at that moment I felt akin to the Sorcerer's Apprentice.

In mid-September, I received a phone call from a documentary filmmaker, Judy Irving. She'd been hearing about me through friends and wanted to talk with me about possibly making a film. I'd been hoping that someone would show interest in making a small film or a video. Two people had talked to me about doing something, but neither one had followed through. I told Judy I'd be happy to meet with her, and we made an appointment for the next day.

I was enthusiastic when I hung up the phone, but later in the evening I started having second thoughts. I was uncomfortable with letting a stranger see the inside of my house. It was small and damp with a lot of weird stuff in it. There were the cages, the rope gym with newspapers underneath, the seed hulls scattered across the floor, the bookshelves piled high with clothing that I couldn't put in the moldy closet, the desk made of milk crates and a door, the recent addition of an old couch whose middle sagged almost to the floor, the refrigerator with a large scab of rust on top, and the kitchen utensils and food stored out in the open. I knew that to most people I looked like an oddball, so I'd kept myself in a position where I didn't have to explain myself to anyone. But if I were to help this woman with a film, it would be impossible to avoid letting her into my life. I started conjuring up images of her as a slick, hard-nosed media type who'd not only be appalled at my living conditions, but skeptical of my ideas and what I was doing with the flock. I wasn't sure now that I wanted to make a film.

The woman who showed up at my door the next day looked nothing like the monster that I'd created in my mind. Judy was tall and athletic-looking, with shoulder-length dark, graying hair, granny glasses, blue jeans, hiking boots, and an Indian-style vest. Her appearance suggested hippie tendencies, or at least a hippie past, so I relaxed a little. She was pleasant but businesslike. We got right down to talking about work. She had excellent credentials. A graduate of the Stanford University film program, she'd been making a living in film for twenty-five years. She and her partner had won both the grand prize at the Sundance Film Festival and an Emmy for best documentary for *Dark Circle,* an exposé on the connection between the nuclear power and nuclear weapons industries.

When she asked what it was exactly that I was doing, I had difficulty explaining. I'd seldom had to describe it cold without the birds as accompaniment, so I stumbled a bit trying to put it into words. I felt her attention start to drift. I had to keep the conversation going single-handedly while feeling more and more inarticulate. Something was distracting her. Finally, the flock came to my rescue, and we went outside. I expected that a feeding would surely break the ice. Most people got excited, or at least *smiled,* but Judy kept a poker face and said almost nothing. I kept talking and talking, trying to fill the void, but everything continued going downhill. After the birds left, she told me she'd think it over. I told her I had to move in a few months, so it might all be for nothing anyway. She said she'd get back to me. "I doubt it," I thought to myself.

A few days later, Judy called. Contrary to appearances, she was interested, but she saw several problems.

"Making a film requires a lot of lead time," she told me. "My film company is a nonprofit, so I have to raise funding through donors rather than investors. I might not be able to raise enough money even to begin shooting by the time you have to move. The thing is, I've been wanting my next film to be my own project. That's going to make a lot of demands on my time and resources, and, frankly, I'm not convinced that there is a film in you simply handing out seeds to birds."

"Well, I'd just as soon not be in the film. I'd like it to be about the *birds.* I think you could make something good that was just about their personalities. Once you get to know them individually, they're fascinating."

"I don't know about that," Judy said. "They all looked the same to me. If they look the same to a live observer, how is a theater audience going to know the difference? Anyway, most people are more interested in other human beings than in animals."

"So what do you want to do?"

"Well, I have an idea I'm working on. I know some children in an experimental acting class. I'm thinking of creating something that revolves around them and the birds, a short fiction film. Do you think the parrots would cooperate if I put some kids on the deck with you?"

"I don't know. It might not be a problem as long as I'm there." I wasn't enthusiastic about her idea, but that didn't matter. I didn't care so much what *kind* of film it was; I just wanted my memory of the birds preserved. Judy said she'd talk to the children's teacher, do some figuring, and get back to me.

Filming was slow to get started, but so was the renovation of the cottage. The date kept getting pushed back. In the meantime, Judy was able to raise a little money and shoot a couple of feedings. As work got under way, she started to get a feel for the parrots and my relationship with them. It turned out that either she'd masked or I hadn't seen her real feelings at our first meeting. The feeding had enthralled her. It took her back to the time when she was a young girl and her grandfather had taught her to feed wild chickadees by hand. She'd loved her grandfather, and it was one of her favorite childhood memories. As we continued working together, I watched her reactions closely. Although she was constantly judging the filmic possibilities, I never had the feeling that she was judging me. I found it easy to trust her.

Judy's initial fund-raising efforts didn't go very well. The subject matter fell outside the guidelines of most foundations, so she was having to seek funding from individual donors, which was a difficult route to take. She decided to throw a fund-raiser. She made contact with a neighborhood organization, the Telegraph Hill Dwellers, who agreed to sponsor it. She booked a local theater, and I prepared a special slide show for the occasion.

A neighbor worked as an editor for the *San Francisco Examiner,* and one day she stopped by to ask if I'd be willing to talk to a reporter. The fund-raiser needed publicity, so I said, "Sure. Send him over." He and I had a long chat, which went well enough, but there was one aspect of the interview that puzzled me: Most of his questions were about *me.* I thought he was there to talk about the parrots, and I kept steering him back to them. After he left, the *Examiner* sent over a photographer, but it was one of the extremely rare days that the flock didn't show up. So that they'd have at least something if the paper decided to use a photo with the article, he took a few shots of me holding and petting Yosemite and Mingus indoors.

The next day, I was walking along Sansome Street. I happened to glance at a newspaper box, and what I saw gave me a jolt. It was a large color photograph of me holding Yosemite and nuzzling the top of his head. The headline read BIDDING FAREWELL TO THE FLOCK. I'd been expecting a small story on a back page, not a front-page feature. I bought a copy and read it on the spot. The main thrust of the article was about me having to move away and leave the flock behind. While it was essentially accurate, the photograph of me holding Yosemite gave the impression that the flock came inside to visit and that I was free to handle them. On the way home, I kept seeing my face staring out at me from newspaper racks. It was very, very strange, especially for someone who for years had been essentially a hermit.

When I got home, the light on my answering machine was blinking persistently. The Associated Press had decided to send the story out over the wire, but they wanted their own photographs. Would I please call immediately? After the AP photographer left, a local television station called, wanting to do the story. The next day, a *New York Times* reporter en route to San Francisco saw the AP article and called me as soon as her plane landed. CNN saw the *Times* article and wanted to do a story. And it just kept on snowballing. I was getting four or five calls a day. All the Bay Area newspapers and television and radio stations wanted stories. So did Reuters, *People* magazine, the *Los Angeles Times,* the BBC, and National Public Radio.

At first, I thought it was humorous. A producer for one well-known television talk show wanted to fly me and one of the parrots down to Los Angeles and have the bird do tricks on air. When I explained that the birds were actually wild, she said, *"Oh,"* and abruptly ended the call. Not owning a television, I'd never heard of half the shows and networks that wanted to talk to me. Things quickly got out of hand. There was no letup, and I started getting cranky from the demands on my time. The most awkward part was that my landlords were being vilified in letters to the local newspapers. My departure from the cottage was being held up as yet another example of what greedy landlords and developers were doing to San Francisco's character and characters. I was as opposed as anyone to what was happening to the city, but my situation was not relevant. I had to write letters to the newspapers defending Tom and Denise.

The publicity generated so much attention and goodwill for the flock that both the mayor and the San Francisco Board of Supervisors got involved, declaring the day of the fund-raiser Wild Parrot Day. At the theater, the line went around the block. Hundreds of people had to be turned away. It was exhilarating to be involved with something that was on such a roll. I gave the show everything I had. I tried to bring the audience into my experience of the the birds as unique individuals, with their own cares and woes. The show was a tremendous success, and the people responded generously. Judy was able to buy the film she needed to start shooting in earnest.

As long as I was there, the parrots were perfectly comfortable with the crew and the children. After three kids' shoots, Judy did a few shoots with just the birds and me. As she became familiar with the individual parrots, her idea about the film began to change. The children's segments had gone fine, but she was getting more and more interested in my relationship with the flock. She also liked the stories I was telling her. Gradually, her idea for the film evolved from a short for children to a feature-length documentary about my friendship with the flock. She started an intense round of shooting aimed at fleshing out the new idea.

To provide material for the sound track, Judy began interviewing me for voice-over. She was constantly peppering me with questions even when the tape recorder was turned off. She kept wanting new stories about the birds and tried to get me to say something clear about the way I lived. I'd never talked with anybody about that—it wasn't merely conversation for me—so I had trouble finding the right words. Judy had worked at a career most of her life, which made it difficult for her to understand why I'd never had one. Americans make such a big deal out of having a real job that whenever I felt the question coming, I flinched. I'd stammer out that I *loved* to work, but that I was incapable of devoting myself to something I didn't absolutely believe in. I pointed out that I'd spent a great deal of time working on things that I didn't get paid for. I could never answer the question to her satisfaction, though, and eventually it became a joke between us. She'd turn to me at random moments and say, "Okay, so tell me again: Why do you refuse to get a job?" The fund-raiser had been so successful, and the film was taking up so much of my time, that Judy decided she could afford to pay me a consulting fee. She offered me $700 a month for four months, which was the equivalent of a year's salary working at odd jobs. I was so burned out on that kind of work that after she gave me the first check, I turned down every job that came my way.

The date for beginning the cottage renovation finally firmed up, with work set to begin in mid-September. I had no idea where I was going. I had a vague wish to end up in rural southern Oregon, but there was so much work to do on the film that I did nothing to prepare for my eventual departure. I just hoped for the best, figuring something would come up before I had to vacate the cottage.

There were two matters I had to take care of before moving. During the media blitz, the San Francisco Commission of Animal Control and Welfare had been deluged with phone calls from people who were concerned about the parrots. The photograph of me holding Yosemite inside the studio had suggested to readers that the flock came inside my house and that they were dependent on me for their survival. I was constantly assuring people that the parrots didn't need my help, but no one believed me. The city was getting all kinds of advice on what to do after I left. Some thought that the flock should be trapped and put in the zoo or adopted out. Others wanted to set up feeding stations on Telegraph Hill where people could put some coins into a machine and get a handful of seeds to feed the parrots themselves—something the flock never would have gone for. There were also the dogmatic nativists who believed the parrots should be exterminated. The commission wanted my opinion. I recommended that the city just let the parrots be. They didn't need to be subsidized. They were fully adapted wild birds who could make it on their own. My concern was that any program whatsoever, no matter how well-intentioned, would in the end lead to the parrots being put in cages, which I was adamantly opposed to. It was my understanding that the laws against cruelty to animals would apply to the parrots, but that they didn't have the protection against being trapped that native birds do. So all I wanted for them was that same legal protection. Pleased that I wasn't calling for a costly program, the commission agreed to see that the parrots got the protection I wanted for them.

My other obligation was to find homes for the four birds I'd been caring for, none of whom could ever be released. A few months earlier, I'd received an e-mail from Nate and Betsy Lott, a couple who ran a sanctuary for abandoned and abused parrots, offering to take them if I could find no other solution. Judy and her partner lent me their van, and we drove the parrots to the Lotts' home. I felt sad saying good-bye to them—I'd grown especially fond of Mingus—but I had no other choice. I was lucky someone was willing to take them.

Throughout the summer, Judy filmed everything she thought she might need to tell the story. Once work began on the cottage, it would be impossible to reshoot anything. By the beginning of September, she was confident she had it all. Then Judy got a *fabulous* idea.

She asked if I'd like to do something she was calling "the Pledge to the Fledge." Her idea was that we'd drive to the nest site in El Coto every morning until a baby took its first flight. She'd film it, and I'd record the sound. I'd always wanted to see a fledge—it was the aspect of the parrots' lives about which I knew the least—and I agreed enthusiastically.

Of the three nests I knew, the easiest to film was the one in the eucalyptus that Mack had shown me. It was near a road, so Judy and I were able to park right next to it and watch for hours from the comfort of the van. We were starting our vigil a few days late, and we were worried that we'd already missed that nest's fledglings. But when we arrived, we could hear the babies still inside. The parents were guarding the nest-hole entrance, and I was able to identify them: Erica and Russell. Although Erica occasionally joined him, Russell did most of the foraging, and each time he returned we could hear a lot of excitement coming from inside the nest. There seemed to be more than one baby. I'd recently learned an interesting fact about that nest hole. A birder told me that it had been used by the very first breeding pair, the parrots that Laurel Wroten called Victor and Inez. She knew the correct year, so her information was solid. I'd seen Erica in that nest before, and as far as I could tell a female used the same nest year after year, so it lent more weight to Laurel's feeling that Erica was the bird she'd called Inez. If so, Erica was the flock's Eve.

The other two nests I knew about were both in Canary Island date palms. One belonged to Olive, the mitred conure, and her new partner, Pushkin. Olive became Pushkin's when he stole her away from Gibson in a fight. Olive had three babies the year before, her first with Pushkin as her mate. The hybrids still fascinated me. Olive always had two types of hybrid babies: one with a crimson patch on its forehead, and another that was entirely green. As far as I could tell, the hybrids with the crimson patch were male and the all-green ones were female. The all-green hybrids were very slow to develop red feathers—at maturity, they had fewer than Olive—and those they had were confined to a narrow band around the eyes. The babies with the crimson patch developed quite a bit of red, but never as much as the reddest of the cherry heads. The hybrid voice was a cross between the two species. In their lower register, they sounded much like cherry-headed conures, while in their higher register they had a metallic shriek that sounded nearly identical to mitred conures. Like mitred conures, the hybrids' legs started out gray and then became pinkish as they matured. The eye ring was halfway between the snow-white of the mitred and the yellowish white of the cherry head.

The third nest belonged to Scrapper and his new mate, Wendell. Wendell was female, and one of the all-green hybrids. I'd wondered for several years whether the hybrids were fertile, and this was the first year that a hybrid was old enough to breed. Scrapper and Wendell's nest was near Erica and Russell's, so I made frequent trips over to check on them. If there were going to be babies from a hybrid mother (the babies would be called *backcrosses*), I didn't want to miss them.

Judy and I would arrive in El Coto before sunrise, set up the camera, tripod, and tape recorder, and then drink tea from a thermos while waiting for the birds to begin their day. I believed that the babies always fledged in the morning, so if nothing happened by afternoon, I'd go back to the cottage to continue packing and feed the flock. We weren't seeing any sign of an imminent fledge, and when I checked my diary it seemed to indicate that the females had gotten off to a late start.

Judy and I filled the hours in the van talking. We discovered that as children we'd both had the same favorite bird: the cedar waxwing. Most of Judy's films had been about the environment, and she said that when we met she'd been looking for a project that could explore ways in which nature and the city could coexist. Originally, she'd seen nature as being "out there"; but more and more, she was seeing it as something that's everywhere, which is precisely the point Gary Snyder had made that had led me to where I was now. Judy and I were both fascinated with the way plants can get a foothold in a crack in a sidewalk. Nature is so strong that given enough time, it could tear down and bury our cities.

We gradually opened up and started telling each other our initial impressions.

"I had you pegged as an eco-feminist lesbian," I told her laughing. "I don't mean that as a put-down. I've had several eco-feminist lesbian friends. That's just what I thought you were."

"I thought you were gay, too," she said, "and a spaced-out hippie who probably couldn't string two full sentences together. That's the reason I came up with the idea of doing a children's film; I thought you'd need to be surrounded by other people to carry the story."

"You seemed distracted," I said.

"Well, I was appalled by your apartment. It was a pigsty! And it stank. The bathroom was the worst. You had all your dirty dishes piled on top of the toilet tank."

"Well, it was impossible to keep the place clean. It was cramped, and the birds were constantly making more mess. I couldn't keep up with it. And there wasn't anything I could do about the mold smell. It was embedded in the carpet."

"Who said anything about mold? I was smelling bird shit."

One morning when Judy picked me up, I could feel that she was unhappy about something. She was usually very even emotionally, which made her bad mood all the more apparent. When we parked, the tension in the van was uncomfortable enough that I asked her what was wrong.

"It's nothing," she said.

There was an awkward moment of silence; then she spoke again.

"I had a problem at home. It's not a big deal. It just put me in a bad mood, that's all. I'd rather not talk about it."

There was another long silence that finally she felt obliged to fill.

"I've been feeling ignored for a long time. He takes me for granted. When I talk to him, I can tell he's not listening to me. It would probably bother me a lot more if I weren't doing the same thing to him. . . . Look, you don't need to hear this."

I shrugged my shoulders as if to say, "Hey, it's not a problem."

"The thing that gets me is that our relationship has become exactly the kind of trap I've always told myself I'd never fall into. He's not abusive or anything. I mean, we're both very polite. But we grate on each other. Whenever I start a project, he always gets into it and tries to take it over. But what should I expect? I mean, we work together, for God's sake. . . . Actually, I think that's the problem— working together. Sometimes I think I'd be better off alone. At least I'd be free to pursue my own projects."

The last remark embarrassed her. She'd said much more than she intended. She was quiet for a moment and then looked at me sheepishly. "So, tell me again: Why is it you refuse to get a job?"

I laughed, and then we both fell silent and drank our tea. Judy stared out the window for a long time, and then she turned to me.

"Okay. I've spilled my guts. Now you tell me something about yourself. You've been doing this for six years. What have you learned from the parrots?"

Consciousness Explained

People often asked what I'd learned from my experience with the parrots. My pat answer was that I'd learned about trust, which was true, but I'd learned other things. I'd learned new skills: how to use computers, how to take photographs, how to do research. And as my research took me into different areas, I gained knowledge about such topics as ecosystems in Ecuador, the history of Telegraph Hill, bird diseases, and the history of bohemian America. I also learned through direct observation about the native birds. But there was one thing I learned that I especially value because it filled a large hole in my understanding.

You could say it all began on the day I told the zoo curator John Aikin that I realized I was anthropomorphizing the parrots. It embarrassed me to say that. It was an awkward moment socially, and, worse, it didn't reflect my real views. I recognized that parrots aren't exactly like human beings, but I believed that each bird is no less an individual personality than I am. But I didn't have a thought-out system to support such a belief. It just seemed self-evident. After John left, I went back into the house feeling the way you do after talking about a good friend behind his back. It forced me to start thinking more deliberately about consciousness in animals.

I knew that in general scientists object to comparisons between animal and human minds, but I was unfamiliar with the exact nature of their argument. So I started reading the science articles I came across in newspapers and magazines. One day, I read a statement that grabbed my attention. A zoologist was complaining about the lack of a sound scientific education within the general populace. He said that one result was the widespread habit of people anthropomorphizing animals. Everything in the universe could be explained through physics and chemistry, he said. An animal is nothing more than a bundle of chemical reactions responding to the instructions of its genes. A whole set of other scientific statements I'd read suddenly fell neatly into place. I realized that there was a way of looking at existence that I'd never considered. Wanting to explore it further, I put down the article, headed out the door, and made my way to a local bookstore. While scanning the science section I spotted the title *Consciousness Explained.* The moment I saw it, I knew I'd found what I was looking for. A quick browse proved me right. I bought the book and took it home.

It was difficult reading—in more ways than one—but I struggled through the opening chapters, taking in what I could while passing over anything I didn't immediately grasp. The author was saying things that gave me a whole new understanding of the word *materialism.* I'd always thought materialism was the love of money and the things money could buy, but it's also the idea that the only thing that exists is the material plane. I know this is elementary to many people, but it was news to me. I'd spent most of my life trying to understand spiritual ideas of reality, so I'd never given much thought to what "nonbelievers" believed. After getting the gist of *Consciousness Explained,* I started examining other books from the same school. I found that while there are differences of opinion (even heated ones) and arcane refinements, all its adherents hold certain key beliefs:

Life grows out of complex material processes. It's random, however—dumb atoms and molecules creating myriad structures, some of which work and some of which don't. This random variation and natural selection are the keys to understanding all biological change. Everything an organism does, it does in order to assure its own individual survival.

All the materialists I read had a special reverence for Charles Darwin. They were unanimous in their belief that before his appearance on earth, humanity was stumbling around in hopeless ignorance and superstition, but that since then we've made tremendous strides. We know now that there is no purpose in life other than the playing out of biological evolution. Nor are there any real mysteries; there are only things we don't understand yet. And true understanding of human nature, like everything else, can come only through science.

The subject of human nature invariably leads to the issue of consciousness—a slippery subject that creates diverging opinions. It's difficult to explain how a thought can move something material like an elbow or an eyebrow. Nevertheless, we know that the brain *is* the mind, and all opposing ideas about the mind come from humanity's long prescientific period of ignorance. Consciousness is generally regarded as the ability to think: "I think, therefore I am." In the materialist view, animals can't think—some say it's because they have no language—so it's difficult to say that they are truly conscious. They're generally regarded as chemical robots. But the extreme materialist position is that human beings are no different. We are machines—extremely sophisticated ones, but machines nevertheless. Since the brain, like everything else, operates solely through the laws of physics and chemistry, there's no reason why one couldn't—at least in theory—build a computer as fully conscious as any human being.

So were my parrot friends merely little green bags of chemical reactions blindly seeking energy from me in order to achieve further combustion? Is that what Tupelo was? Is that what Dogen was? And what was my love for them?

There are two views on the fundamental nature of reality: One says that it's material, and the other says that it's spiritual. From the material point of view, consciousness arises from matter. From the spiritual point of view, matter—or perhaps one should say the *illusion* of matter—arises from consciousness. To a materialist, a belief in something spiritual is purely a matter of faith, and since matters of faith can't be measured, tested, or proven, they're unworthy of serious consideration.

During the period I lived with my sister, before I got kicked out of the van, my entire life was absorbed in meditation. From the start, I found meditation to be a difficult and awkward struggle. I felt like I was pushing against immovable inner walls. Then one day, while digging around inside myself, I unexpectedly sailed right through one of those walls. I felt astonishingly bright and clear. I had a strong urge to be at the top of a hill, so I went up to Coit Tower. When I reached the hill's summit, I walked to the edge of the parking lot and looked out over the long expanse of San Francisco Bay. It was a sunny morning in late winter and unusually warm and windless. I was in the state of mind where the world looks timeless and fresh. It could have been any year in history. The sky was deeper than I'd ever seen it and my vision was astonishingly acute. As I stood there, I felt a great turning, and the entire material plane seemed on the verge of dissolving. For just an instant, I glimpsed the shadow of something that I knew intuitively to be the yin and the yang, the two spiritual forces whose interaction is said to generate all visible reality. The vastness and beauty of what I saw was so riveting that for that moment nothing else existed. I had no wishes, no complaints, no distractions. But I couldn't hold onto the vision. I noticed myself noticing, and the moment I did, it vanished, and I became just some guy standing in a parking lot.

I feel fortunate to have had such a glimpse. It hasn't been my only experience of the spiritual realm, but it was my first strong one. After that, I could never doubt its reality. There were rebellions—the spiritual path is difficult and demanding—but they were short-lived. Over the years, as I ran through the implications, I saw that since religion is supposed to describe how the universe functions, there can be only one true religion. Eventually, I came to understand that the one true religion isn't Zen or Taoism. And it isn't Hinduism, Judaism, or Sufism. Nor is it Christianity. The one true religion doesn't have a name. All the religions with names are derived from the one true religion, which is here and now, eternal, the living law of what actually is. Christ and Buddha and every other real spiritual teacher saw the same thing. There is nothing else to see. But all of them had to speak to the people of their time and culture, which is why they sound different to us. But the source is the same. Aldous Huxley called the one true religion the Perennial Philosophy, a handy term that I will use here.

The Perennial Philosophy is what's true for everyone, everywhere, always. It's not the creation of a particular culture; it's a description of how the universe actually operates. When you strip away the accretions of cultural myth, all religions say the same things. Karma is the same thing Christ was talking about when he said, "As you sow, so shall you reap." It's the universal principle of cause and effect. Heaven is the same as nirvana. All religions stress that life is short and death is momentous and that we shouldn't fritter away our time seeking pleasures or wealth. All stress the importance of telling the truth. All say—if they are true—that we shouldn't harm each other because we're all brothers and sisters. When Christ said that one must be born again, he was speaking of the enlightenment experience. The goal of life is the realization of God. Ultimately, you can't get it out of a book; you have to experience it directly. The kingdom of heaven is within.

A principal tenet of the Perennial Philosophy is that everything is God. God is not some old man with a beard and robes living outside of his creation. God is the All; God is the universe. Many Christians insist that this isn't true, that God is separate and created us. But in the Gospel of Thomas, a book that conventional Christianity, for no good reason, long ago rejected, Christ says, "You split the wood and I am there. You pick up a stone and I am there." God is everywhere.

This principle was just a bunch of words to me until one day when I was out feeding the flock. I was absentmindedly handing them seeds while trying to come up with a concept of what their minds are like. I was looking at their eyes when I remembered that everything is supposed to be God. If that is true, then, logically, the parrots are God, too, and their consciousness is part of God's consciousness. Every set of eyes is part of God's vision, and every viewpoint in the universe is God's viewpoint. I'd heard this idea many times, but this was the first time I was able to envision it.

As soon as the flock left, I went inside and pulled *Zen Mind, Beginner's Mind* off the shelf and started reading at random. Sentences that had never made sense to me in the past were suddenly simple and clear. I don't call it a moment of enlightenment or spiritual realization, which comes only with practice. I was too unsettled at the time to have a practice. What I found was only an intellectual understanding, but it was sufficient for what I needed at the time. It opened up new territory for me, and I spent months working through elaborations of the idea. It allowed me finally to take on the issue of anthropomorphism.

When I say that Connor has a regal personality, the philosophical materialist insists that I'm projecting a human idea onto a bird. Actually, if there were only material reality, to describe anyone at all as being regal would be delusional. There'd be no basis for any kind of spiritual qualities whatsoever. But if existence is spiritual, then *regalness,* or nobility, is a universal characteristic, not something strictly human. And if all minds are one, then all creatures partake of the same universal qualities. Some creatures may express a broader range than others, and each will have different qualities emphasized, but consciousness is consciousness. There is only one.

This isn't to deny the existence of the material plane or to say that science is useless and its understanding totally off base. Nor am I denying the function of the brain. Buddhism uses the terms *big mind* and *small mind,* with big mind representing the universal mind and small mind representing the individual brain. The brain contains the memory and all the other biological processes that an individual organism needs in order to function in the material plane. The material plane does have its laws. I have no doubt that life evolved from microorganisms and that human beings are closely related to apes. But I think the Darwinists are wrong about the mechanism of change—as are the creationists. One scientist writes affectionately of "good, old dumb evolution." He's referring to random variation and natural selection. Everything in the universe is in constant change; but in the spiritual view, all change follows strict inner laws. If everything is God, what can be beyond the reach of God? A scientist looking at a starfish clinging to a rock that is being pounded by waves will say that the starfish is a separate organism being affected by things outside of it. Science seeks to reduce everything to individual components. At one level, the scientist's observations will be accurate, but at another level, they will fail, because individuality is not absolute. The starfish, the rock, and the waves are also a single structure, which is, in turn, part of a greater single structure.

In Western science and philosophy, consciousness is usually equated with intellectual capacity. But intellect is only one aspect of consciousness. One of the goals of meditation is to quiet the chatter of the thinking mind. That which watches one's thoughts come and go is conscious. To be aware of your awareness is not always desirable. An animal might be lonely, but it won't conceptualize about it, nor will it complain. But it will *be* lonely.

Some believe that language is essential to consciousness, but there is meaning even without language. When I was studying Italian, I met an Italian woman who was both extraordinarily attractive and extraordinarily arrogant. She was used to getting whatever she wanted. She admitted it. She once told me that she *never* lost, that she hated losing.

One day, I walked into a sort of communal apartment where some Italian friends of mine were staying and found Laura playing a game of chess. Laura was so notoriously competitive that the game had drawn a crowd. While all that attention was focused on her, Laura's opponent suddenly put her in checkmate. Nobody saw it coming. Laura was stung. I felt very clearly her rage surge upward, and then, just as clearly, I felt her squelch it. There was a brief pause, and in that pause the thought "I am not amused" passed through my mind. Immediately afterward, she said, "Non la trovo divertente"—literally, "I don't find it amusing," the Italian equivalent of the English phrase. That was a telepathic experience. We all have them, but if we don't believe in them intellectually, we don't call them that. The interesting thing is that what passed through my mind was not the Italian syllables, but the thought translated into English. The phrase "I am not amused" has a particular sense that goes beyond the individual words. There is a haughtiness to it. What I picked up on was the meaning beyond our two languages. That meaning has representations in both languages, but it is a meaning that exists before language. My mind translated her meaning into the language I knew best.

I've had other experiences with wordless transmission of meaning. One example is Tupelo's death. She communicated to me that she was dying. I felt her fear and loneliness and her wish to be comforted, but I was too dense to realize what was happening. In several instances, I've translated what I thought the parrots were saying to each other. To an outsider, that might seem like a stretch, but once I became familiar with the individuals, they weren't so difficult to understand. All living creatures are personages, and the issues among us are similar. I wrote of feeling someone staring at me, turning around, and seeing Connor at the window. All of us have had that experience. It's stubborn to ignore it.

Watching the parrot flock in flight, I've often wondered how the group is able to make sudden turns in unison. Scientists look for an outer signaling system, but I think the birds have such a "flock sense" that at times they are of one mind. I picked up some of that flock sense, and at times it was uncanny. I almost always knew when there was a major development in the flock. Even when they were in front of me in large numbers, my eyes frequently knew to look at a particular bird to learn what had changed. One time I saw a parrot sitting alone in the garden, which wasn't at all unusual, but something inside of me wanted to take a closer look. I walked over to where the bird was perched and saw that it was Gibson. One of Gibson's eyes was covered with blood. The next day, I discovered that Pushkin had stolen Gibson's mate, Olive. This kind of thing happened repeatedly. How did I know that Dogen was gone? I had no reason to think so; I'd seen her just an hour earlier. The flock was deep inside of me; it wasn't something conscious or willed. And I think I was inside of the flock. I have no idea how one would do it deliberately. I think it came about naturally, through mutual affection. The parrots were aware of and responsive to my moods, even at subtle levels. Once I had to reach into Yosemite and Ginsberg's cage at a moment that I was feeling speedy and scattered. When my hand entered the cage, they both panicked and started bashing up against the cage bars trying to get away from me. Worried that they were going to hurt themselves, I stopped moving my hand, but their level of anxiety was just as high as when my hand had been moving. I became aware then of my psychological state and consciously relaxed. As soon as I did, they did, too. Nothing changed outwardly. It's what people used to call vibes. At feedings, when the birds were in a highly anxious state, I felt it inside of me, so much so that it could make me very uncomfortable.

These are examples of small minds—brains and nervous systems—communicating with each other through the medium of the universal mind. We tap into it best when we're relaxed and focused. Sometimes it happens in dreams, like the two that I had about the parrots. The one in which I was bowled over by the giant babies anticipated by just a couple of hours the arrival of the year's first fledglings. I had no idea they were due. That was the first breeding season I witnessed, and at the time I assumed they weren't even breeding. I believe that that same dream also anticipated the burden the babies put on me as they fell ill. The second dream, the one in which four birds and a hairy mammal were sharing the dining room table, anticipated my taking care of four birds in the house. It also reminded me that I am an animal, too.

What we call intuition is our brain tapping into big mind. The time that strange man stepped out of the garden and I instantly knew he represented a danger to the flock is an example of the brain having access to something beyond observable data. I don't know how it works. I can speculate, but how it works isn't so important. Science doesn't tolerate this kind of mysticism, though. The widespread assumption nowadays is that accumulating facts about the material plane—knowledge—is more important than understanding the depth of being—wisdom. To the scientist, everything I'm saying is purely a matter of faith (or, depending on the scientist, sheer idiocy). But faith isn't about guessing or believing in something you can't see. It isn't difficult to know that Spirit is real; you just have to look at the truth without compromise. Now, scientists insist that that's precisely what they do. But they ignore the inner world, which they dismiss as subjective. But the connection to the spirit is within, and if you refuse to look there, you will *never* see it. If you examine the true content of what's within your mind at any given moment and keep going to the next thing, all paths lead to the understanding of the spiritual nature of reality. There's nothing cheap or insulting to your intelligence in following what's true, but you have to stay with it no matter where it takes you. You can't be swayed by ambition or fear. The test of faith is not whether you believe there is a spiritual plane; it's whether you'll live by that knowledge once you've caught a glimpse of it.

There is a difference—obviously—between the abilities of humans and animals. But what? Pure consciousness is absolutely serene and without fear, but the consciousness of the brain is consciousness after it has been conditioned by the material plane. Biological beings fear injury, death, and starvation, and they experience jealousy, anger, and greed. When people talk about human nature, they're often referring to selfishness. But that's not human nature; that's egotism, and we are capable of transcending egotism. That's the teaching of real religion. When psychologists talk about the human mind, they're usually talking about the neuroses of the small mind. Being selfish cuts you off from the big mind because the big mind includes everything.

Our true nature can be found only through deliberate effort. I think that's the real difference between animal and human nature: We have much more free will. It's only through free will that we are able to reach beyond our fears and grasp the roots of consciousness. This is what Buddha and Christ accomplished. Our capacity for free will does make us superior to the other animals. But all kinds of misunderstandings arise when you say that. Our superiority doesn't make animals worthless, and superiority doesn't confer upon us a special privilege to exploit them. It is the obligation of the superior to *serve* the inferior. That's the spiritual understanding. But we're superior not merely by having the capacity to transcend our animal nature, but by actually transcending it.

One Darwinist doctrine that I have little patience with is the notion that everything an animal does is for the sake of its own survival. This ignores their transparent affection for one another and their play. I've written a lot about the violence that the parrots inflict on one another, especially on the sick, but it never seemed to me as though they were "culling out the weak." I don't know with certainty why they do it, but my sense is this: Much of each day is a frantic search for food, and then they're more high-strung than usual. They're hungry. During these frenzied periods, if they see a bird in a vulnerable position, they go for it. I've seen birds get bitten simply because they had their back to another bird or were bent over. They were bitten because they were available to be bitten. And in spite of the level of violence within the flock, there's also a tremendous amount of cooperation. Whenever I got caught petting a bird, the others came to its defense. I even saw examples of interspecies support, like when the scrub jay chastised me for seizing one of the parrots. We all know that when we feel vulnerable, we're more likely to come under attack from others—even from friends and family. This is our animal nature. We have the freewill choice not to do it, but the animals have less control over themselves. They are more impulsive when they're angry. But at least when they're angry they don't become mass murderers.

It was my embarrassment at telling John Aikin that I knew I was anthropomorphizing the parrots that started me thinking seriously about the issue of consciousness in animals. Tupelo's death intensified it. I wanted to tell her that I loved her, and I kept asking myself if she could still exist in some way, which led to more questions about consciousness and death. What happens to the personality after death? Mainstream culture provides two models. One is popular religion's idea of a heaven where our individual souls spend eternity happily resting. The other is the tough-minded (or hardheaded) materialist approach: "You just die; you cease to exist." I don't buy either idea. Nor do I believe in the reincarnation of the individual personality. But what does happen? Short of dying, can you know?

In *Zen Mind, Beginner's Mind,* Suzuki-roshi tells a story about a trip he took to Yosemite. While there, he stopped to watch a waterfall. It was one of the very tall ones, and he noted that when the stream at the top of the ridge hit the cliff, it split into many individual droplets on its way to the bottom. There, the individual droplets came back together into one stream. I'd read that story many times without comprehending his point. At a basic level, it's quite simple: There is one river until it hits that cliff, which is life. The one river then breaks up into many individual living beings—humans, animals, and plants—until we hit the bottom of the cliff and become one river again. Each droplet loses only its identity as a single drop. But nothing is really lost. It's all still there. I'd encountered this idea in different ways many times over the years, but I'd never grasped it. It's an elementary idea, and not so difficult to understand. But my problem was that I'd been thinking about consciousness solely in human terms. It wasn't until I considered the minds of the parrots that my outlook broadened. So my problem was not with anthropomorphism; rather, it was with *anthropocentrism,* which is seeing human beings as the center of the universe. The parrots broke through that delusion. The understanding that ultimately came to me from looking in the parrots' eyes was that their consciousness is one with mine. We are all one consciousness, and each finite being embodies a little piece of it. This is the preciousness of all that lives.

A Late Fledge

J udy and I drove through the predawn darkness to El Coto every day. We could hear the muffled yelping of at least one baby, but after a week we hadn't caught even a glimpse of him. Filming nature requires a great deal of patience, and after a few days the wait grew tiresome. For all we knew, there was only one baby in that nest, and if so, we'd get only one chance at filming a fledge. Having no idea when it would come, we had to keep our attention constantly focused on the nest hole.

In the midst of our vigil, word came that the contractor was ready to start gutting the cottage. For the sake of closure, I gave a last feeding. It was a large group of parrots that came to see me off. I did shed a few tears, but they were all from laughter. When another parrot landed on Snyder's branch, he removed the interloper by giving him a straight-legged kick that sent me off into hysterics. It was appropriate. Laughter—joy—had been the essence of the experience for me. The only sad part of the feeding was seeing the state that Connor had fallen into. He looked old, and he was covered with pinfeathers again. Connor had been avoiding my touch for months, but he allowed me one last stroke of his chest. Seconds later, the flock abruptly bolted. It was the time of the annual hawk migration, and the sky had been filled with raptors in recent days. The parrots must have spotted one. I watched them fly north toward Fisherman's Wharf until they disappeared from view.

It was difficult to explain to others how I felt. Mostly, I was relieved to be done with it, but nobody wanted to hear that. The image people had of me and the parrots was very appealing, and no one wanted it to end. For me, it had started out as a lark and then turned into something serious and involved. I'd loved being with them, but as a permanent way of life the intensity was unsustainable, and I'd reached the end of what I could endure. I knew I'd miss the birds—the hardest part would be not knowing the day-to-day details of what was happening—but the way I saw it, they'd come from mystery, and now they were returning to it.

The next day, I moved my belongings. Everybody assumed that after all the publicity I'd gotten, I had it made. But I was old news, and my position was no different than it had been before all the media attention. A couple whose house I used to clean offered to put me up until the end of the "Pledge to the Fledge," but after that I had no sure place to stay.

Judy and I continued to wait for the fledge, and on September 17, more than two weeks after it typically got under way, we caught our first glimpse of a baby in Erica and Russell's nest. He stuck his head up into the nest-hole entrance and started making a lot of noise. He was restless, so Judy and I jumped out of the van and got ready to shoot. But apparently Russell didn't believe that the baby was ready. He flew from a nearby branch and stuffed the baby back down inside the hole. Judy and I named the baby Do (pronounced "doe," like the first note of the major scale). As soon as it became clear that Do wasn't fledging that day, I ran over to Wendell and Scrapper's nest to see what, if anything, was happening there. Their baby was visible now, too. He was perched between two palm fronds and gazing down upon the world with big, kindly baby eyes. I named him Ace. He was proof that the hybrids were fertile.

The next morning, we arrived in El Coto convinced that this had to be the big day. Do climbed up the tunnel to the nest-hole entrance several times, but Erica and Russell still refused to let him out. I'd always imagined that the babies had to be coaxed out, but that wasn't the case. His parents were actively blocking him. So Do didn't fledge that day, or the day after.

Early in the morning on September 21, it finally happened. Erica was perched on a limb near the nest hole where Russell was busy stuffing Do back inside. The baby was bleating insistently when Russell suddenly left the hole and joined Erica on her branch. It was foggy, and because Judy couldn't see much through the camera's viewfinder in the dim morning light, I had to be her eyes. It was my responsibility to choose the right moment for her to start rolling. She was using a small hand-wound Bolex set for slow motion that allowed her to film only eight seconds of real time per wind. If she waited too long to start shooting, she'd miss the moment of the fledge; and if she started too soon, she could miss it while rewinding. When Russell left the nest hole, I hesitated. I managed to blurt out just in time that the nest hole was open. Judy pushed the button at the very moment Do burst out of the hole. When Do jumped, so did Erica and Russell. The two parrot parents took the lead, and Do followed them on big, ungainly wings for a short loop around the grounds. They quickly returned to the big eucalyptus, and Do's first-ever landing was nearly a failure. He hit the branch with too much forward momentum, and he turned his wings like a crazy windmill until he was upright and still. Judy and I were both ecstatic—she for having gotten the shot, and I for having witnessed my first fledge. We slapped palms and shouted out loud in triumph.

When we returned the next day, Do was still perched in the eucalyptus. I'd always thought that the babies came around to the cottage immediately after fledging, but so far he'd taken only a few short escorted flights around El Coto. As we watched Do, we heard another baby bleating from inside the nest hole. We named this one Re. Like Do, Re was eager to fledge, but Erica and Russell were restraining this one, too. Several days passed, and Re's yelping grew louder and louder. Re fledged four days after Do. It happened without warning. Re was out of the nest before Judy could pull the trigger. She'd put me on a second camera, wide, and I started a hair late. Although we both missed the moment that Re left the hole, Judy was able to track the baby's maiden flight around the grounds. Erica and Russell had just the two babies, Do and Re, so we weren't going to get the chance to film a Mi. But Judy was confident that she had enough footage between the two fledges to build a sequence for her movie.

Three days later, Judy and I made another trip to El Coto. Our intention was to take one last look around and film some pick-up shots, but we got more than we came for. Judy noticed Pushkin clinging to a palm frond and liked the image, so she stopped to film him. While watching Pushkin through the viewfinder, she noticed one of Pushkin and Olive's babies in the background poking his head out of the nest hole. She reframed and started running film through the camera. An instant later, Pushkin leaped into the air and the baby followed him—a fantastic stroke of luck.

If I'd only gotten to see some babies fledge, it would have been a wonderful ending to my years with the parrots. But something else took wing that September, something I didn't see coming: Judy and I fell in love.

I'd always imagined that when love arrived, the clouds would part and flaming chariots would descend from the sky. But it wasn't that way at all. I *liked* her. She has a young heart that feels cozy without being overly sentimental. She's smart as a whip and *tough,* but she loves to laugh. Judy is present in a way that I often am not. I have a tendency to get lost in my thoughts when I'm out walking, while she has the eye of a cinematographer and notices everything around her.

On a day when I think everything looks gloomy, she'll cheerfully point out the loveliness and delicacy of the mist. And then I try to see it the way she sees it, and . . . oh yes, how beautiful! She's self-confident, considering herself the equal of everyone she meets. I've never seen her impressed by wealth or fame. I'm always startled at the ease with which she meets strangers. It usually takes me awhile to get comfortable with new people, but Judy is always immediately there with them. I asked her about it once, and she told me that she regarded each new person she met as a friend whom she didn't know yet. She'd worked that magic on me. Her interviews with me for the film's voice-over had drawn me out in a way that I'd always resisted. I saw it as part of my job anyway, but she made me feel so comfortable that it was easy to be open with her. I wasn't hoping to win anything or afraid of losing anything, and it led to a closeness that I'd never had with anybody else.

But it was the flock that brought us together. We'd spent hours and hours standing side by side watching them and talking about them. As she learned to recognize individuals, I told her each bird's story. I loved having someone with whom I could share the flock lore. No matter how much I went on about them, she'd want to hear more. Eventually, she got to know the parrots almost as well as I did. That's how we fell in love.

Although it wasn't what you would call a *torrid* romance, our coming together was not without drama. Judy was living with somebody else. Their relationship was at a standstill and had been for years, but she hadn't wanted to face that, and once she did, she couldn't see a way out. They owned an apartment and a business together, which made the situation painfully complicated. I felt deficient in that I couldn't provide us with a place to live. I was homeless again and living in one of the most expensive cities in the world. But I no longer wanted to leave San Francisco. Although it hadn't been easy for her to accept them, Judy understood my explanations of why I'd been living the way I did, and she didn't give up on me. Neither one of us knew what to do, but we decided to stick it out and see where the path led.

Five days after our last shoot in El Coto, Judy and I went to film the ruins of my old cottage. We parked the van near the Greenwich Steps, and as we were climbing out we spotted a red-tailed hawk perched on a nearby chimney. Judy needed some close-ups of a hawk, so we quickly pulled the gear out of the van and set up. She managed to get a shot off just as the big raptor flew away.

We packed up her gear and hauled it down the Greenwich Steps. All that was left of the cottage now were the four walls, which were surrounded by big piles of debris. The low autumn sun cast an especially eerie light on the wreckage of my old home. While Judy set up the camera, I tried to absorb the reality of it. As I was taking it all in, I heard the flock approach. They landed in some trees right next to where we were standing. Connor was in a plum tree just a few yards away, and Judy and I were both shocked by what we saw. He'd deteriorated markedly since the last feeding. He looked feeble and lost; he was barely moving. Judy shot some film of Connor while I searched the lines and limbs for others I recognized. Suddenly, everybody bolted from the trees in a mad panic. Two red-shouldered hawks had eluded the watch parrots and flown low into the garden, catching the flock completely by surprise. The hawks got so close that they were able to dive into the main body of the flock, which scattered the parrots in every direction. Seconds later, the red-tailed hawk that Judy and I had seen on the street joined in the attack. I'd never seen anything like it. I was terrified for the flock and swearing furiously at the three hawks, while Judy swore and swung the camera around trying to follow the action. The parrots were screaming hysterically and flying back and forth in confusion, while the hawks emitted their spooky high-pitched calls. Fortunately, all three hawks came up empty, and the parrots made their getaway.

Immediately after the parrots left, I went down to the bottom of the hill to get some coffee. James Attwood, a man who lived on the Filbert Steps, was standing in line next to me, and I started telling him what I'd just seen. I was still rattled by the intensity of the attack and couldn't stop talking about it. Two hours later, James would witness an attack that was far worse.

Just as I was running out of places to stay in San Francisco, I bumped into the girlfriend of one of my old buddies from my street days. It had been nearly ten years since I'd last seen Joe and Lisa, so we had some catching up to do. The encounter turned out to be an incredible stroke of luck. When I told Lisa about losing the studio, she offered to put me up in their house across the bay in Piedmont. They ended up giving me my own room, telling me that I was welcome to stay for as long as it took me to finish my book.

For someone who was technically homeless, I was doing an incredible amount of work. I'd get up before dawn, write until noon, and then rush down to the underground train to San Francisco, where I'd help Judy with the chore of logging in tedious detail every single shot in the thirty-five hours of film footage. It was more than an excuse for us to be together; I was the only one who could reliably recognize the birds and understand what was going on. We'd wrap up at six o'clock, and I'd head back across the bay, where I'd collapse into bed, and then start up the cycle again the next morning.

A couple of weeks after filming the cottage ruins, Judy and I returned to Telegraph Hill to film the cutting down of the mirror plant—the bush that the hand feeders used to perch in. During a break in the shoot, I went up the hill to a grocery store and I ran into an old neighbor. He told me about James Attwood witnessing a second hawk attack, and that this time the red-tail had killed one of the parrots. I scrambled to a pay phone and called James to get the details. He told me that he hadn't seen the actual attack; he'd seen the hawk on a chimney holding the parrot in his talons, while the flock circled and chastised the red-tail. The parrot was still alive—he saw it twitching—but the flock had been so noisy that he couldn't tell whether it was making any sound. James had taken some photographs, and I was welcome to come look at them, but he warned me that they didn't reveal much. He'd used a cheap camera and been far from the action. All you could see was the green of the parrot's body, he said; there wasn't any red visible. I guessed that it was one of the babies—they wouldn't know much about avoiding hawks yet—but on my way to James's house, I ran into another old neighbor who made me think otherwise. Gary lived on the Filbert Steps and had been putting out peanuts for the parrots for several years. He told me that since the day of the hawk attack, he hadn't seen his most regular customer—the parrot with the blue head.

James had six photographs. In the clearest photo, the hawk has the parrot underfoot with his wings held high in victory. There seemed to be some blue in what may have been the parrot's head, but I couldn't be sure. But because he was so weak that day and because he hadn't been seen again after the attack, I had little reason to doubt that it was Connor.

I went back to the Greenwich Steps and told Judy what I'd learned. The news hit her hard. Connor had been her favorite. He'd been almost everybody's favorite. She started crying, and I tried to console her. I didn't feel the same sorrow, and I wasn't sure why. I'd loved Connor from the moment I first saw him. I explained away my reaction as my having gotten used to the fact that wild birds have relatively short lives. I told Judy that if there was a tragic aspect, it had more to do with his life than his death. He should have been left in the wild in Argentina with other blue-crowned conures where he would have had a mate. Instead, he'd ended up frustrated and alone. I said that I accepted Connor's death as nature's way. But nothing I told Judy satisfied her, and it didn't really satisfy me either, given that lately I'd been having a problem writing or even thinking about Dogen without having to fight off tears.

Over the next months, Judy and I occasionally returned to the garden to get more shots of the parrots. She was the first to voice it, but I'd been noticing it, too: After Connor's death, the flock felt like a different entity. He was a loner who'd been kept to the fringes, yet there was something about Connor—something ineffable—that gave the entire flock its character. We both could feel its absence very clearly.

A year after I moved to Piedmont, word came through the grapevine that the trustee for the compound of cottages next door to my old studio on Telegraph Hill was looking for me. She wanted to know if I was interested in being a caretaker. The proposition was a familiar one: She needed someone to live in the main house while she consulted a lawyer. I wouldn't be staying there long, just for the few months it would take to resolve some legal issues so the property could be sold. The very next day I was back on the Greenwich Steps.

It was a real house, with a kitchen, a bedroom, two bathrooms, a living room, and a washer and dryer. Like my old studio, it was old and crumbling. The bedroom ceiling leaked and the building leaned so much that some doors couldn't be shut, but I had all the solitude and quiet I needed to write. Actually, it wasn't always so quiet. Nearly every day, the parrots would land in the Monterey cypress, which was just twenty feet from my door, and start up a prolonged flock scream. Sometimes they were so noisy that I couldn't focus on writing about them. Just as I'd assumed, the flock had done fine without me. It seemed to be even larger than when I left. I was very curious to know who was still alive, but they were too high up in the tree to pick out individuals, and I didn't see any place on the property to which I might lure them down. But I didn't think I wanted to start feeding them again anyway.

After I'd been in the house for a few months, it became apparent that the legal process had gotten bogged down and that I wasn't going to be moving anytime soon. That I had a place to stay created a possibility that Judy had to consider. Her life at home had become untenable. She and her partner had been heading in different directions for a long time. When she'd left her parents' home, her dream had been, like mine, to do creative work. But by working as part of a team for more than twenty-five years, she'd lost touch with her vision of herself. The relationship had deteriorated to little more than a business partnership, and it didn't look to her as though it were ever going to change. Judy still felt affection for her partner and hated the idea of causing him any pain, but a door was open, and she had to make a difficult choice. What do you do? Do you turn away from that door and stay in a familiar rut for the rest of your life, all for the sake of a false and dissatisfying peace? Or do you take a risk in the hope that you'll find what your heart seeks and endure the consequences? Judy chose to move in with me.

The breakup was stressful. The lives of everybody involved went through a tremendous amount of upheaval. But over time things settled down and took a shape. A new world opened up for Judy and me.

One of the most appealing aspects of living on Telegraph Hill for her was its proximity to the South End Rowing Club, where she'd been a member for years. Founded in 1873, it's the oldest athletic club on the West Coast and part of the real San Francisco. In spite of its name, it's on the north waterfront and caters more to swimmers than rowers. Judy is an avid bay swimmer, and there was no way that I could be in this relationship without giving bay swimming at least one try. The water seldom gets warmer than sixty degrees, and in winter it dips below fifty. So I was squeamish. My ankles hurt as I waded in, and when I finally immersed myself, I was gasping for breath. But the shock wore off, and I found myself enjoying the silkiness of the salt water. The setting, which is near Alcatraz and the Golden Gate Bridge, is gorgeous. Judy swam alongside me, pointing out what the tide was doing. It was pushing me much harder than I realized, and it frightened me a little. It was the Great Mother in her most elemental and uncompromising mode. But I ended up liking the swim so much that I joined the club. I'd never been a swimmer, but I took it up with enthusiasm. In the cove, I was encountering sea lions, harbor seals, and many species of waterbirds. I liked the waterbirds even more than the native land birds. Judy taught me their names: cormorant, brown pelican, tern, egret, and night heron.

One day, I read Judy the statement by Gary Snyder that had affected me so strongly: "The city is just as natural as the country, let's not forget it. There's nothing in the universe that's not natural by definition. One of the poems I like best in *Turtle Island* is 'Night Herons,' which is about the naturalness of San Francisco." She asked to read the poem. I'd never been sure where in San Francisco the poem takes place, but Judy recognized it immediately: It was along the cove at Aquatic Park, the very cove we were swimming in. She knew the tree that the night herons roosted in, and one day she pointed them out to me. There they were: large black-and-white birds, perched in a sycamore. They looked silly up there. They didn't look like the kind of bird that belonged in a tree. I must have walked by them hundreds of times without ever noticing them. But that's typical of the urban dweller's experience of nature: It's all around us, and we don't see it. When, years earlier, I first read Snyder's statement and tried to make a study of the local ecology, I'd never thought of San Francisco Bay as being part of it. For me, the bay had always been purely aesthetic— something nice to look at. But the bay *is* the ecology. I was too spaced out to see what was right in front of me! It occurred to me that after living in San Francisco for nearly thirty years and spending most of that time waiting to leave, I'd finally arrived.

One morning while I was writing, Judy came in to check on my plans for the day. In the middle of the conversation, she paused to take a long look out the window. It's a marvelous view, with several Monterey cypresses in the near foreground and San Francisco Bay behind them. She turned back to me, her eyes lit.

"You know what? You got what you wanted," she said.

"What do you mean?"

"Your three wishes. You got all three of them: a girlfriend, work you love, and a place in the country."

I'd told her when she was interviewing me for the voice-over about the three things I'd decided I needed to be content.

"Well, this isn't the country," I said.

"In a way it is. The place you imagined was in the mountains with a forest and a river. Telegraph Hill is your mountain; the cypresses are your forest; and the bay with its tides—that's your river."

I raised my eyebrows and laughed. Maybe so. But the house wasn't ours, I reminded her. I was still homeless. Actually, we both were now.

One day, I went to answer a knock at the door and found three men in business suits. They were real estate agents there to look at the property in preparation for putting the compound on the market. I hadn't been told they were coming, so I was off balance and a little nervous. They kept trying to get me to say that I wasn't a tenant, that I was only a caretaker. Obviously, there was some concern that I'd raise a stink about leaving. Judy and I had been dreading this day, and as soon as they left, I called her office to tell her what had happened. I was upset. I'd been making steady progress with the book, and I didn't want to break my momentum. Judy was surprisingly calm, though.

"Well, we're just going to have to buy the place then," she said.

The property consisted of seven separate units, a collection of run-down cottages, some of which had been built even before my old studio. Judy had put together a tenants in common, or TIC, once before. It's a fairly common arrangement in San Francisco: A group of people buy a multiunit building and live there. She and her ex had recently sold their apartment so Judy had some cash, but she needed to find others to go in on the deal.

One day, I was in the dining room talking on the phone to Judy when I noticed a hawk on top of a telephone pole on the Greenwich Steps. It was tearing at something with unusual intensity. There was a scrub jay perched just a few feet away from the hawk shrieking hysterically. I abruptly ended the call and ran around the house looking for binoculars. I couldn't find them, so I grabbed a camera with a zoom lens and ran outside. Even before looking through the lens, I knew it was one of the parrots. It was screaming helplessly, in despair and disbelief.

The hawk carried his catch to the garden, where the parrot continued its hopeless, mournful wailing. I ran down and tried to find them. I wanted to stop the attack, but they were high up in the trees. The parrot was doomed. I went back up to the house, still hearing its horrible cries. It left me shaken, and I realized then that this was the way it must have been for Connor. I couldn't hate the hawk, but I knew that if I'd witnessed Connor's death, it would have been extremely difficult to tell myself that this was simply nature's way.

Thinking back, there were probably two reasons that it took me so long to grasp the reality of his death. One was that austere front of his, which discouraged sentiment. The other is that at the time of his death, my life was in such flux and I was moving away from the flock.

The reality of Connor's death hit me again not long after I saw the hawk kill the parrot. I was listening to a piece of music that Chris Michie, the composer for Judy's movie, had written about Connor. As I listened to the piece, I began to visualize Connor, old and alone. I remembered what his presence was like—how noble and gentle he was—and how much I'd loved him. It finally got through to me that my old friend really was dead, and I cried.

While Judy handled the day-to-day details of putting together a group of buyers, I continued work on my book. One day, during a break, I stepped outside and saw the flock perched in a cherry tree that grew right next to the bedroom. The tree limbs hung over the flat bedroom roof, and I saw that the roof would be a perfect platform from which to feed them. It had been a year and a half since the last feeding, and I was very curious to see whether they'd still remember me.

I bought a bag of sunflower seeds, and the next morning, as I'd hoped, the flock made a pit stop in the cherry tree. When I heard them arrive, I went outside and climbed up onto the roof. I made a slow, cautious approach. Every eye was focused on me, and as I got close, they started up the nervous cawing sound they make when they see danger. I stopped to give them a chance to relax. Looking them over, I couldn't recognize a single bird. After a minute, they calmed down, and I started moving toward them again. They were still anxious, but they allowed me to get within three feet. I slowly extended my seed-filled hand toward the closest bird. Nobody moved. Suddenly one of the parrots fluttered down from an upper limb and landed on my right forearm. It was Patrick! He'd gone to the very same spot that he used to feed from. After Patrick, Bo came to a nearby branch and started taking seeds. And then the floodgates opened: Gibson, Olive, Pushkin, Miles, Scrapper, and Wendell. Erica! Erica was still alive. Then I saw Sophie, which surprised and pleased me. I'd assumed that if any parrot depended on my handouts and protection, it was Sophie. She was just as clumsy as when I left, but still hanging in there. None of the birds born since my departure joined in the feeding, but all my old hand feeders ate freely and without fear. The feeding was no different than any I'd ever given. The birds were all over me squabbling for position, while I laughed and laughed. It must have been a strange sight for the young birds.

In the days that followed, I continued to feed them. After watching the older birds get free handouts, some of the youngsters overcame their fear, and I started making new friends. As much as I enjoyed being back with the flock, I decided that I wouldn't feed them every day. And I made a rule that on the days I did feed, I wouldn't do it more than once. I wanted to stay in touch, but I wanted to keep my involvement at a moderate level. I liked the idea of being able to watch them for the rest of my life, to see what would happen to them over the long haul. I'd already discovered that their old yearly pattern had changed somewhat. They were seldom in a single group anymore. There were probably too many of them now for it to be manageable. One day, I counted a minimum of eighty-five parrots. They'd also expanded their range slightly, moving farther south past Walton Square to a waterfront park. One of the biggest changes was the level of hybridization. Olive and her offspring were having great success in the nest. But if I were to continue with this as a lifelong study, we had to buy the house, and Judy was having a lot of trouble putting a deal together.

Our competition was slight—people had been passing on the property because it was so dilapidated and inaccessible—but Judy's partnerships kept falling apart. It was all very complicated. She finally put together a group that made an offer, but then a developer with deep pockets came along. His offer was accepted, and Judy and I received an eviction notice.

The rejection of our group's offer threw both of us into a tailspin. For two months, we lived under the gun, waiting for the sheriff to serve final notice. But the developer's deal fell through, and at the last minute the eviction was rescinded. It took us fifteen months and three separate tries, but in the end we got the property.

For many years, I'd felt as though I were on a death march across an endless desert. And although, in the end, I received everything I asked for, I know that life is not about getting what you want. You can want the wrong things. Because I'd once invested all my energy into becoming something I wasn't suited to be—a musician—I lost my way for the longest time. Each of us has a true nature, the real laws of our being, and that inner nature will always receive what is appropriate to it as long as we're honest with ourselves.

If I'm to be in a city, there really isn't any other neighborhood in this world I'd rather live in. Even before leaving the Pacific Northwest, I'd felt drawn to Telegraph Hill as the most magical part of San Francisco. I know that nothing in life is permanent; nevertheless, having a home is a real change for me. I feel different now. I have a place, and work to do. And I have found somebody to love.

"When you find your place, practice begins."
—DOGEN

❧❧❧

ACE The offspring of Scrapper and Wendell. Wendell was a hybrid, which made Ace a backcross, or double-hybrid.

AMAROU Paco's mate, she was unusually aggressive for a female. I had little contact with her. Amarou was named after a character in the Van Morrison song "Caravan."

ANDITSON The offspring of Guy and Doll. Anditson was a female and the mate of Mingus. She was one of the birds who, as a juvenile, contracted the mysterious disease.

BLAKE Probably a female, she was the hybrid offspring of the mitred conure, Olive, and the cherry-headed conure, Gibson. Exceptionally friendly with me, Blake lived only a few weeks as a free bird. She was named for the poet William Blake.

BO One of the most timid males in the flock, he had a peculiar obsession with the sick parrots I kept in the house. He lost his first mate,

Stella, to disease, and his second, Mandela, in a fight. He finally became a parent with his third mate, Sticky Chest, aka Murphy. He received his name when he was courting Stella. I kept referring to him as "Stella's beau," and eventually he became just Bo.

BUCKY I brought Bucky, a blue-crowned conure, into my household at a time that one of my flock favorites, Connor, also a blue crown, was single. I wanted Connor to have a mate. An exceptionally robust bird, Bucky had been a pet bird for many years, and was somewhat neurotic and clingy on account of it.

CATHERINE Connor's blue-crowned conure companion for several years. She was the most timid bird in the flock, but one of the most good-natured. Her name comes from one of my unrequited loves.

CHAUNCEY One of the juveniles who contracted an unknown, crippling disease, Chauncey was in my care for a few months and then escaped. He survived only a couple of weeks after that in the wild. He was named for the character Chauncey Gardiner, from the novel *Being There*.

CHOMSKY The offspring of Sonny and Lucia and a sibling of Mandela and Stella, he was fond of perching on top of my head. Chomsky was a victim of the illness that afflicted the juveniles. He was named in honor of the brilliant intellectual and dissident Noam Chomsky.

CONNOR A blue-crowned conure and one of my two favorite parrots in the flock. Connor was regal and handsome, but unhappy because of the poor treatment that the cherry heads made him endure. I named him Connor because of its similarity to the word *conure*.

COSTANZE The offspring of Eric and Erica, her name was originally

Mozart. I changed it to Costanze, the name of the real Mozart's wife, when I realized she was female. I had very little contact with her. She was Gibson's mate for a short time.

DO The offspring of Erica and Russell. Do was the first baby I ever saw fledge. Re was Do's sibling. She was named for the first of the solfeggio syllables (do, re, mi . . .).

DOGEN Originally named Smith, Dogen was a female cherry head and my favorite bird in the flock. I found her intolerably feisty until I got to know her. She was the offspring of Guy and Doll and the sibling of Jones. Dogen was a survivor of the mysterious illness that used to strike the juveniles every spring and summer. She was named in honor of the Japanese Zen master Dogen.

DOLL The mother of Dogen and Paco and the mate of Guy. I named her Doll so that the couple would be called Guy and Doll. She was an aloof bird who had little curiosity about me. She died with her mate when the palm tree they nested in fell over in a wind storm and crushed them.

ERIC A banded male cherry head, he was the strongest and most respected bird in the flock during his lifetime. Although he never

seemed afraid of me, he's the only bird I remember refusing to take seeds from my hand. He may have been the parrot that someone else named Victor, the founding male member of the flock. His mate was Erica. I named him for Eric the Red, the Viking.

ERICA A female banded cherry head, she may have been the bird that someone else named Inez, the flock's Eve. She was, like her mate Eric, an elusive bird who preferred to have nothing to do with me. After Eric died, she took up with Russell.

GEORGIA The offspring of Sonny and Lucia, she was a bird with whom I had little contact, but may have been the bird that I later

named Tupelo. Her name was taken from the song "Georgia on My Mind."

GIBSON He may have been the bird that I once called Rascal. If so, he was born in the summer just before I began to observe the flock close up. He was generally friendly with me but could be quite aggressive. He was Olive's mate for two years and the father of four hybrids: Picasso, Blake, Snyder, and Wendell. He had an orange tinge to the feathers on top of his head that reminded me of the finish on a friend's guitar. The brand of the guitar was Gibson.

GINSBERG A cherry head who fell ill with "the virus." A sweet-natured but severely crippled bird who never completely lost her fear of me, she was in my care until my departure from the hill. She was named in honor of the poet Allen Ginsberg.

GUY An aggressive male cherry head, the father of Dogen and Paco. He was prone to pushing his flock mates aside to steal their seeds, so I had to restrain him constantly. Nevertheless, he seemed to like me. Before he had a name, I kept saying to him, "Hey, guy." So he became Guy. His mate was named Doll.

HENRY One of the stronger birds in the flock. He usually ate at the seed bowl, so I had little contact with him. He was named for the writer Henry Miller.

INEZ The flock's Eve. She was named by the husband of Laurel Wroten. Laurel was an observer of the flock when it was just beginning. Inez may have been the bird that I called Erica.

JONES Dogen's sibling. His parents were Guy and Doll. I named him Jones at the time that Dogen was called Smith. Jones was one of the few birds who didn't claim a particular spot to feed from. He followed my hand everywhere, which led to his having constant altercations with the others. Jones may have been female. If so, I think she was briefly the mate of Pushkin.

KRISTINE The mate of Sam. I had very little contact with her. She was named for a girl who enchanted me when I was five years old.

LUCIA Sonny's mate, a female cherry head. She was the mother of Mandela, Stella, Chomsky, and perhaps Tupelo. Like Sonny, she was generally aloof from me, but came to me when she was in need. She was an especially anxious bird who was named for Lucille Ball (a redhead).

MANDELA A female cherry-headed conure, and the first bird to land on me. Playful and curious, she was one of the friendliest birds toward me in the flock. She was briefly in my care after a cat attacked her. Her parents were Sonny and Lucia, and her siblings were Chomsky and Stella. She was named for Nelson Mandela before I knew she was female.

MARLON Born just months before I began observing the flock, he was the first baby I recognized as an individual. Originally a very cool customer, he became quite ornery as he matured. His mate was Murphy (female). He was named for the actor Marlon Brando.

MARTHA Martha was the first bird I saw contract the mysterious disease that afflicted the juveniles. I knew her only a very brief time. She was a sweet and shy bird named after a girl I had a brief crush on in high school.

MATTHEW The offspring of Sonny and Lucia. He (or she) may have been the bird I later named Tupelo. His name was taken from the Book of Matthew.

MENDELSSOHN The offspring of Eric and Erica. I had little contact with Mendelssohn. He was probably killed by a cat when he was a year old. He was named for the composer Felix Mendelssohn.

MILES The offspring of Bo and Sticky Chest. An unusually handsome and friendly bird, he liked to perch on my shoulder and take seeds from my lips. He was named for the jazz trumpet player Miles Davis.

MINGUS Someone's pet cherry head who, I believe, was deliberately released into the flock. Against my wishes, he took up residence in my house. He was extraordinarily infuriating and lovable, just like his namesake, the jazz bass player and composer Charles Mingus.

MONK The offspring of Bo and Sticky Chest. When he was just a baby, he smashed up his beak very badly. Although already weaned, his parents resumed feeding him until the beak healed. Monk later came down with the mysterious disease and died in my arms. He was named for the jazz piano player Thelonious Monk.

MOZART See *Costanze.*

MRS. HENRY The mate of Henry. She seldom ate from my hand, so I never got to know her well. She was named for the Bob Dylan song "Please, Mrs. Henry."

MURPHY A female cherry head, she was Marlon's mate and the first parrot to touch me deliberately. She had little curiosity about me. Her primary interest was food. She was named after Jack Murphy, the man who built the house I lived in on Darrell Place. Later I changed her name to Sticky Chest.

NOAH The first bird to take a seed from my hand. She was a frisky

bird who made a game out of biting me and then hightailing it. She was, as I learned later, a female. Her name was a mistake on two counts; I meant to call her Adam.

OLIVE The flock's sole mitred conure, and a former pet, she was the mother of all hybrids. She was extraordinarily nervous and high-strung. She had two mates, Gibson and Pushkin. She was first called Oliver after a bookstore, Oliver's Books. When I learned she was female, I changed her name to Olive.

PACO The offspring of Guy and Doll, Paco injured his wing on his first flight and was given to me to care for. Although I had him from the time that he was a baby, he never really tamed down. He was rambunctious and yearned to fly free. He was the mate of Amarou. He was named for the flamenco guitarist Paco de Lucia.

PATRICK One of the most colorful birds in the flock. Often single, he had several short-term mates, but never parented any babies. He was named for a neighbor who gave me an encouraging word when I sorely needed one.

PICASSO The first hybrid I ever saw, his parents were Olive and Gibson. From practically the first time we met, he was surprisingly friendly. I always had the impression that he wasn't too bright, though. He was, for a time, my favorite in the flock. Picasso was a strong bird who even as a baby dominated many of the other birds. He was named after Pablo Picasso.

PUSHKIN A woman stealer, and a great father. After his first mate, Jones, died, Pushkin stole Mandela from Bo. After Mandela's death, he stole Olive from Gibson. One year, I had to take in Olive when she fell ill, and Pushkin raised, single-handedly, the three babies they had in the nest. He was named for the Russian poet Aleksandr Pushkin.

RASCAL A bird who used to taunt Marlon. I think he may have been a bird whom I later called Gibson.

RE The second baby I saw fledge, she was the sibling of Do. Her parents were Erica and Russell. She was named for the second of the solfeggio syllables.

RUSSELL He became Erica's mate after the death of Eric. Russell was primarily a bowl bird, so I had very little contact with him. He was named after the American Indian Movement leader Russell Means.

SAM The mate of Kristine. Sam was one of the toughest birds in the flock. He once severely injured his beak, but acted as though it were nothing. He was named after my father's uncle, one of my favorite relatives.

SCRAPPER A male cherry head, he was in the first group of five parrots who ate from my hand. He was a small but self-assured bird who minded his own business. His first mate was Scrapperella. He got his name because I thought his missing feathers were the result of fighting. In fact, his mate was plucking them out. He later paired up with Wendell.

SCRAPPERELLA A cherry-headed conure, presumably female. She was an in-the-wild feather plucker. The other birds picked on her often simply because—I'm convinced—she looked so weird. Her mate was Scrapper. I named him first, and her name was derived from his. They were the first pair I ever saw get a divorce.

SEBASTIAN The offspring of Marlon and Murphy. Sebastian was a frisky bird like his father. He was named after the explorer Juan Sebastián del Cano.

SMITH See *Dogen.*

SMITTY A spunky little budgie (parakeet) who was in the flock for one summer, and became Connor's constant companion.

SNYDER A male hybrid who adored his sister, Wendell, he was utterly distraught when she took a mate and left him. Like most of the hybrid males, he seemed to easily dominate most male cherry heads. The offspring of Olive and Gibson, he was named in honor of the poet Gary Snyder.

SONNY A banded male cherry-headed conure, and one of the orneriest birds in the flock. His first mate was Lucia. Later, he paired up with Dogen. He was named after Sonny Corleone of *The Godfather.* His band number was OJG 943 (perhaps 343).

ƧOPHIE One of my favorites. She was feisty, strong-willed, and a real sweetheart. Sophie was one of the juveniles who fell ill from a crippling disease. She was in my care for a few months, and then picked the lock on her cage and escaped. I thought she was doomed, but she still survives in spite of her disability.

ƧTELLA A female cherry-headed conure, she was the offspring of Sonny and Lucia. Her siblings were Mandela and Chomsky. She was unusually large, and even as a baby she seemed matronly. She was a victim of the disease that used to strike the juveniles in the spring and summer. Because there was a bird named Marlon in the flock, I was reminded of the film *A Streetcar Named Desire* and the character Stella.

ƧTICKY CHEƧT See *Murphy.*

TUPELO A juvenile in my care who had come down with the same unknown disease that until 1998 struck some of the juveniles every spring. A sweet and helpless bird who was utterly dependent on me, Tupelo was one of my favorites. She was probably the offspring of Sonny and Lucia. Her name was taken from the Van Morrison song "Tupelo Honey."

VICTOR The flock's "Adam," the first breeding male cherry head. He was named by the husband of Laurel Wroten. Laurel was one of the earliest observers of the flock. Victor may have been the bird whom I called Eric.

WENDELL A female hybrid, the offspring of Olive and Gibson, and the sibling of Snyder. As a baby, Wendell was a biter whom I always had to keep an eye on. She was the mate of Scrapper and the first hybrid to have babies. Wendell was named in honor of the poet and farmer Wendell Berry.

YOSEMITE A victim of "the virus," he was named after the cartoon character Yosemite Sam on account of his orneriness. He paired up with Ginsberg, with whom he liked to hang by his beak from his cage bars for hours at a time.

About the Author

❦

MARK BITTNER was born and raised in southwestern Washington State in the shadow of a volcano. After graduating from high school, he hitchhiked through Europe, trying to decide what to do with his life. Upon his return to the United States, he briefly moved to Seattle and then to San Francisco, where he made a failed stab at a career in music. While spending the next several decades pondering his next move, he fell in with a gang of parrots. He still lives in San Francisco on Telegraph Hill.

$13.95/NATURE—BIRDS & BIRDWATCHING
(Canada: $21.00)

—— A *San Francisco Chronicle* Bestseller ——

Like a lot of young people in the 1970s, Mark Bittner took the path of the "dharma bum." When the counterculture faded, Mark held on, seeking shelter in the nooks and crannies of San Francisco's fabled bohemian neighborhood, North Beach. While living on the eastern slope of Telegraph Hill, he made a magical discovery: a flock of wild parrots. In this unforgettable story, Bittner recounts how he became fascinated by the birds and patiently developed friendships with them that would last more than six years. When a documentary filmmaker comes along to capture the phenomenon on film, the story takes a surprising turn, and Bittner's life truly takes flight.

"A healthy dose of inspiration . . . the perfect read for anybody who believes that success means more than a corner office." —*Elle*

"[A] charming memoir. For devoted birders everywhere."
—*Reader's Digest,* Editor's Choice

"[An] inspirational saga of one man finding his life's meaning in the most serendipitous way." —*San Jose Mercury News*

"Instructive, surprising, sweet." —GARY SNYDER, author of *Turtle Island* and *Mountains and Rivers Without End*

 MARK BITTNER is the subject of a documentary film, also titled *The Wild Parrots of Telegraph Hill,* directed by Judy Irving. He still lives in San Francisco on Telegraph Hill.

Visit the book's website at www.markbittner.net and the film's at www.pelicanmedia.org.

Cover design: JENNIFER O'CONNOR
Cover photograph: COURTESY OF THE AUTHOR
Author photograph: JUDY IRVING

THREE RIVERS PRESS
New York
www.crownpublishing.com

NATURE—BIRDS & BIRDWATCHING
U.S. $13.95/$21.00 CAN
ISBN 1-4000-8170-X

5 1 3 9 5

9 781400 081707